The Ideology of the New Right

The Ideology of the New Right

Edited by Ruth Levitas

Polity Press

© Polity Press, 1986

First published 1986 by
Polity Press, Cambridge, in association with Basil Blackwell, Oxford.

Editorial Office:
Polity Press,
Dales Brewery, Gwydir Street, Cambridge, CB1 2LJ, UK.

Basil Blackwell Ltd
108, Cowley Road, Oxford, OX4 1JF, UK.

Basil Blackwell Inc.
432 Park Avenue South, Suite 1505, New York, NY 10016, USA.

British Library Cataloguing in Publication Data

The Ideology of the new right.
  1. Conservatism—Europe 2. Right and left
(Political science) 3. Europe—Politics and
government—1945-
I. Levitas, Ruth
320.94 JN94.A91

  ISBN 0-7456-0190-1
  ISBN 0-7456-0191-X Pbk

Library of Congress Cataloging in Publication Data

The Ideology of the new right.
  Bibliography: p.
  Includes index.
  1. Liberty—Addresses, essays, lectures.,
  2. Conservatism—Addresses, essays, lectures.
  3. Liberalism—Addresses, essays, lectures.
  I.Levitas, Ruth. II. Title: New right.
  JC571.I34 1985 320.5'2 85 – 19119

  ISBN 0 – 7456 – 0190 – 1
  ISBN 0 – 7456 – 0191 – X (pbk.)

Typeset by Graphiti (Hull) Ltd, Hull
Printed in Great Britain by Bell and Bain Limited, Glasgow

Contents

Acknowledgements

Notes on Contributors

Introduction: Ideology and the New Right   1

Ruth Levitas

1   The Political Economy of Freedom   25

    Andrew Gamble

2   The Free or the Good   55

    David Edgar

3   Competition and Compliance: The Utopias of the New Right   80

    Ruth Levitas

4   Culture, Nation and 'Race' in the British and French New Right   107

    Gill Seidel

5   Moral and Maternal: The Family in the Right   136

    Miriam David

6   The New Right, Social Order and Civil Liberties   167

    Andrew Belsey

Bibliography   198

Index   203

Acknowledgements

The idea for this book emerged from a seminar on the New Right which took place in Bristol in February 1984 and which was convened by Robert Moore; particular thanks are therefore due to him for that initiative, and for his continuing encouragement while the book has been in preparation. In any such project, the contributors incur individual debts, too numerous to list, to their families, friends and colleagues for various forms of help and encouragement. As it has been very much a collective venture, I would like to thank the contributors themselves, not just for what they have written and for their tolerance of editorial interventions, but for their commitment to the whole enterprise. Those nearest at hand, Andrew Belsey and Miriam David, have contributed much more than their own chapters to the completion of the project including invaluable help with indexing. I am grateful to Steve Fenton, Tony Giddens, Theo Nichols and Jackie West for their comments on individual chapters; and to Pauline Tilley and Jackie Bee for typing sections of the manuscript and for their forbearance on a day to day basis. Above all, I am indebted to Robert Hunter for his comments on the entire manuscript and for his unstinting intellectual, emotional and practical support.

Ruth Levitas, May 1985

Notes on Contributors

Andrew Belsey is a lecturer in the Department of Philosophy, University College, Cardiff. His main academic interests are the philosophy of science and political philosophy. He is a member of the Executive Committee of the Society for Applied Philosophy.

Miriam David is a lecturer in the Department of Social Administration at the University of Bristol. Her publications range over feminist scholarship, the family, education and social policy in Britain and the USA. They include *The State, The Family and Education* (1980), 'The New Right in the USA and Britain: A New Anti-Feminist Moral Economy' in *Critical Social Policy* (1983) and *For the Children's Sake* with Caroline New (1985).

David Edgar is a playwright whose work includes *Destiny, Mary Barnes* and *Maydays*. He has written about the British and American Right in a number of journals, including *Race and Class* and the *New Statesman*. His analysis of Thatcherism, 'Bitter Harvest', was first published in *New Socialist* and subsequently in *The Future of the Left*.

Andrew Gamble is Reader in the Department of Political Theory and Institutions, University of Sheffield, where he has lectured since 1973. His publications include *The Conservative Nation* (1974), and *Britain in Decline*, 2nd edition (1985). He is currently working on a book on Thatcherism entitled *The Free Economy and the Strong State*.

Ruth Levitas is a lecturer in the Department of Sociology at the University of Bristol. Her research is in the fields of gender relations, social policy and utopias. She has published numerous articles including 'Sociology and Utopia' (1979), 'Feminism and Human Nature' (1983) and 'New Right Utopias' (1985).

Gill Seidel is a specialist in political discourse, and lectures in French and discourse studies at Bradford University. She also leads a Paris-based international research team (CNRS − National Council for Scientific Research) investigating the vocabulary and discourse of the contemporary Right. She has published in *Langage et Société* and *MOTS* (Paris). Her recent books include an edited collection of feminist papers, *La Nature de la Droite* (1986) and *The Holocaust Denial* (1986). She is currently preparing a book on the language of the Right for Benjamins (Amsterdam).

Introduction

Ideology and the New Right

RUTH LEVITAS

Is there a New Right?

The title of this introduction raises several questions currently under discussion by those who wish to understand and to combat the rise of right-wing ideas and policies that has occurred since the mid-1970s. The first set of questions concerns whether such a phenomenon as the New Right actually exists, or whether it is simply that the old Right is enjoying a new ascendancy. All the contributors to this volume agree that there is something new to be examined, but its relationship to the old Right and the far Right requires clarification. This cannot be done purely with reference to Thatcherism, because even in Britain the New Right is broader and more varied than a particular set of policies or style of government, and because there are parallels to the British experience throughout the capitalist industrialized world, especially in France and the USA. The second set of questions (interwoven with the first, as issues of description and analysis always are) concerns how far this New Right is to be understood in terms of its ideology, and the relationship of ideology to political practice both for the Right and for the Left in its strategies of opposition. These questions relate to long-standing disagreements among Marxists and others about the role of ideology in the social process in general, and to current debates about the 'new social forces' (the women's movement, the peace movement, anti-racist movements) and their relationship to the organized working class in the shape of the trade union movement.

Even among those who use the term the New Right there is little consensus about its meaning. Some writers, notably Nick Bosanquet, use the term New Right to refer solely to a form of neo-liberal, laissez-faire economism informed by authors including Adam Smith, de Tocqueville, Schumpeter, Hayek, Milton Friedman and Keith

Joseph; others, including the authors of *The Politics of Thatcherism*, refer both to this neo-liberalism and to a form of authoritarian conservatism which has also enjoyed a resurgence in recent years.[1] Since part of the object of *The Ideology of the New Right* is to explore the relationship between these strands, the contributors to this volume use the term New Right to include both, and to include certain forms of repressive puritanism which have also become more apparent. It is worth examining these contributory strands in more detail before considering their relationship to one another.

For Bosanquet, the New Right is based 'in economics and on ideas about individualism and markets' and is to be contrasted with the old Right which was based 'in political philosophy and on ideas about tradition and hierarchy'.[2] Bosanquet summarizes this form of New Right thinking in a series of propositions under two headings – 'thesis' and 'antithesis'. The thesis refers to the integrating force of the market within society, producing order, justice, economic growth and constantly rising incomes, including those of the poorest; inequality is the inevitable (and beneficial) outcome of individual freedom and initiative. The antithesis refers to short-term stresses generated by this long-term progress towards utopia – stresses which produce politicization and interference in the workings of the market, and in which democracy is a major culprit. Or, as Andrew Gamble puts it in his contribution to this volume, the view can be summarized as 'markets good, governments bad'. This is not just an empirical, but a metaphysical claim. Society is seen as 'a battleground between the forces of light working in the longer term through the economy and the forces of darkness working through the political process'.[3] Schumpeter, who is discussed by both Bosanquet and Gamble, argues that 'since we are dealing with a process whose every element takes considerable time in revealing its true features and ultimate effects, there is no point in appraising the performance of that process, *ex visu* of a given point in time';[4] while Hayek says 'our faith in freedom does not rest on foreseeable results in particular circumstances, but on the belief that it will, on balance, release more force for the good than the bad'.[5] This is paralleled by the present British government's insistence that its policies will in the long run reduce unemployment; no measured level of unemployment could demonstrate this to be false, since the claim is intrinsically impervious to empirical evidence. The thesis is thus protected against invalidation by its emphasis on the long run (which is why Keynes said that in the long run we are all dead).

Gamble shows that even neo-liberal New Right thought is an amalgam of three strands, which, while united by the 'markets good, governments bad' assertion, vary in significant ways. The first is traditional laissez-faire economics, the second extreme libertarianism (which logically implies an almost total lack of constraint of individual activity by the state), and the third Austrian economics which contributed Schumpeter and Hayek. This third strand is explicitly anti-socialist, and contributes greatly to Bosanquet's 'antithesis'. In so far as Hayek's position, as Andrew Belsey argues in chapter six, is effectively antipathetic to individual liberties, there is already a conflict within New Right thought.

The ideas involved here are, of course, by no means new. Some of the pressure groups which propagate neo-liberal economic theories and oppose trade union organization were founded before the Second World War. These groups include the Economic League (founded in 1919), Aims of Industry (1942) and the Institute of Economic Affairs (1957), as well as the more recent Centre for Policy Studies (1974), the National Association for Freedom (1975) and the Adam Smith Institute (1979). But groups of this kind merely took over from earlier organizations which date back to the 1880s and 1890s; private capital has always defended itself against socialism and organized labour in this way. In addition, the political shift marked by NAFF's influence on Thatcher in the years before the 1979 election was mirrored by a plethora of groups with a more popular base (including the National Association of the Self-Employed) which appealed to the middle class substantially on the grounds of economic individualism. These groups claimed a membership of about half a million people in 1975.[6] The pressure groups declined, but the importance of economic liberalism to government policy did not. Particular forms of monetarism derived from opposition to Keynesian intervention and from the policy of floating exchange rates. Not only were old ideas newly ascendant, but they were accompanied by a qualitative shift in both policy and ideology *against* government intervention, which was condemned as collectivist, socialist and economically misguided.

The rise of ideas and groups supporting neo-liberalism is in itself an important phenomenon, not least because of their influence upon the Conservative Party from the mid-seventies, and particularly from 1975 when Thatcher became Party leader. This alone might be grounds for arguing that the New Right differs from the old. However, this shift was paralleled by a resurgence of ideas closer to those Bosanquet calls the old Right. This second strand, of neo-conservatism, is included by most commentators in the term 'New Right'.

It is necessary to refer to these two strands as neo-liberalism and neo-conservatism to distinguish them from what has passed as liberalism or conservatism during much of the twentieth century, especially the period of the so-called post-war consensus. For neo-liberalism wishes to separate itself sharply from 'pseudo-liberalism',[7] a social democratic liberalism corrupted by the welfare state and the New Deal; this neo-liberalism is not to be confused with a socially concerned liberalism, and does not necessarily imply a libertarian attitude to personal conduct and individual freedom. Neo-conservatism, too, must be distinguished from the conservatism of the post-war consensus, which included a commitment to welfare capitalism. Exponents of both strands of New Right thinking would claim, in fact, to be returning to their original nineteenth-century forms, prior to contamination by the 'socialist' ideals of the welfare state. It should however be noted that the neo-conservatives are 'returning' to a particular construction of nineteenth-century Toryism, owing more to Lord Salisbury than to Benjamin Disraeli; they are selecting, rather than embodying, a tradition.

Neo-conservatism, like neo-liberalism, was accompanied by the formation of new groups, notably the Conservative Philosophy Group (1975) and the Salisbury Group (1977), a group of Cambridge academics closely connected with Peterhouse. These gave rise to a volume of *Conservative Essays* in 1978, a concerted attack upon the neo-liberal emphasis on freedom, and subsequently to the journal *The Salisbury Review*, edited by Roger Scruton, one of the most vociferous exponents of neo-conservatism. These academics, and most particularly Scruton, are good illustrations of Mannheim's point that 'the discovery of the conservative idea' did not take place within the ruling class itself, but 'became the work of a body of ideologists who attached themselves to the conservatives'.[8]

Since these writers emphasise hierarchy, authority and nation, it can again be argued that there is little new other than the fashionable status these ideas enjoy, and their political influence. Indeed, it is easier to argue this in relation to neo-conservatism since there was in Britain no clearly related popular movement comparable to the National Association of the Self-Employed in the mid-1970s. There were, however, a number of movements such as the Festival of Light, the Society for the Protection of the Unborn Child, and the National

Viewers and Listeners Association (formed by Mary Whitehouse). Moral issue campaigns have recently achieved two important victories (or inflicted two such defeats). The first was the passage of the Video Recordings Act, misleadingly referred to as the 'video nasties bill', which confers extraordinarily wide powers of censorship upon an appointee of the Home Secretary.[9] The second was Victoria Gillick's success in securing a judgement in 1984 that it is illegal for doctors to prescribe contraception for children under sixteen without parental consent, the implications of which are discussed by Miriam David in chapter five. This strand of overt opposition to personal freedom, particularly in sexual matters, has been more dominant in the USA than in Britain. The USA has seen concerted efforts by born-again Christians to reverse, through the Moral Majority, all the attitudes and legislation of the permissive sixties. There have also been terrorist attacks on family planning and abortion clinics; of over twenty such attacks in 1984 three were on Christmas Day, and were explained as 'a gift to Jesus'. Similar attitudes have led to the cancellation of US aid to countries permitting legal abortion. Thus authoritarianism and sexual repression constitute two different strands of neo-conservative thought, with different weights in Britain and the USA. Again, none of the ideas are particularly new: they echo the objections made to the passing of the permissive legislation of the fifties and sixties, as well as older political themes.

The meaning of the designation New Right becomes even more complex in an international context. In France, the New Right is overtly racist, and cannot easily be distinguished from the racist and fascist groups which in Britain would be termed the far Right. In the USA, there are, as in Britain, a number of different strands in the New Right. These are discussed by Miriam David in chapter five. In spite of the fact that the political groupings are slightly different, so that the term neo-conservative does not mean quite the same thing in the American context, both she and David Edgar demonstrate that there are very close similarities, and indeed links, between the New Right in the USA and in Britain.

Considerable debate has taken place about the hypothesis that what is new about the New Right is not just that all these various (old) right-wing ideas are enjoying a new ascendancy, but that they have been welded together into a new ideological synthesis, whose political expression in Britain is Thatcherism. This is the position argued in *The Politics of Thatcherism,* in which the contributors share the assumption that Thatcherism exists as a new conjuncture whose novelty lies in the fusion of neo-liberal and neo-conservative ideas. Thus:

> The New Right is the seedbed from which Thatcherism has grown and is composed of two rather different strands. There is the revival of liberal political economy, which seeks the abandonment of Keynesianism and any kinds of government intervention; and there is a new populism – the focusing on issues like immigration, crime and punishment, strikes, social security abuse, taxation and bureaucracy. . . The real innovation of Thatcherism is the way it has linked traditional Conservative concern with the basis of authority in social institutions and the importance of internal order and external security, with a new emphasis upon re-establishing free markets and extending market criteria into new fields.[10]

Given the self-evident contradictions between freedom and authority, the claim that a new ideological synthesis has been forged bears closer inspection. A central theme of *The Ideology of the New Right* is the relationship between the ideological strands of neo-liberalism and neo-conservatism and an exploration of their coincidences and contradictions, both theoretically and in relation to political practice. Other authors, notably Jessop et al., are clearly right to remark on inconsistencies.[11] The two strands initially seem to imply, as chapter three shows, rather different forms of society. They also depend upon very different conceptions of human nature, the neo-liberal view having close parallels with sociobiology which is increasingly invoked in lay explanations of social inequalities. Neo-conservatism takes a much less biologically determined view of human nature, seeing it as essentially constructed by, and expressed in, social institutions, and defends this by mystical references to intuition. But both strands rely heavily upon 'human nature' as a legitimation of their political claims. In one respect, this does not distinguish the New Right from other political ideologies; all have implicit or explicit models of human nature, so that debates in this field always have politicial relevance.[12] In the case of the New Right, the references are explicit and involve contradictory positions. Several of the contributors to this volume show, however, that such contradictions do not necessarily lead to conflicting outcomes at the level of policy; and there are many areas where surface contradictions mask deeper continuities.

Adam Smith's view of the role of government is often cited as justification for the 'minimal state':

According to the system of natural liberty, the sovereign has only three duties to attend to . . . first, the duty of protecting the society from the violence and invasion of other independent societies; secondly, the duty of protecting, as far as possible, every member of society from the injustice or oppression of every other member of it, or the duty of establishing an exact administration of justice; and thirdly, the duty of erecting and maintaining certain publick works and certain publick institutions which it can never be for the interest of any individual, or small number of individuals to erect and maintain, because the profit could never repay the expence to any individual or small number of individuals, though it may frequently do much more than repay it to a great society.[13]

However, such a view, while not placing the same emphasis upon nation and patriotism as traditional conservatism does, has always allowed for a strong state in the areas of national security and law enforcement. The neo-liberals, being concerned primarily with economic matters, generally leave this implicit rather than explicit; yet the views of the Adam Smith Institute reveal few differences of substance, extending the concept of national security to include the promotion of national economic interests. For both strands, the Cold War is a vital ingredient. The national interest is situated within the NATO alliance, and opposed to the 'Red Menace', both in the form of the enemy without (the Soviet Union) and the enemy within. Andrew Belsey shows how, even in theory, major strands of neo-liberal ideology are hostile to the civil liberties of individuals, not because they are subordinate to the national interest as neo-conservatives would claim, but because they are subordinate to the preservation of the (natural) order of the market; and both Andrew Gamble and David Edgar similarly argue that the market can be seen as a source of discipline rather than freedom. In relation to family policy too, the neo-liberals are less explicit. But their unstated model of the family, albeit underpinned by a different theory of human nature, leads as Miriam David shows, to policies virtually identical with those of neo-conservatives; and this is true for both Britain and the USA. On all these matters, where polices do coincide, they coincide in ways which override the libertarian strand in neo-liberalism in favour of authoritarianism, bearing out Edgar's claim in 'Bitter Harvest' that despite the contradictions 'in the final conflict, it is the authoritarians who will win'.[14] Indeed, the conflict between libertarianism and Thatcherism is reflected in the disquiet in the Conservative Party at the increasing prominence of extreme libertarians in the Federation of Conservative Students.

In 'Bitter Harvest' and in his contribution to this volume, Edgar's discussion sheds some light on the relative silence of neo-liberals on social issues, particularly that of race, and thus contributes to an understanding of the differences between the New Right and the far Right. The logical position for both libertarians and free-marketeers is to oppose immigration controls and restrictions on the free movement of labour, but not to prevent discriminatory decisions by individuals. Enoch Powell tried to reconcile nationalism and free-market liberalism in terms that were, intellectually at least, less than convincing. Such reconciliation in relation to race has not since been a highly visible phenomenon. Edgar attributes this to the 'messy collapse' of the Monday Club following infiltration by the National Front in the 1970s, and the consequent determination of the National Association for Freedom, founded shortly afterwards, to avoid becoming embroiled in such issues. NAFF concentrated on economic issues, and 'went to great lengths to distance itself from racism and the National Front'; in so doing, it insisted on a basic political division, frequently reiterated, between individualism and collectivism, which equated communism and fascism and opposed free market liberalism to both.[15]

Neo-liberal silence on the issue of race has continued. It is much harder to detect implicit models of race in the *Omega File* than to do so for gender. Sociobiology of course, at least in some versions, has racist implications.[16] The main boundary to be examined between the New Right and the far Right — the overtly racist Right — is thus the distinction between neo-conservativism and racist groups and ideas. What is clear is that the neo-conservatives also seek to distance themselves from the National Front. The connections claimed by the television programme *Panorama* on 30 January 1984, between individual members of the Conservative Party — indeed, some Tory MPs — and overtly racist groups, would not belie this. The reaction of the Conservative Party to these allegations confirms its anxiety to insist upon its distance from the ideas and the disreputable tactics of the far Right. Gill Seidel's argument in chapter four suggests that the organizational links, or lack of them, are less important in terms of the effect on public consciousness than the continuities of discourse between New Right and far Right, and that the presence or absence of racist intent is substantially irrelevant; and even though contributors to the neo-conservative *Salisbury Review* seek to disown racism, their use of the concepts of culture and nation, and indeed the form of their denials of racism, facilitates the spread of racist sentiments. Such denials rest upon a redefinition of terms which itself involves levelling the charge of racism at the Left, a strategy encapsulated in the election slogan 'Labour says he's black, Tories say he's British'. The unacceptability of overt racism distinguishes the neo-conservative New Right from such groups as the National Front and and WISE (Welsh, Irish, Scottish and English), as indeed do other aspects of their policies; but this should not, as Seidel makes clear, lead to complacency. The New Right may not in itself be evidence of a major mobilization behind racist ideas, but may nevertheless contribute to a situation in which such mobilization would be possible. And the power of covert, cultural racism is demostrated by Margaret Thatcher's decision − reported in the press on 30 September 1985 − to invite Ray Honeyford to an exclusive high-level meeting at 10 Downing Street to discuss educational policy.

A further reason for arguing that there is something that distinguishes the New Right from the conservatism of the post-war era is the suggestion that it differs in the class composition of its main exponents, if not in the class interests that it serves. Thus the editorial in *The Sunday Times* on 12 May 1985, commenting on a caucus of Tory 'rebels' which it described as 'the grouse brigade' and as being 'distinguished for their wealth, wetness and country pursuits', continued:

> Britain's decline owes too much to the feeble efforts of our faded gentry for us to yearn for their return. If Mrs Thatcher has one virtue, it is to show the grit, energy and determination of the upwardly mobile on whom this country's fortunes depend . . . Mr Pym and his friends . . . are of a bygone era, when the grouse moor and the old school tie set the tone. That day is gone.

There are echoes in this of the New Right's own 'new class' model, which David Edgar discusses in chapter two, and which counterposes producers and parasites, the latter including both the old aristocracy and the whole of the public sector. In spite of the fact that some of the free-market pressure groups of the mid-1970s were clearly rooted in the middle classes, it is not possible to account for the different strands of neo-liberalism and neo-conservatism by invoking an obvious class difference in their proponents. It would appear to be true that the ideologues of the Adam Smith Institute, several of whom attended St. Andrews University, are indeed upwardly mobile; but then so is Roger Scruton, albeit via Oxbridge. An analysis of the Tories newly elected to Parliament in 1983, compared with previous cohorts, again showed a difference in class background, suggesting an element of upward mobility there too, a marked decline in the proportion educated at public school and/or Oxbridge and virtually no association with farming.[17] And the strand of repressive puritanism has also been shown to be rooted in a particular sector of the lower middle class.[18]

Upward mobility is however hardly an adequate explanation. Examination would undoubtedly show that most of the critics of the New Right have also experienced this. Nor is it sufficient to argue that the New Right is in some sense expressive of middle-class interests. The ideologies designated New Right have become extremely pervasive; substantial numbers of the unemployed voted conservative in 1983. There is no one-to-one relationship between social location and ideology, or even 'interest'; for the social role of ideology, as is discussed below, is precisely to interpret experience and to construct those interests. To some extent, the question of the social support for particular ideas and the question of whose material interests are actually served by them, are separate issues. It is precisely because New Right ideology, in its various forms, has become influential beyond obviously definable social groups, that it is necessary to combat it in its own terms, as an ideology.

The Left and the New Right

Whether the continuities between neo-liberals and neo-conservatives are sufficient to confirm the notion of a new synthesis, or whether the remaining contradictions refute this, is not merely a matter of empirical description. For what is also in dispute is the role of this new ideology in producing the electoral results of 1979 and 1983, and more generally, the characterization of such explanations as forms of idealism. Thus, Jessop et al. criticize the contributors to *The Politics of Thatcherism*, and Stuart Hall in particular, for attributing Thatcher's victories 'to the initiatives of the New Right in constructing a new hegemonic project and mobilizing popular support for a right-wing solution to the economic and political crisis', and call this a 'celebration of Thatcherism'.[19] They argue that this both overstates the degree of support for the New Right among the electorate, and the importance of ideology to the policies of, and support for, Thatcherism.

The criticism is important, for Gramsci's concept of hegemony has been used both by the Left and by the New Right to describe what is taking place; and it is a concept which can mislead its users into placing too much emphasis on the role of ideology in the social process. Misappropiated by the New Right, it is taken to mean that culture is the real arena of struggle; misunderstood by the Left, it can imply that the real problem of Thatcherism is simply that the Right won this battle of ideas.

Gramsci did indeed stress the role of ideology in class domination. In so doing, he made a distinction between state and civil society which is complex and not altogether consistent, complicating the notion of hegemony. It is a view which places great emphasis upon ideological struggle, but it does not reduce class struggle to a battle of ideas. The concept of hegemony has however been taken from Gramsci and used to refer to ideological dominance in a way which is quite compatible with the idealist view that social and political change derives from ideas. Curiously, even the critics of 'ideologism' occasionally fall into this trap; one of the objections made by Jessop et al. to the 'celebration of Thatcherism' is that it overlooks the inconsistencies in New Right thought. Yet is it only from an idealist position that it could appear even remotely plausible that logical contradictions in themselves undermine the strength of Thatcherism. And even from such a standpoint, given the lack of logical coherence required by common-sense ideologies, contradictions may be a strength rather than a weakness, enabling the New Right to switch the grounds of its legitimations at will. It is in fact only where the logical contradictions produce conflicts at the level of policy that the strength of Thatcherism would thereby be reduced.

Although there are dangers in focusing on the ideology of the New Right, particularly the danger of at least appearing to share an idealist position with the New Right itself, it remains the case that that ideology does need to be examined and combated on its own terms. An interpretation of the New Right derived from Hall's work, and thus indirectly from Gramsci, argues that the New Right has adopted an explicitly ideological strategy and has been successful in mobilizing at least sufficient support from a range of social groups to remain in power. Its political defeat requires an understanding of how the New Right has managed to do this, and how that process might be reversed.

There are three other areas in which the celebration of Thatcherism has been argued to concede too much to the New Right itself. Firstly, the claim that the rise of the New Right is attributable to the failure of socialism. Secondly, the claim that it addresses people's real needs and experiences in a way which the Left fails to do. And thirdly, the suggestion that the New Right has succeeded in its hegemonic project so that we are all Thatcherites now. It is my contention that left-wing commentators on the New Right do at times inadvertently make such concessions – and indeed that the success of the New Right in setting the political agenda makes it difficult not to do so. It is instructive to examine the ways in which members of the Left thus give hostages to fortune; but, as we shall see, this does not mean that their analyses are fundamentally invalid, nor, of course, that they are closet supporters of the New Right.

The Politics of Thatcherism in fact locates the rise of the New Right in Britain in an historical context whose key features are the crisis in the world capitalist economy and Britain's long-term decline in relation to that economy, the resumption of the Cold War and the breakdown of the post-war social democratic consensus. It is in relation to the last factor that serious misconceptions are being promulgated. The breakdown of this consensus is attributed to the failure of the welfare state, equated with a failure of socialism, or at least 'state socialism'. The problem is the characterization of the post-war consensus as 'state socialism'. In 1979, before the election of the first Thatcher government, Hall characterized the post-war era as one of state monopoly capitalism.[20] More recently, commentators including Hall have tended to refer to it, as the New Right does, as a period of state socialism. The problem is compounded by the fact that the New Right has hi-jacked left-wing criticisms of the limitations of the welfare state – its bureaucracy, its intrusiveness, its failure to help those most in need – for its own purposes, making it difficult for the Left to voice such criticisms in ways which do not lend support to the New Right's own project of dismantling the welfare state. This leads to disconcerting similarities between commentators on the New Right and the New Right itself.

Thus, in a special issue of *New Internationalist*, Dexter Tiranti argues that negative experiences of the welfare state have been widespread and crucial:

> far too many people have experienced [the extension of the welfare state] not as helping them but as an intrusion on their personal

freedom . . . what they remember from their everyday experience of welfare is the way they are reduced to a client status. They remember real or imagined humiliations. They remember waiting.[21]

David Held and John Keane, in an article which sets out to explore socialist alternatives to the welfare state, go further. The 'dwindling popularity' of the Keynesian welfare state, or what they call 'state-administered socialism', derived from the 'actual experience of those in daily contact with the welfare state'. Socialism encouraged the passive consumption of state provision and undermined people's confidence to direct their own lives: 'this "passivity" was necessary to the achievement of socialism by gradually extending networks of intrusive state power into civil society'. Their most extreme claim is perhaps that 'socialists who call for less bureaucracy have failed, with few exceptions, to recognise that some positive things can be learned by engaging the New Right, which has taken the lead in popularising the demand for less state action'.[22]

Such descriptions are familiar, and familiar above all from the New Right's own descriptions of the failure of the post-war consensus/welfare state/socialism and Keynesian economics. It is ironic that the New Right repeats criticisms of that welfare state which have come from the Left over many years. This can be seen clearly in the opening sections of the Adam Smith Institute's report *The Omega File: Health Policy* (and Tiranti includes the National Health Service among the 'pervasive and giant welfare systems' to which he claims there is 'increasing hostility',[23] in spite of the fact that widespread public support for the NHS forced Thatcher to insist that it was safe in Conservative hands). The ASI's argument is that the only justification for any welfare services, including the NHS, is that they aid those who could not afford to buy such services for themselves; but stress is laid on the fact that it is not the poor, but the middle class, who make greatest use of the NHS. Titmuss himself is invoked in support of this claim:

> the higher-income groups know how to make better use of the NHS. They tend to receive more specialist attention, occupy more of the beds in better-equipped and staffed hospitals; receive more elective surgery; have better maternity care, and are more likely to get psychiatric help than low-income groups – particularly the unskilled.[24]

The report draws attention to queues for operations such as hip replacements, deaths through inadequate provision for renal dialysis, and regional inequalities. It even notes, albeit in the past tense, the fact that 'health problems of the poor arose from their inability to build up and sustain good health by the purchase of an adequate diet',[25] making the elimination of poverty a priority; and argues that the NHS has not produced a measurable improvement in the nation's health. Like Tiranti, the report blames the bureaucratic nature of the system and, following Illich, the 'fact' that it is therefore run in the interests of administrators rather than patients. 'People on all sides' it says 'are agreed about its shortcomings'[26] – so let us privatize it. Held and Keane of course would not dream of advocating the privatization of the NHS, and their intentions are quite different from those of the ASI; but the example they use of allowing parents to set up their own schools, initially at their own expense, is in some respects not too far distant from the ASI's own proposals for the education system, discussed in chapter three.

'Bitter experiences of the welfare state' have almost certainly been less dominant in relation to the NHS than the benefits system, where there has been much dissatisfaction. But it is dangerously wrong to follow the New Right in attributing this to the failure of socialism. The 'post-war consensus', the framework within which the welfare state was established, was never a socialist consensus; there was never, as Tiranti claims, 'agreement that equality was a good thing'.[27] Indeed, many socialist criticisms of the system hinged precisely upon the contradiction between the goals of welfare, in particular the abolition of poverty, and the capitalist context which requires that there be no more than a limited alleviation of poverty. Failures of the welfare state, from this point of view, are failures of welfare capitalism, not failures of socialism. It is salutary to remember, however, that if the achievements of welfare capitalism have necessarily been limited, they have also been real. The welfare state has afforded working people genuine protection against destitution resulting from unemployment, illness, or old age; constructed a health service free at point of use; and provided the possibility of free education to degree level and beyond. True, the funding has been inadequate and the benefits grossly unevenly distributed. But it has been a real defence, nevertheless; and its dismantling is a real attack. The attack on welfare provision, in which sections of the Left are inadvertently colluding, is an integral part of a more general anti-socialism, fundamental to the Thatcherite argument that 'there is no alternative'. This operates on a national and international scale, so that there is an intrinsic connection between Cold War rhetoric and the domestic hegemonic project. The ASI thus argues that we should defend ourselves against the 'Russian Threat', since the economic inefficiency and failure of socialism is likely to lead the Soviet Union to seek to undermine Western economic development. Because of the role of anti-socialism in New Right ideology, there is a danger of concessions like those of Held and Keane, and Tiranti, turning into something of an 'own goal' for the Left.

Further parallels between the Left and the New Right can be found in the argument that the success of the New Right can be explained by its addressing the real needs of ordinary people, in a way the Left has failed to do. Thus Tiranti says that the New Right's success results from the fact that it has 'addressed deep-seated needs of ordinary people', and argues that the appeal of the free market, the return to Victorian values, monetarism and nationalism lay in the fact that they provided solutions to problems the Left could not tackle. 'People's own experience' of supermarkets and the consumer culture 'showed the market could provide, and it was popular'. The appeal of authoritarianism and Victorian values was 'grounded in very real fears of social chaos'. And in the fight against inflation, the New Right could wheel in 'the intellectual coherence of Milton Friedman and von Hayek'.[28] But the Right claim exactly the same thing. Thus Alfred Sherman, erstwhile advisor to Mrs Thatcher, wrote in *The Guardian* on 11 February 1985 that 'Ideas from Hayek and Friedman . . . were assimilated precisely because experience had already created a place for them by convincing people that neo-Keynesian economics, trade-union hegemony and the permissive society had failed'. This position is sometimes attributed to Stuart Hall, not least, perhaps, because Tiranti's editorial appears to be largely a superficial rehash of an earlier article by Hall in *Marxism Today*;[29] Hall's position however, is, as we shall see, different in important respects, and considerably more sophisticated.

In so far as the anti-welfarism of the New Right has a popular appeal, it emphatically does not have this appeal because it provides solutions which meet people's needs or speak directly to their experiences. Such an interpretation misconstrues the nature of 'needs' and 'experiences'. Tiranti implicitly but uncomprehendingly concedes this in the phrase 'they remember real or imagined humiliations';[30] it is not events in themselves which expose needs to which solutions can be offered. Rather, experiences and needs are constructed through the interpretation of events so that they are always mediated by ideology. This does not mean that events are irrelevant, and needs and experiences fantasies. But for solutions to appeal, they must be preceded or accompanied by descriptions of experiences and needs which render the solutions apparently relevant. Hall recognizes this process, and is adamant that what is involved in the appeal of New Right ideology is the *misdescription* of needs and experiences in order to impose *pseudo-solutions* which are in fact deleterious to the interests of the people concerned. Thus while he does argue that the Right has been able to 'connect its message with some of the actual, real discontents which people were experiencing under Labour',[31] and includes among these discontents the fact that the welfare state 'is experienced by masses of ordinary people, in the very moment they are benefiting from it, as an intrusive, managerial, bureaucratic force in their lives',[32] he recognizes the parallels between this claim and the claims of the New Right, and the consequent dangers. The experience of the state is contradictory; and while the dissatisfactions are real enough, the New Right has been able to harness 'these popular discontents to its cause' because 'Thatcherism . . . misdescribes and misexplains them' and 'its remedies for the problem are fictitious'.[33] The connections that are made by the New Right are not 'natural' or necessary, for 'they represent an attempt to inflect and expropriate and absorb what are often democratic currents into free market channels'.[34] It must be said that Hall comes perilously close to the position adopted by Held and Keane, and by Tiranti, but is redeemed by the explicit recognition that the New Right's connection with need and experiences is illusory.

Similarly, the Right's arguments in favour of greater discipline (imposed either through policing or through the family), to which David Edgar refers, did not in any simple sense relate to 'very real fears of social chaos'. Those fears had first to be constructed, and indeed this process of construction was analysed in *Policing the Crisis*.[35] While it has subsequently been argued that both the risk and the fear of crime should be taken more seriously by the Left, there is little doubt that such fears, especially the fear of general social breakdown, are exaggerated and cultivated by media coverage of events like the 1981 riots and the mass picketing of the 1984-5 miners' strike, and are used to justify policing methods involving serious erosions of civil liberties.

It is arguable that even Hall's argument overstates the success of the New Right's hegemonic project, if it is taken to imply that (even though we have been misled) we are all Thatcherites now. Plenty of evidence can be cited to show that this is not true, from the publication of survey data on British social attitudes at the time of the 1983 election,[36] and much subsequent opinion-poll data, through widespread protests against privatization in the NHS, to the massive resistance of mining communities, followed by the teachers' industrial action. It is myopic to draw too much comfort from this evidence of opposition. Hegemony does not require that all of the people are convinced all of the time, only enough of the people enough of the time. The argument that there is no dominant ideology because it can be demonstrated that different people believe different things, and moreover the same people believe different things in different contexts, and act in ways that are at odds with the views expressed to survey researchers, misses the point. A dominant ideology is dominant not just by its receipt of a majority vote, but because it is propagated and supported by the institutions of civil society and the state. It requires a degree of assent, which it is well placed to elicit; but more importantly, it must prevent the formation of coherent counter-ideologies. The centrality of anti-socialism to the New Right project is not fortuitous. On these criteria, the hegemonic project of the New Right must be deemed to have had some success even if large numbers of people are ignorant of, or indifferent or antipathetic to, aspects of New Right ideology.

The process of delegitimation of socialist alternatives is crucial, and explains otherwise strange phenomena. In chapter four, Gill Seidel demonstrates the ideological reversals whereby contributors to *The Salisbury Review* accuse their opponents of racism. The function of this, especially in Scruton's ostensibly whimsical *Times* columns, is not to make out a serious and convincing case that, for example, the proponents of multicultural education are racist; it merely operates to discredit critics, using whatever means are available. The New Right's success in delegitimating socialism is such that Hall himself has argued for a rethinking of socialism in terms of the 'new impetus towards choice, the new spirit of pluralism and diversity, which has become such a driving force of the masses under advanced capitalism'; for 'why else should the toiling masses under capitalism ever commit themselves to an alternative which offers them *less* than they can currently get?'.[37] Is it really true that even state socialism or welfare capitalism offer the masses something less desirable than what is currently available — mass unemployment, increasing poverty, progressive de-industrialization and all the other effects of Thatcherism? Does Thatcherism really offer them more choice?

Clearly, there is a problem of analysts of the New Right 'celebrating' Thatcherism, and even reinforcing the views they set out to criticize. But these dangers are certainly not inherent in a mode of analysis which pays attention to ideology. Hall's argument that the New Right has adopted an ideological strategy to mobilize electoral support is quite consistent with the recognition that 'Thatcherism is not universally popular' and has 'never commanded universal assent on the political scene'.[38] Far from implying that this means the Left must make concessions to a new right-wing consensus, Hall argues that what is required is a counter-hegemonic project to create an alternative vision of a socialist future and establish an alternative socialist common sense. Over the last few years, there has been renewed debate about the potential role of utopian constructs. The strength of such a view is that it recognizes the explicit intentions of the New Right, and recognizes that, since needs and experiences are constructed, there is no natural constituency for socialism, that support for socialism has to be built, and that the role of ideology in this is central. The weakness is that it is vulnerable to charges of idealism or 'ideologism'.

Firstly, it can be alleged that Hall's thesis equates Thatcherism with its hegemonic project and implies that all policies derive from the ideology. But the thesis is not, in fact, an explanation of policies at all; rather, it is an explanation of how the electorate has been persuaded to give sufficient support to a set of extremely damaging policies which are not in their interests, and which represent an attack on the living standards of large sections of the population, both immediately and in the forseeable future. Secondly, it can be argued that the stress on creating an alternative vision gives ideology a privileged role in the politicial process. This is to misunderstand the nature of ideology and hence the nature of both the Right's hegemony and the Left's necessary counter-hegemonic project. Ideologies become rooted in communities by their capacity to order daily practice. Ruling groups consequently have a head start over the rest of us, not only because they control (though they may) the institutions of civil society but because their control of the state exerts a (sometimes coercive) control over the range of practices available. This is not simply because certain forms of activity are illegal: more importantly, the economic and social constraints of daily life derive from both state and civil society. Hegemony is rooted in both.

The implication of this is that the counter-hegemonic process is of necessity rooted in practice as well. Constructing a positive image of socialism is not an abstract exercise, but one necessarily rooted in political struggle – although it does not automatically arise out of that struggle. The capacity of the 1984-5 miners' strike to create an alternative common sense about the economics of pit closures, and collective rather than individualistic means of coping with extreme hardship, is a clear example of this relationship. The difficulty of extending that common sense beyond the mining communities, even within the organized labour movement, and of mobilizing active support for the strike, demonstrates the extent of the ideological work which, over a period of decades, has not been done because ideology was not taken seriously. Raymond Williams has pointed to the need for a new vision of socialism to be rooted in democratic practices and in the struggles in which people are actually engaged. Hall's discussion of the Greater London Council – not just its policies, but its procedures – supports this view.

One of the reasons why the position adopted by Hall and Williams is contentious is that it has implications for the role of the 'new social forces', and consequently for the much-debated issue of 'alliances' against Thatcherism. Williams says that the process of constructing a new socialist vision 'must be deeply sited among women, or it will not . . . occur at all'.[39] Hall commends the GLC for acknowledging 'the necessary autonomy of the different social movements – blacks, women, neighbourhood groups, welfare rights organisations, gay people' and others; and remarks of Neil Kinnock 'no one who thinks feminism and the women's movement is a bit of a joke will lead Labour towards socialism in this century'.[40] For some writers, emphasis on the 'new social forces' is predicated on disillusionment with the prospects of the working class carrying out its historic role as the midwife of socialism. Consequently, there has also been reassertion of the importance of class politics and the key role of the trade union movement, as opposed to the dubious reliance upon these new movements.[41] What is at issue here, as Hall observes, is the composition of the working class, which is diverse and constantly changing; and whether the energies of the 'new social forces' can be absorbed into and subordinated to existing structures of the 'organized working class' (i.e. the trade union movement), or whether those structures must themselves change. Hall says 'It is impossible to forsee a point when all those struggles and movements come into line inside the already established hierarchy of social forces that constitute the existing labour movement . . . and resolve in the great scheme of things to . . . wait in turn, women behind men, blacks

behind women, gays behind everybody'.[42] The counter-hegemonic
project involves the construction and communication of a vision of
an alternative way of life which recognizes and reconciles, but does
not subordinate, the interests of different groups.

Conclusion

Recognizing that the struggle is not *just* a battle of ideas means
recognizing also the limits of this book. In examining the structure
of the New Right's ideology, we are not suggesting that this is all
that needs to be said, still less that the logical contradictions between
its various strands will be its downfall. Understanding the ideology
is a necessary, but by no means sufficient, condition for combating
it. If the ascendancy of the New Right is to be even undermined,
let alone destroyed, by internal contradictions, these will be
contradictions not at the level of legitimations, but at the level of
policy; and several of the contributions to this volume show that
the conflicts here are less acute. And even at this level, the conflicts
of policy would have to coincide with conflicts of interest between
different key sectors of support for Thatcherism, particularly
different fractions of the ruling class itself, in order to have a
disruptive effect. To focus upon the ideas which sustain the New
Right is not to underestimate the importance of the economic context
in which they occur and the class interests which they defend.

This is particularly important in understanding the international
dimension of the New Right. It is an international phenomenon in
more senses than one. Similar ideological and political trends can
be located throughout Western Europe and the USA (though
interestingly they are much less apparent in Canada). This is not just
because all are affected by the crisis of world capitalism. There are
also deliberately cultivated links between the organizations and
ideologues of the New Right: both between intellectuals through such
bodies as the Mont Pelerin Society, and between politicians, as in
Thatcher's International Union of Democrats (IUD) – that intra-
uterine device to prevent the conception of socialism in the womb
of capitalism. The ideological differences, such as the much greater
dominance of evangelical Christianity in the USA, relate primarily
to the characteristics of the different markets to which New Right
policies have to be sold; but since the ideology is not *just* a marketing

device, this does have an effect upon outcomes as well. The common themes of nationalism, anti-Sovietism, surveillance and suppression of 'subversion', neo-liberal economics and anti-feminism are fundamental to New Right ideology throughout the Western world. In addition, despite rhetorical variations, the repressive and moralistic elements hitherto more prevalent in the USA are becoming increasingly central to the New Right project in Britain, as Miriam David demonstrates. A close examination of New Right ideology suggests that if the Left fails to develop a successful counter-hegemonic project, the implications are worse than even current Thatcherite practice would indicate.

Although the chapters in this book can be read separately, they are designed to be read in the order in which they appear. The first chapter, by Andrew Gamble, examines the different strands of economic thought which constitute the neo-liberal strand of the New Right; little mention is made here of the authoritarianism of the neo-conservatives, as this is the central theme of David Edgar's argument in chapter two. This division of labour does not represent a disagreement between the authors about the significance of both strands. The third chapter explores the contradictions and continuities between these two strands, with particular reference to recent reports produced by the Adam Smith Institute; it shows that although there are surprising overlaps between neo-liberals and neo-conservatives, including their common reliance on 'human nature' as a legitimation, they take very different views of what human nature is. The issue of racism is taken up by Gill Seidel in relation to neo-conservative thought (epitomized in *The Salisbury Review*) which is compared with the racism of the French New Right. The last two chapters, by Miriam David on the family, and Andrew Belsey on civil liberties, explore the implications of New Right thought in its various manifestations for politics in these crucially important areas.

Since the contributors are discussing current events, the situation will inevitably have changed by the time this book is published. Almost every edition of *The Guardian* reports a further erosion of civil liberties. Although the Thatcher government is, since the 1985 budget, doing rather worse in the opinion polls, the picture nevertheless looks bleak. For even if the Conservative Party were to lose the next election, not due until 1988, the institutional havoc

which has already been wreaked is appalling; and the ideological shift
which the New Right has brought about remains to be reversed. The
purpose of this book is to contribute to an understanding of the New
Right – and thus to contribute to that reversal.

Notes

1 N. Bosanquet, *After the New Right* (Heinemann, London, 1983);
   S. Hall and M. Jacques (eds), *The Politics of
   Thatcherism*(Lawrence and Wishart, London, 1983).
2 Bosanquet, *After the New Right*, p. 1.
3 Ibid., p. 7.
4 Ibid., p. 13.
5 Cited in E. Butler, *Hayek* (Temple Smith, London, 1983), p. 27.
6 A number of the groups existing in the mid-1970s, both neo-
   liberal and moral reform groups, are discussed in R. King and
   N. Nugent (eds) *Respectable Rebels* (Hodder and Stoughton,
   London, 1979).
7 F. A. Hayek, *Law, Legislation and Liberty*, vol. II (Routledge
   and Kegan Paul, London, 1976), p. 44.
8 K. Mannheim, *Ideology and Utopia* (Routledge and Kegan Paul,
   London, 1936), p. 208.
9 See M. Barker (ed.), *The Video Nasties*, (Pluto, London, 1984).
10 A. Gamble, 'Thatcherism and Conservative politics', in *The
   Politics of Thatcherism*, ed. Hall and Jacques; pp. 113 and 121.
11 B. Jessop et al., 'Authoritarian populism, two nations, and
   Thatcherism', *New Left Review*, 147 (1984), pp. 32-60.
12 This point is elaborated and illustrated in I. Forbes and S. Smith
   (eds), *Politics and Human Nature* (Frances Pinter, London,
   1984).
13 A. Smith, *The Wealth of Nations*, bk. IV, ch. ix. (Clarendon
   Press, Oxford, 1976), pp. 687-8.
14 D. Edgar, 'Bitter Harvest', in *The Future of the Left*, ed. J.
   Curran (Polity Press/New Socialist, Cambridge, 1984), p. 40.
15 Ibid., pp. 41-3.
16 See M. Barker, *The New Racism* (Junction Books, London,
   1981).
17 'Tory MP's: The new breed', *Labour Research*, Aug. 1983.
18 D. Cliff, 'Religion, morality and the middle class', in King and
   Nugent (eds), *Respectable Rebels*, pp. 127-52.

19 Jessop et al., 'Authoritarian populism', pp. 32-3.
20 S. Hall, 'The great moving Right show', *Marxism Today*, Jan. 1979, p. 18.
21 D. Tiranti, 'The big clampdown', *New Internationalist*, 133 (Mar. 1984), pp. 7-8.
22 D. Held and J. Keane, 'Socialism and the limits of state action', in Curran (ed.), *The Future of the Left*, pp. 170-72.
23 Tiranti, 'The big clampdown', p. 8.
24 *The Omega File: Health policy* (Adam Smith Institute, London, 1984), p. 3.
25 Ibid., p. 7.
26 Ibid., p. 2.
27 Tiranti, 'The big clampdown', p. 7.
28 Ibid., pp. 8-9.
29 S. Hall, 'The culture gap', *Marxism Today*, Jan. 1984, pp. 18-22.
30 Tiranti, 'The big clampdown', p. 8.
31 S. Hall, 'Faith, hope or clarity', *Marxism Today*, Jan. 1985, p. 17.
32 S. Hall, 'The state – socialism's old caretaker', *Marxism Today*, Nov. 1984, p. 24.
33 Ibid., p. 27.
34 Hall, 'The culture gap', p. 22.
35 S. Hall et al. (eds), *Policing the Crisis* (Macmillan, London, 1978); see also the analysis of the concept of 'genuine fears' in Barker, *The New Racism*, ch. 2.
36 R. Jowell and C. Airey (eds), *British Social Attitudes: The 1984 report* (Gower, Aldershot, 1984).
37 Hall, 'The state – socialism's old caretaker', p. 28.
38 Hall, 'Faith, hope or clarity', p. 17.
39 R. Williams, *Problems in Materialism and Culture* (Verso, London, 1980), p. 272.

40 S. Hall, 'Face the future', *New Socialist*, 19 (Sept. 1984), p. 37; S. Hall, 'Labour's love still lost', *New Socialist*, 15 (Jan./Feb. 1984), p. 7.
41 B. Fine et al. (eds), *Class Politics: An answer to its critics* (Leftover Pamphlets, London, 1984). For a discussion of this position, see E. Hobsbawn, 'The retreat into extremism', *Marxism Today*, Apr. 1985, pp. 7-12.
42 Hall, 'Faith, hope or clarity', p. 19.

Chapter One

The Political Economy of Freedom

ANDREW GAMBLE

The Flight from Political Economy

There are few fields where New Right ideas have had such impact as economic policy. Their influence has been particularly marked in Britain and the USA. Most well-known of all New Right ideas is the doctrine of monetarism, which has been widely disseminated in recent years. Although the term originated within a technical debate on the role of money in the economy, it is often now used as the label for a much wider set of New Right economic analyses and prescriptions. It has been attacked strongly as a result. Some monetarists object to the broader implications of the label. Samuel Brittan complains that 'the campaign of vilification has been so successful that many educated citizens believe the principal tenet of "monetarism" to be support for Latin American dictatorships employing torture. Those of a more charitable disposition suppose it to be a label for hardships deliberately imposed on people by governments to punish them for laziness or poor productivity.'[1]

Others have urged that monetarism is as value-free as any other doctrine in economics and can logically be accepted by left-wing socialists as well as right-wing conservatives. From this standpoint New Right economics is not about economics at all but about politics. It is merely a coincidence, it is suggested, that many leading monetarists happen to be advocates of free market solutions to problems of economic policy while many Keynesians favour government intervention. The confusion arises because of the desire of most economists to hold to a distinction between political economy and economic analysis; between the principles which should govern public policy and value-free generalizations which form the body of knowledge of scientific economics.[2] In the last hundred years, with the organization of economics as a profession and its international acceptance as an academic discipline, most economists have concentrated on economic analysis and ignored political economy as part of the prehistory of the subject.

New Right economics marks the rediscovery and reinvigoration of a crusading liberal political economy on the one hand, as well as explicit attempts to associate economics as an academic discipline with a new consensus on key policy issues. This project requires that Keynesian economics and all forms of socialist economics be discredited and that there is a conscious return not only to the key themes of nineteenth-century liberal political economy, but also to the emphasis which neo-classical economics placed on microeconomics.

Neo-classical economics is a vague term most often applied to the pre-Keynesian orthodoxy which dominated economics for fifty years after 1880, and which owed much to the independent development of 'marginalism' by Jevons, Walras, and Menger. The 'marginal revolution' led to a significant redrawing and consequent narrowing of the boundaries of the subject.[3] The historical and institutional analysis which played an important part in classical political economy was filtered out and economists began to concentrate on deductive theory − the working out of the logic of choice for the self-interested, utility-maximizing and hence rational individual. The new subjective theory of value that arose not only overthrew all cost-of-production and labour theories of value; it allowed the nature of the economic problem and therefore the subject-matter of economics to be stated with much greater precision. Economics became the study of scarcity, how scarce means with alternative uses could best be allocated between various ends. As Lionel Robbins expressed it:[4]

> From the point of view of the economist, the conditions of human existence exhibit four fundamental characteristics. The ends are various. The time and the means for achieving these ends are limited and capable of alternative application. At the same time the ends have different importance.

In this way economics could aspire to universality, and develop an analysis that was neither time-bound nor place-bound − a science of the economic aspect of action.

This development in economics has often been described by Marxists as a retreat from the problems of analysing the nature of capitalism as a particular historical economic system, with its own laws of development and internal structures that made it different from other systems. Concentration instead on how the price system effected the co-ordination of the immensely complex division of labour allowed capitalism to be presented as a rational and socially beneficial system. Since its reasoning was entirely circular on the relationship between value and price, the new subjective theory of value gave legitimacy to the existing distribution of income, and in particular to the share of income accruing to the owners of capital as dividends, interest and rent, as their just and necessary reward which permitted an efficient allocation of resources. It gave no basis for criticizing existing economic institutions such as private ownership of capital. Many Marxists were scornful of the turn from historical and institutional economics. Bukharin regarded marginalism as economics for rentiers.[5]

Yet the motivation of those who developed marginalist analysis was not aimed at providing a new legitimation for capitalism or an answer to the socialists. The Austrian school, the followers of Carl Menger, were most active in trying to refute socialism. For most of the neo-classical economists marginalist analysis was welcomed precisely because it appeared to offer an escape from the problems of deciding the principles that should guide public policy and how to justify existing economic arrangements into pure logical analysis of a set of abstract problems.

The Collectivist Challenge

The increasing division between liberal political economy and economic analysis did not spell the end of the former. It remained the most influential doctrine in practical policy-making, but it came under increasing challenge from other doctrines of political economy which rejected economic individualism and laissez-faire. The most thorough-going attack came from the socialists who rejected private ownership of the means of production and called for the abolition of wage labour, money and commodity production. But the principles of liberal economy were also challenged by many other critics. As the problems of modern economies multiplied, so the arguments for laissez-faire and economic individualism were discredited. State intervention came to be justified in an ever-increasing number of cases to tackle particular problems for which markets seemed to have no solution. Many groups in Britain contributed to the elaboration of the case for collectivist and governmental solutions to problems of economic and social policy. The Fabians and the New Liberals were particularly prominent.[6]

The doctrines of laissez-faire were tenacious and were never completely defeated. But in several areas of policy they were significantly modified or rejected in the first half of the twentieth century. A combination of the new collectivist doctrines, the political pressures of an enlarged democracy and the particular problems with which policy-makers had to deal, favoured the adoption of collectivist measures and institutions. The battles were fought over welfare and poverty, over unemployment, over industrial efficiency and social justice. The supporters of economic liberalism were gradually isolated. To many of them the collectivist advance seemed unstoppable.

In Britain leading Liberals like Keynes and Beveridge were key figures in making the case for an extension of public intervention in particular areas. The doctrines of sound money and of the balanced budget were discredited. The case for state provision of welfare services and state redistribution of income and wealth gained increasing acceptance. The need for governments to regulate modern industry either through monitoring agencies or through direct public ownership was also advanced. The result was a steady if rather incoherent and uncoordinated growth in public responsibilities, public agencies and public spending. By the 1950s the foundations of capitalist economy were still intact but the system had been greatly modified by the extensive role for public intervention that had developed. Governments were responsible for the general economic condition of the whole economy, for the public provision of many goods and services and for the transfer through the tax system of many incomes. The limits of government involvement in the economy were hotly disputed, but that government should have a major interventionist role was not. Those who kept alive the ideals of liberal politicial economy seemed to belong to a different age.[7]

Post-war collectivism fell far short of socialism, but it was an important modification of free market capitalism. Yet the new institutions and policies received considerable support from neo-classical economists. Apart from the Austrian school the dominant strands of neo-classical economics had never denied the economic rationality of socialism. True to their conception of the universal nature of the economic problem, some neo-classical economists were happy to apply their analytical techniques to the problems of resource allocation and price determination in a socialist economy, defined as one in which all means of production were publicly owned, as well as to analysing the case of market failure in a competitive market system.[8] The neo-classical notion of an equilibrium to which a market always returned was often attacked as ideological. But although it was often used to justify the existing economic system, it could also be used to direct attention to the way in which real world markets failed to clear (to balance demand and supply) and how this made government intervention legitimate. The very absoluteness of the assumptions of neo-classical economics meant that in the real world, government policies could be justified to create artificially the conditions which would exist under a regime of perfect competition. Such arguments were used to challenge the notion that markets were naturally harmonious and self-adjusting, further weakening the policy of laissez-faire.

The picture should not be overdrawn. The ideological ascendancy of Keynesianism and collectivist welfare policies was always much greater than their domination in practice.[9] The market economy continued to function and, although the state played a much larger role, the basic institutions of the economy remained capitalist.[10] With the onset of the Cold War the onslaught against socialism resumed, and a sharp distinction in both political economy and political sociology was drawn between the limited collectivism of the capitalist democracies and the totalitarian order of the Soviet bloc.

Such qualifications are necessary to make a proper estimation of the rise of the New Right. The great collectivist tide which the ideologues of the New Right love to depict themselves swimming against was never as mighty as they pretend. Focusing on which ideas and which doctrines are intellectually fashionable at any one time can be very misleading. The network of institutions, the structure of social relations and the impact of contingency and circumstances are all more important in determining how policies emerge and are implemented.

The Revival of Liberal Political Economy

New Right economics has become a broad and rapidly expanding field. At the forefront is the revival of the doctrines of liberal political economy and a wholesale attack upon all collectivist systems of political economy. From the start this has had a strong policy focus. The New Right has set out to change the agenda in economic and social policy. New Right economists argue for market solutions to economic problems and reject governmental ones. Their general catechism – markets good, governments bad – unites all strands of economic liberalism.

The revival of liberal political economy has gone much further however than the advocacy of free market policies. It also encompasses broad philosophical and theoretical discourses about the nature of the economy and its relationship with the state. Three major strands may be distinguished, although they overlap at times. The first is the most straightforward and easily understood. It is the doctrine of economic individualism which has always ·flourished so vigorously in the USA. This is traditional laissez-faire economics which assumes without question that markets are beneficial and governments harmful and that individual freedom and government action exist in inverse ratio to each other. The best-ordered economy is therefore one in which scope for individual choice is greatest and scope for government responsibility smallest. The level of taxation is the most important measure of this. The more taxed citizens are, the less free. Such notions connect with ideas of self-help, self-reliance, competition and personal responsibility. Few of these ideas are new. Herbert Spencer expressed most of them with brutal clarity: 'Is it not manifest that there must exist in our midst an immense amount of misery which is a normal result of misconduct, and ought not to be dissociated from it?'[11]

A second strand is libertarianism, which bases its case for laissez-faire capitalism on moral grounds. One of the best-known statements of this position is made. by Robert Nozick.[12] He argues that the minimal state, the state which protects the lives and property of its citizens, can be justified, but nothing beyond the minimal state. Any use of the state's coercive powers beyond this minimum infringes individual rights. Under this definition all taxation becomes forced labour. Other libertarians go further and argue against even the minimal state on the grounds that not everyone is willing or able to pay for protection of life and property by state agencies and that therefore collective provision of these things involves illegitimate coercion by the state. Libertarianism carries hostility to government to its furthest extreme. Its concept of the economy is constructed on the basis of the absolute character of the property rights of the individual. The logic of this position means justifying free markets in heroin and pornography as well as opposing controls on immigration. This, as is argued elsewhere, conflicts sharply with the authoritarian strand of the New Right, but also with traditional economic individualism with its celebration of the sanctity of the family.

The third strand in this revival of liberal political economy is Austrian economics. This approach stems from the work of Carl Menger and his students, F. von Wieser and F. von Böhm-Bawerk. Later prominent members of the school have included Joseph Schumpeter, Ludwig von Mises, and Friedrich A. Hayek. Although its origins go back to the work of one of the founders of marginalist analysis, Austrian economics was always distinct from the rest of neo-classical economics. It refused to accept the methodology of positive economics or the focusing of attention upon the problem of equilibrium. But its greatest importance for an examination of contemporary New Right economics was that many of its leading figures remained deeply concerned with questions of political economy. Von Mises and Hayek in particular emerged as implacable opponents of socialism. They argued from the 1920s onwards that there was no middle way between capitalism and socialism. There was no possibility of rational economic calculation under socialism, once private ownership of the means of production had been abolished and the market suspended.[13] Any socialist economy would be highly inefficient because the modern economic order was too complex to be centrally planned.

During the last thirty years the laissez-faire, the libertarian and the Austrian perspectives in liberal political economy have been undergoing a major revival. But what has also occurred is an attempt to re-knit economic analysis with liberal political economy, by claiming that the findings of modern positive economics provide support for free market economic policies. This is where monetarism has been so important. The problem of inflation in the 1960s and its acceleration in the 1970s created an opportunity for both practical and ideological intervention. What might have been merely a highly technical argument between macroeconomists about how the economy worked and how it might be stabilized became a much more general debate about the rights and wrongs of intervention and the success of Keynesianism.

Many of the advocates of monetarism, like Milton Friedman, were long-standing advocates of economic liberalism. Monetarism did not make them economic liberals. It was the other way round. Friedman's early declaration of faith in the free market, *Capitalism and Freedom*, was published in 1962 and was based on lectures first

delivered in the 1950s. Yet even with Friedman the influence of
Keynesianism was such that much of his early work was conducted
within its framework. Only gradually did Friedman come to reject
the framework and develop his own, one much more in tune with
his laissez-faire principles.[14]

What shaped Friedman's intellectual evolution was his increasing
preoccupation with inflation and the apparent inability of Keynesian
policies to control it. In the 1950s Friedman had already offered a
new definition of the quantity theory of money and he followed this
with empirical studies of the actual course of monetary history in
the USA.[15] In so doing he offered a non-Keynesian interpretation
of economic development; in particular he disputed the Keynesian
account of the Great Depression in the 1930s, arguing that the slump
was caused by the decision of the banking authorities to contract
the money supply too quickly. Armed with these arguments Friedman
began to deploy a far-reaching criticism of Keynesianism. He claimed
that a monetary counter-revolution was in progress and he began
to explore in detail the consequences for policy.

At first, support for these new ideas was confined to a few centres.
Chicago, the London School of Economics, and Manchester were
particularly prominent. Monetarism first began to be widely
discussed outside the academic journals in the late 1960s,[16] and as
inflation accelerated and Keynesian policies proved ineffective, so
more economists became convinced that the monetary approach to
economic management needed to be revived, while politicians and
commentators came to accept monetarism on pragmatic grounds as
the only policy capable of containing inflation and satisfying financial
markets, without introducing extensive and permanent wage and
price controls.

Monetarism

The triumph of monetarism in the 1970s and its widespread adoption
as the new orthodoxy, was presented not as a modification of
established principles of economic management, but as a decisive
shift involving the overthrow of previous conceptions and
assumptions. The more this view was taken, the more not just post-
war economic management, but the principles of social democracy,
began to be questioned. Monetarism was the battering ram that made
the breach. The result was a considerable widening of the political
agenda.

Yet initially monetarism was merely one position in a technical debate on how best to stabilize the economy. Throughout the period of maximum Keynesian influence, there was a debate among economists about whether monetary or fiscal instruments were more effective in influencing demand and ensuring that governments' objectives of full employment, stable prices and rising living standards were met. Keynesian economics was a factor here but more important was the shape of the post-war economic order. Each national economy remained heavily protected for a time with non-convertible exchange rates linked to the dollar. Great emphasis was placed initially on keeping interest rates low and maintaining domestic demand. Fiscal policy was the preferred instrument. As world trade revived, so liberalization proceeded, controls were relaxed and the importance of money as the principal means of co-ordinating an unplanned market economy increased.

In Britain, monetary policy was revived in the 1950s as a major instrument of policy. However, the persistence of fixed exchange rates still meant that there was considerable scope for domestic stabilization policy using fiscal instruments. By varying tax rates and spending plans, national governments could hope to influence the total level of demand and therefore the amount of economic activity. Monetary measures such as raising interest rates or directly curtailing bank lending were also used, but the main target of policy was to fine-tune the pressure of demand in the economy.

Monetarism grew in favour as the liberalization of world trade and the internationalization of production proceeded. The difficulties of maintaining external balance and fixed exchange rates and a high level of domestic activity increased. The simple trade-off between inflation and unemployment no longer seemed to be available by the late 1960s. Both had started to rise. The additional policies to supplement demand management and contain cost pressures, such as prices and incomes policy, seemed to work well only for brief periods. In the meantime the financial imbalances in the world system, caused by the rising US deficit, exacerbated by US spending in Vietnam, were making it impossible to hold the system of fixed exchange rates in place. In 1971 the dam cracked and by 1972 all the major currencies were floating.[17]

A regime of floating exchange rates greatly strengthened the practical and theoretical case for monetarism. Fixed exchange rates had forced monetary control on national governments, since the result of excessive domestic expansion of the money supply would be to create inflation and a deficit of trade, which would have to be corrected if the established parity of the currency were to be preserved. Under floating exchange rates this external financial discipline was removed. The prospect loomed of unrestrained domestic monetary expansion and an acceleration of inflation. If no external financial discipline existed, it followed that governments needed to adopt definite rules on money supply so as to reduce inflation and currency fluctuations. Monetarism became the international policy to which all governments committed to an open world economy felt obliged to subscribe. This need for financial discipline was reinforced by the behaviour of the financial markets. Because of the increasing liberalization of capital movements, tight money policies became the test of confidence in a national economy. Domestic reflations, or doubts about the commitment to reduce inflation, could trigger a flight from the currency. In the period of floating exchange rates and world recession, governments have found themselves obliged to adopt monetarist policies or contemplate stringent controls on trade and capital flows to insulate the economy from the world economy.

The rise in influence of monetarism has to be understood against this background. Monetarism would have remained a technical debate among economists if conditions in the world economy had not altered so dramatically in the 1970s and made the control of inflation the top priority for government economic policy.

The theoretical case for monetarism was based on a revival of the quantity theory of money, one of the oldest ideas in economics and one of the most commonsensical. It suggested that the level of prices was directly related to the quantity of money in circulation. Increases in the money stock, or increases in the speed at which money changed hands, would lead to a rise in prices if output of goods and services remained constant. In policy terms a revival of the quantity theory of money meant that 'money matters'. The Keynesians were credited with the idea that money does not matter, that what counted was always the 'real economy', the actual output of goods and services and actual levels of investment and productivity. Money flows adjusted passively to changes in the real economy. For the monetarists, money was an independent power which could influence conditions in the economy, so a neglect of monetary conditions could have the most serious consequences for the real economy.

This debate could have been conducted within Keynesian parameters. Keynes after all had been a noted monetary theorist.

The break with a Keynesian framework and the polarization between Keynesians and monetarists was dictated by the political need to reassert the principle of sound money, to restrict government intervention and to give less importance to other economic objectives. What monetarists wanted was for inflation to be recognized as the major problem whatever its rate. There was no question of governments assessing whether inflation or unemployment was the greater evil which required policy action. Sound money had to become government's main priority again; without sound money no other objective − such as full employment or faster growth − could be achieved.[18]

The political significance of monetarism was that in placing sound money once more on a pedestal above all other objectives of economic policy it rejected Keynesian modes of intervention. The objectives of Keynesian policies were derided as far too ambitious. Governments could not choose how much unemployment or inflation or growth they wanted and then engineer it. In the monetarist world the only policy governments needed to have was a policy for controlling the money supply. If governments delivered sound money then the economy would be stabilized. The amount of employment and the rate of growth both depended on the conditions prevailing in particular markets. They could not be altered by injections of demand from the centre. This crucial monetarist idea was developed by Milton Friedman and others in the doctrine of the natural rate of unemployment.[19] This stated that imperfections in the labour market produced a level of unemployment which could not be reduced by government action to stimulate demand. Such increases in spending would only lead to increases in inflation. The trade-off in the Keynesian world is between inflation and unemployment. In the monetarist world the choice for governments is between price stability and inflation.

In its revival of the quantity theory of money, monetarism was hardly a very original doctrine. Its main claim to novelty was the crusade against Keynesianism which monetarists mounted and the actual techniques which monetarists proposed for controlling the money supply. Sound money had traditionally been associated with the gold standard and its automatic imposition of financial discipline on national governments. Some monetarists have indeed recommended reimposition of the gold standard,[20] but others have followed Friedman in advocating floating exchange rates. Under floating rates an alternative mechanism is required for controlling money supply. This led to the idea of setting monetary targets, preferably for several years ahead, a medium-term financial strategy, fixing on one or more definitions of money as the appropriate variable to control.

The imposition of such targets is geared in Friedman's writings to the gradual slow-down in the rate of inflation until price stability is approached. The slow-down is associated with some transitional unemployment. The time-lags between changes in money supply and changes in output and later in prices have been variously estimated by monetarists as between nine months and twenty-four months. This makes testing of the theory hazardous. To ease the strains and conflicts of the period of counter-inflation policy, Friedman has advocated such measures as the indexation of all prices, wages and taxes, in order to limit the gains and losses for different social groups.[21] Governments have been very reluctant to follow this advice.

Most monetarist writing evades the question as to why governments should ever permit inflation if there is a simple technical cure for it. In many of his early pronouncements Friedman encouraged a politically naive view of the causes of inflation and how it could be stopped. One of his most quoted statements on inflation was 'Inflation is always and everywhere a monetary phenomenon in the sense that it is and can be produced only by a more rapid increase in the quantity of money than in output'.[22] Friedman suggested at times that governments were merely the victims of bad economics and wrong advice. If the advice were changed inflation would be halted.[23]

This was never a view shared by Hayek, who together with Friedman became a fashionable New Right economist in the 1970s. Hayek put forward a much more complex view of the causes of inflation. He did not dispute that inflation could be halted by monetary means, but he concentrated his analysis on the political difficulties preventing governments from pursuing sound money policies.

Hayek's interventions helped to broaden the monetarist attack on Keynesianism. For him inflation was not just a matter of poor economics or misguided advice, but was the most visible symptom of a long period in which market principles had been undermined and an interventionist policy regime installed. Hayek put the greatest emphasis in his analysis on how the economy had been politicized; more and more economic decisions had been transferred to the public sphere or interfered in by public agencies. The huge growth in public expenditure and taxation had created an army of public agencies and continued expansion of government spending. This was further exacerbated by the growth in the power of the trade unions and the multiplication of pressure groups within mass democracy. Strong trade unions and mass political parties have exerted continual pressure for collectivist policies and government intervention in free markets.[24]

According to Hayek, trade unions have a legitimate role as voluntary associations, but this role is strictly limited. In large-scale organizations, collective agreements on rules governing differentials and promotions as well as the conditions of work, may assist the smooth running of the business. Hayek also allows that unions can act as friendly societies insuring their members against sickness and unemployment. The problem with unions for Hayek is that they have been allowed and encouraged to develop far beyond these functions and now pose a major threat to the survival of a free society:[25]

> Public policy concerning labour unions has, in little more than a century, moved from one extreme to the other. From a state in which little the unions could do was legal if they were not prohibited altogether, we now have reached a state where they have become uniquely privileged institutions to which the general rules of law do not apply. They have become the only important instance in which governments signally fail in their prime function – the prevention of coercion and violence.

Hayek claims that unions have become private monopolies able to pursue their objectives only by the coercion of some of their members or other workers. He argues that unions 'cannot in the long-run increase real wages for all wishing to work, above the level that would establish itself in a free market'.[26] If this is so, it follows that where unions seek to raise wages above this level they can only permanently improve the position of some workers by harming that of others, by lowering their wages or making them unemployed. Hayek concluded from this that if unions did not have the power to coerce and intimidate through picketing and the closed shop, backed up by legal immunity from prosecution, they would never get all workers to assent to it voluntarily.

Hayek claims that the existence of national and industrial, rather than company or plant unions, causes major damage to the economy; it distorts relative wages, restricts the mobility of labour, deters investment. Trade unions are therefore a major cause of slow growth whenever they interfere with management's right to manage, and Hayek argues that in countries where unions are strong the general level of real wages is lower than it would otherwise be.

In Hayek's view, trade unions are not directly responsible for inflation. But they do increase unemployment, and if governments respond by increasing money supply so as to maintain the level of demand, the result is an artificial boom and higher inflation. Curbing trade union power by removing trade union legal immunities, and outlawing picketing and the closed shop, are therefore seen by many on the New Right as a major step in the long-term cure for inflation by removing some of the political pressures on government to expand the money supply.[27]

Inflation for Hayek is a symptom of government interference in the market and specifically in the post-war period in Britain a product of social democracy. The political forces that pressed for full employment policies and collectivist welfare policies are the forces that established a political system in which it appeared natural for governments to take responsibility for economic outcomes and to be prepared to intervene whenever particular market outcomes appeared undesirable.

In this way Hayek directed attention to the foundations of a free market system and the ways in which social democratic institutions and policies violated it. He knitted together the monetarist explanation of inflation with a much broader sociological and political account of why it was that governments constantly infringed the principles of a market order. Between them Friedman and Hayek ensured that the debate over monetarism would not stay at the level of macroeconomic models but would re-ignite the debate on the principles of political economy which had seemingly been settled by the triumph of social democracy and rise of interventionist governments.

The Main Themes of New Right Economics

The main propositions of this new liberal political economy may be summed up as follows: intervention doesn't work; all alternatives to markets are deeply flawed; government failure is more prevalent than market failure; government intervention is unjust.

All these themes can be found in the writings of most prominent New Right economists, but inevitably the emphasis placed on them varies. They will be reviewed in turn.

The claim that intervention doesn't work is the most potent and widely disseminated idea in the political economy of the New Right. It has long been the standard case of economic liberals against each and every proposal for government intervention in the market economy, from the factory acts to incomes policy. It is the central theme of Milton Friedman's writings.[28] What Friedman offers in his writings on political economy as distinct from his more technical contributions to economic analysis, are common-sense maxims for business people. Every area where government has responsibility is shown to be inefficient and to have failed. The market solution is then unveiled. The emphasis is placed throughout on the empirical evidence that proves the market non-interventionist solution to be the one that works.

Much of the policy output of New Right economists and New Right think-tanks such as the Institute of Economic Affairs, the Adam Smith Institute and the Centre for Policy Studies, is devoted to analysis of particular policy areas from this perspective. This approach long predates the concern with inflation and covers welfare, distribution, nationalized industries and the impact of controls. Anything that restricts competition is exposed as inefficient. Rent control, industrial subsidies, agricultural protection, are all attacked on these grounds. Controls, it is argued, are ineffective because they are always evaded and because when they have an effect they distort behaviour into patterns which produce results less beneficial than the state of affairs which already existed. So controls on rents are said to have the effect of keeping the rate of return so low that landlords fail to maintain their property or withdraw it from the market. There is a progressive deterioration in the quality and quantity of the rented stock.

Similar analyses are made of state welfare services. Costs are alleged to be much higher than in the private sector because of the lack of competition and resulting waste and inefficiency. The solution is privatization of services and the ending of direct government responsibility for them. The case for bringing taxes down hinges on the presumed effect of taxes on incentives. The economy, it is suggested, would be much more prosperous if taxes were lower, because individuals would work much harder and high earners would spend less of their energies in finding ways of avoiding paying taxes.

The same empirical bent is evident in the treatment of inflation.

The main charge against Keynesianism is that it failed. Inflation accelerated, unemployment soared and growth disappeared. The main advantage claimed for monetarism is that it works; it brings inflation under control, restores confidence to the financial markets, and reduces the burden of public debt.

This is one of the reasons why New Right economics appeals to a certain kind of politician. It directly expresses their prejudices and intuitions about economic policy. It is a popular common sense about the way markets and governments work, dignified with the label of economic realism. Friedman's many axioms such as 'there is no such thing as a free lunch' illustrate the style.

Friedman's trust in this kind of argument stems in part from his faith in positive economics – his belief that propositions in economics can be proved to be true. He believes the evidence can show conclusively whether a governmental solution or a market solution works best. In almost every case he assumes it will be the latter. In deploying such arguments New Right economists are continuing a long tradition, and reasserting the superiority of market solutions which, if never entirely eclipsed, were at least overshadowed for a time in some areas by state solutions. In no areas were market policies thought to have failed more completely than in the field of economic management, and specifically in the prevention of mass unemployment. This again pinpoints the importance of monetarism. By attacking Keynesianism as a discredited and failed theory New Right economists were trying to knock out the lynchpin on which so much of the justification of post-war intervention in the economy rested. But this was by no means the only attack that was made. For many New Right economists, asserting the superiority of monetarism over Keynesianism on the basis of experience alone was too fragile. They sought additional theoretical grounds for rejecting intervention by government in markets.

The second theme in New Right economics is the argument that all alternatives to markets are deeply flawed. The shortcomings of the political analysis of the monetarists helped legitimate a range of other positions in the political economy of the New Right. In particular it led to a revival of the Austrian perspective.[29]

The most important contribution made by Austrian economists to New Right economics stemmed from a long-standing and implacable hostility to socialism. The Austrian system had from an early stage engaged in a bitter confrontation with Marxism. A great deal of Austrian effort was devoted to demonstrating firstly that the basic ideas of Marxism contained logical flaws and that secondly socialism was not a rational means of economic organization.[30] In its defence of modern capitalism the Austrian school asserted that only an economic system based on private ownership of the means of production could be rational in the economic sense, i.e. could achieve an efficient allocation of resources and the greatest possible increase in wealth and productivity.

This argument was based not on outcomes but on first principles. The Austrians asserted that modern economic institutions such as the market and money were the spontaneous creation of individual agents and had evolved over a very long period. The only way in which they could work effectively was if their nature was respected. The great superiority of markets over all other forms of economic organization was the way in which they co-ordinated all economic activity through the division of labour *and* created opportunities for continual experimentation and improvement. While the neo-classical economists were most concerned with analysing economies in equilibrium − the way in which co-ordination of all activities was achieved and maintained − the Austrians placed great emphasis on markets as a discovery process. What was discovered were new needs, new tastes, new technologies, new methods of organization, new products.

The condition for markets to function as a discovery process was that they should be as decentralized as possible. The more knowledge was dispersed throughout society the more opportunities for creative entrepreneurship existed. But such entrepreneurship depended naturally on access to capital, hence the Austrian stipulation that only an economic system based on private ownership of the means of production could be dynamic. Many of the neo-classical equilibrium theorists had admitted that theoretically a socialist economy might be more successful in achieving equilibrium in the economy and eliminating market failure and imperfections. The Austrians retort that this ignores the main benefit of markets − the raising of economic productivity and living standards as a consequence of the constant search for new ways of making profit. They argue that no economy can ever achieve perfect competition. In the economy as it is, free markets are much more successful than central planning in coping with uncertainty and rapid social and technological change. A central planning authority could never know as much as the knowledge dispersed in a market among all its agents, and it would have no means of assessing whether its planning decisions were efficient or not, since prices were no longer set by the forces of demand and supply set in motion by the competition between the multitude of individual producers and consumers.[31]

The key idea in the Austrian system is that the institutional form of the modern economy is not optional. It cannot be changed by political decree without endangering the basis of modern civilization itself. This is why the Austrians see socialism as atavistic, encouraging dreams of bliss and revenge amongst the ignorant, the disadvantaged and the unsuccessful. Far from being a higher stage of civilization it is a throwback to a lower one. It ignores all the complexity of the modern economic institutions which have sustained economic progress.

Socialism is thus declared wholly illegitimate and the sanctity of private ownership of capital is vigorously asserted. But the Austrians go even further. For they also have very strong objections to any form of government intervention in markets. Since the state can never know more than markets because of the way in which knowledge is dispersed in a modern economy based on division of labour, all forms of intervention are likely to be harmful and destabilizing. Governments and individual economic agents all act in conditions of uncertainty. The trial-and-error approach of markets is always likely to be more successful than government decisions, since amidst the innumerable calculations and decisions made by individuals the best course of action will spontaneously emerge. It will often be one which a central government agency would not have chosen and could not have predicted beforehand.

An approach which has much in common with the Austrian perspective is supply-side economics.[32] It has been specially influential in the USA. Like the Austrian economists supply-siders reject the notion of perfect competition as unobtainable and unrealistic. The main feature of capitalism for them is the process of innovation, the launching of new enterprises, the activity of entrepreneurs. Competition will always be imperfect because the economic process depends on incomplete knowledge, and uncertainty and risk are unavoidable elements of the economic process. Capitalism is about the creation of wealth by individuals taking risks and launching new enterprises. Real aggregate demand in the economy is an effect of production not of policy. Governments, it is argued, are powerless to affect real aggregate demand through policies of taxing and spending. What they can do is encourage or discourage entrepreneurship and the creation of wealth by changing incentives through tax policy.

Such an approach gives rise to the best-known idea of the supply-siders – the Laffer curve. Laffer argues that lower tax rates can so stimulate business and weaken the attraction of the black economy and tax evasion that they actually bring in higher tax revenues. A policy of cutting taxes substantially could therefore be pursued without first seeking expenditure cuts or incurring extra debt or printing more money. By concentrating on profitability, investment and incentives, rather than on monetary aggregates or levels of effective demand, governments would unleash a virtuous circle of expansion spearheaded by the private sector. Supply-siders are therefore opposed to either Keynesian demand management or monetarist management of the money supply becoming the centrepiece of economic policy, because both can be used to justify continuing high levels of taxation. Lowering taxes for the supply-siders is the key to a revitalized capitalism.

A third theme in New Right argument is the assertion that government failure is more prevalent than market failure. The Austrian emphasis on the superior rationality of unregulated and unfettered markets is taken further by the approach known as the economics of politics, or public choice. It represents a major recovery of self-confidence by economists. During the period of the marginalist revolution, economics contracted both its boundaries and the definition of its subject-matter; the economics of politics sees it expanding once more. The tools of economic analysis are now applied to the analysis of politics and governments; this follows the recognition that, since economizing is defined as a universal feature of human behaviour, there is no area for social life which is not in principle amenable to economic analysis.

The main contribution of the public choice theorists to New Right economics is the argument that for too long debates on public policy have contrasted the failures of the market with a supposed omniscience of the state. Furthermore, in Keynesian and social democratic legitimations for government action, public power appears enlightened, disinterested and wholly committed to serving the public good. The main purpose of the economics of politics is to puncture these myths.[33]

The early work in this field concentrated on demand-side analysis – examining how electoral choices were made and how parties competed on the analogy of markets, consumers and firms. The shortcomings of political markets compared with economic markets were exposed. The results showed, it was claimed, that individual voters did not have to bear the full cost of policies they voted for and the political parties had an interest in outbidding one another in promising collective expenditures. Hence there was a continual bias in a democracy for increases in spending by governments.

More recently attention has switched to supply-side analysis. The focus has been on how politicians and bureaucrats, as normal rational, self-interested agents, behave. Again the general conclusion is that there is a massive 'over-supply' of government services. Expenditure soars, bureaus expand, and governments become more and more inclined to intervene in the market economy. A network of client groups and vested interests springs up which consolidates and legitimates government spending programmes. In these ways a continual upward bias is given to public spending.

Such analyses suggest that, from the side of demand and supply of government services, there is constant pressure for governments to expand their spending and increase the range of their interventions. But from the standpoint of the model, such expansion in the role of government is undesirable and irrational because it is a result of the inadequacies in the public-choice mechanism for ensuring that individual preferences can be properly weighted and taken account of, and that government agencies are disciplined by competition and subject to 'voter sovereignty'. On these grounds it is concluded that government failure in the economic sense is a far more serious problem than market failure, because markets do work efficiently some of the time, while government — because it is not organized as a market — cannot work efficiently any of the time. The policy conclusion is that in our present state of knowlege it is better to trust markets than governments and that governments should be restricted as much as possible.

A fourth theme in New Right economics is that government intervention is unjust. Government intervention is variously described by New Right economists as inefficient, illegitimate and irrational. There has been much cross-fertilization between the different approaches. The libertarian New Right extends the argument still further and condemns all state intervention as unjust. One of the main Austrian arguments for resisting intervention was that once intervention had begun in a capitalist economy it was very difficult to stop it, so more and more areas passed under the sway of the state. Intervention, of even the mildest kind, therefore led directly to socialism. There was no possible middle ground or middle way between capitalism and socialism. This theme was the centrepiece of Hayek's 1944 tract *The Road to Serfdom*. The main stimulus to these gloomy forebodings was the experience of the war economy, when the process of intervention had indeed encompassed more and more fields as the war progressed, although private ownership of the means of production was not affected.[34]

The argument that intervention in a capitalist economy even by right-wing or mildly reforming governments should be strongly opposed because it leads straight to socialism, has never been the most plausible argument in the New Right armoury, although attempts have been made to apply it to incomes policy and the drift into corporatism in the 1970s. A much more robust line of argument has been developed by the libertarians, who attempted to show that there are no moral arguments that can justify government transfer of wealth or income from one citizen to another except where public order is concerned. All redistributive policies are therefore illegitimate. The significance of Nozick's arguments for New Right economics is that they justify the same view of distribution taken by Hayek. Hayek rejects the notion of social justice. There is nothing just or unjust, he argues, about market outcomes.[35] What matters for Hayek is not the pattern of distribution established through the market, but that there should exist a market order, based on general rules, which guarantees everyone maximum opportunities. Actual distribution will be a lottery depending on skill and effort to a limited degree, but predominantly on chance — the chance of genetic and material inheritance and the manner in which opportunities arise.

Hayek defends the lottery on the grounds that no better system can be devised. There are no principles of justice available that would permit a central authority to redistribute income more fairly. Redistribution undertaken by the state would be as arbitrary as the system it sought to replace, and by politicizing the distribution of income and wealth it would help legitimize all manner of intervention in the economy.

Nozick's justification for the lottery is rather different. He argues from first principles. If you accept his premises it is hard to fault his conclusions. He starts from the assumption that in the state of nature there are individuals who have rights and that there are things no person or group may do to them without violating their rights. These rights include a right to property. Nozick then argues that individuals will be prepared to give up to a protection agency their right to punish violations of their rights. Once formed, however, the power of this protection agency will be such that it will be obliged to extend protection to non-clients as well as clients so as not to violate their rights. This means there will be a measure of redistribution between clients and non-clients – those prepared to pay for protection and those not. In this way Nozick justifies the minimal state of classical liberalism. But no further redistributive measure, from welfare benefits to foreign aid, can be justified except as acts of individual charity and benevolence. The existing distribution of wealth and income is just, so long as it arises from an original distribution that was just, and so long as every succeeding exchange has been voluntary and has not violated anyone's rights.

Like all state-of-nature theories, Nozick's is a historical fiction since there is no way of determining whether existing holdings were acquired justly in the first place.[36] Nozick uses it to argue for an entitlement theory of justice – the justice of a given set of holdings depends purely on how those holdings have been acquired and not on whether they conform to a particular desired pattern of distribution. Nozick's most important conclusion for New Right economics is that if individuals are granted an inviolable pre-social right to property, then any principle of justice that seeks a particular pattern of justice will involve continual violation of people's rights and interference in people's lives. In a socialist society he argues the state would have to forbid capitalist acts between consenting adults.

The implications of this kind of approach are far-reaching. Nozick defines taxation as a form of forced labour, and this has been echoed by other libertarians. Murray Rothbard for instance, a prominent representative of the American 'Austrian' school, argues that the free market economist must oppose all actions of the government whatsoever, since all such acts involve taxes and therefore illegitimate redistribution. The government, including the one under which we are 'forced to live', takes on the 'status of an organization of banditti'.[37]

Conclusion

Such extreme libertarian attitudes jar with political realities. Can this be the New Right of the Moral Majority and the rearmament lobby who loyally support politicians such as Ronald Reagan and Margaret Thatcher? The paradox dissolves on closer examination. New Right economists love to parade as 'libertarians', but the libertarianism of most of them is meagre. They apply it as a remedy to the ills of contemporary society only in miniscule doses. Few are libertarian about life-styles, or gender relations, or race, or defence issues, or crime and punishment. There is a libertarian wing in the New Right but it is not dominant. The few genuine libertarians stand out among the rest.[38]

For most New Right economists, libertarian attitudes to economic policy are quite compatible with neo-conservative attitudes on many other issues. They willingly exclude the application of libertarian principles from two key areas — the family, and internal and external security. The 'individuals' in New Right economics turn out not to be individuals at all but households represented by the male, wage-earning, head of the family. In supply-side texts like George Gilder's *Wealth and Poverty*, patriarchy is defended as normal and inevitable and the basis for psychological and economic achievement. The 'individualism' of the New Right is not a creed of universal opportunity for all individuals whatever their sex or age or race. It is primarily a creed of opportunity for male heads of families who receive the rewards of enterprise and in return are made responsible for their dependants — women, children and old people. Maintaining the solidarity and cohesion of families by non-market means is seen as an essential prop for a free market economy.

The need to provide for 'his' dependants is seen as the greatest incentive each individual has to work and to be enterprising. Collective welfare programmes and the high taxation they require necessarily reduce the incentives for individuals and undermine their commitment to their families. On these terms the individualism of New Right economics is perfectly compatible with the individualism of many conservative politicians who proclaim the family as the foundation of social order and social discipline. The farther reaches of the New Right may have thrown up some exotic flowers. The British Conservative Party now has an ideological fringe which favours privatizing the fire service and decriminalizing heroin. But no one would put an early date on a Conservative government adopting such policies. The Conservative Party has never been disposed to determining its attitudes on policy as a result of arguments from ideological principles and it is not likely to begin now.

The reasons why the ideas of foreign ideologues like Milton Friedman and Friedrich Hayek should have been taken up by an influential section of the Conservative leadership, and their authors and acolytes patronized and honoured, is one of the curiosities of recent British political history.[39] One explanation stresses the need of the new Thatcher leadership in 1975 to distance itself politically and intellectually not only from the Labour government but also from the previous Conservative leadership and the ethos of post-war Toryism. New Right economists supplied an intellectual framework for thinking about policy problems which offered a break with past policies and a return to 'fundamentals'. The monetarist emphasis on sound money made the control of inflation the central object of economic management and overturned Keynesianism. To make the financial strategy work, large cuts in public expenditure and taxation were advocated, a cause certain to unify the party. To make cuts in public expenditure permanent, the Thatcherites began exploring ways of privatizing public services and selling public assets. To revive the spirit of enterprise, new ways of curbing trade union power were devised and plans were drawn up for reducing the controls on business activity.

None of these policies were new for the Conservatives. They accorded with many of the traditional beliefs and prejudices about economic organization and economic policy that were widespread in the party. Margaret Thatcher herself clearly trusted far more to her grasp of the simple truths of personal responsibility, hard work and thrift, than to anything she read in Hayek or Friedman. She did not need (nor, apparently, does she have) any precise understanding of the doctrine of 'the natural rate of unemployment' in order to oppose reflationary policies. An instinctive distrust of borrowing and credit was enough. Her concept of a free economy has always been of networks of families − self-reliant, hard-working, living within their means, independent, patriotic and respectable.[40]

Thatcher's main contribution to the spread of New Right ideas within the Party was her insistence that they be presented in populist terms − as a set of simple common-sense maxims about how the economy worked and how it should be organized. She knew also the ideas which would rally support among conservative MPs and at Conservative Party Conferences − promises to cut taxes, to sell council houses, to privatize state industries, to control inflation and to curb trade union power.

A few Conservative leaders, like Keith Joseph, were persuaded by the intellectual case put forward by the New Right and became ideological converts to it. Joseph recognized in the mid-1970s that Keynesianism and social democracy were both weakening, and that an anti-socialist position could be advanced much better from the ground of neo-liberal economic principle than from the fashionable middle way of post-war conservatism.[41] Why choose a middle way between socialism and capitalism when it was capitalism you wanted all the time? Hayek had long argued that there was no secure resting place between the mild intervention and full socialism. This idea was adopted by Joseph. It enabled him to interpret the whole post-war period as a steady progress down the road to serfdom which the Conservative Party had failed to halt.

All the arguments adopted by Thatcher and the leadership group she slowly assembled around her had been anticipated by Enoch Powell in the 1960s.[42] Powell at that time had had few ideological supporters within the leadership, and after his departure from the Shadow Cabinet following his Birmingham speech on immigration in 1968, he gradually became more and more isolated from the Party. What made possible the rise of Thatcherism in the 1970s was the widespread perception in the Party that the Heath government had been a failure, and that Britain was becoming ungovernable. This coincided with the onset of world recession and increasing alarm about the implications of Britain's continuing relative decline. The climate of failure and indecision that clung to British governments in the 1960s and 1970s gave the political opportunity for a sharp break with both the rhetoric and the practice of post-war economics. The New Right, through its many think-tanks, pundits, journalists and academics, supplied a wealth of arguments as to why the change should be made and the consensus abandoned. Many of the doctrines of New Right economics such as monetarism and supply-side economics, became fashionable and attracted many new supporters.

They also attracted much opposition, not least within the Conservative Party.[43] Many of the critics suspected that the policies would have to be reversed after six months because of the opposition they would arouse and the harmful effects they would create. But the critics underestimated the determination of Thatcher herself to persevere with the policy despite temporary unpopularity, and to reconstruct her Cabinet to weaken and isolate dissent.

The alliance that was forged under the Thatcher leadership between the populists and the ideologues in the Conservative Party proved a powerful one. It allowed the New Right project to become installed as a framework within which thinking about policy could go ahead. It was accepted that to reverse Britain's relative economic decline, a major break with post-war social democracy and its attendant ideologies and doctrines, such as Keynesianism, had to be carried through. It was the vision of a new social order and the faith that it could be brought about, which sustained the New Right and made the Thatcher government appear radical even when its actions were cautious.

The vision which animates the New Right is the ideal of a social market economy or market order. All New Right theorists seek the reassertion and extension of market principles in areas where social democracy has encroached and set limits to the market or suspended it altogether. Hayek's idea of a market order is a potent one – an economy in which economic power is decentralized, the division of labour co-ordinated, and income distributed, through the free operation of market forces. The role of government is confined to the enforcement of those general rules, for example on contract and property, that define the market order and make market relations possible. It needs to be vigilant and strong to enforce competition and outlaw private coercive power, but it has no role in, and no justification in, seeking to intervene directly in the decisions individuals take in the market.[44]

As an ideal the social market economy has deep roots in liberal tradition. But the term has been used in very different ways. Originally coined by German liberals who favoured a strong state to destroy concentrations of private capital and construct a market economy composed of small property owners, it was adopted as the slogan for the economic policies of the post-war Christian Democrat governments in the Federal Republic and later by the opposition Social Democratic Party to signify their acceptance of competition and the free market and their abandonment of Marxism. In Britain it was adopted by the Thatcherites in the Conservative Party to describe their new perspective in 1975, and in 1983 it was adopted by the recently formed Social Democratic Party.[45]

The concept signifies acceptance of markets as the most efficient means of allocating resources and co-ordinating the economy. It therefore signifies also acceptance of the basic institutions associated with markets, in particular private ownership of the means of production and a rejection of central planning. Beyond this, however, there is much disagreement on the actual scope of market forces, and on the definition of government's minimum functions. New Right libertarians favour extending market principles to the furthest extent possible, embracing both the family and defence and greatly reducing the numbers of actions to be labelled criminal by the state.

New Right social democrats favour full application of market principles in the private sector but argue that welfare services such as education and health should be run on different principles and should continue to be provided by the state.[46] The mainstream New Right view knits together the views of economic liberals and neo-conservatives. The application of market principles is restricted to the economy. The family, national defence and traditional morality remain protected domains from which the corrosive power of markets is to be excluded. The reduction of private coercion is confined to restriction on trade unionism; little enthusiasm exists for tackling corporate power or the power of professional associations. Unlike New Right social democrats, however, the mainstream New Right favours major reductions in collective welfare, extending privatization to all public welfare services.

The New Right in Britain and the USA as well as in some other countries, has been seeking to establish a new agenda for economic policy. It is an agenda which makes sound money a major priority for any government. It enjoins major reductions in public expenditure and taxation; a major de-regulation of private industry and privatization of public enterprises and services; a major reduction in trade union power and legal immunities; and constitutional changes to impose limits on what any democratically elected government can do in the field of economic policy.

Under the leadership of Margaret Thatcher in Britain the Conservative Party has become committed to all the elements of this programme except the last. Since 1979 the monetarist commitment has been central to the Government's policy and image. The Treasury team of ministers has been selected only from those who were declared monetarists. Yet apart from a spectacular slump in 1979-81, caused by mismanagement and external factors rather than deliberate policy, the success of the Thatcher government in achieving its economic goals has been limited.[47] Public expenditure and taxation both rose rather than fell between 1979 and 1983 and the economic recovery when it came was slow and hesitant. The problem that the Thatcher government encountered was the difficulty of changing attitudes and behaviour quickly. It found itself forced to rely on more authoritarian and repressive measures in order to introduce greater 'freedom' to the economy. The price of forcing the market to be free is a strong state. If the policies are resisted and if the consensual basis of economic policy is disrupted, major conflicts can erupt as public opinion becomes more polarized, creating a climate in which major breakdowns of public order become commonplace.

Whatever the fate of the Thatcher government, however, the New Right will survive it. In its impact on British policies and economic policy it has already been remarkably successful. The traditional post-war argument between different kinds of interventionism has been replaced by a much broader debate. The hope of the New Right is that eventually the debate can be shifted onto ground where all the protagonists accept the primacy of market principles, and all other positions are ruled illegitimate.[48] But they still have a long way to go.

Notes

1 S. Brittan, *How to end the Monetarist Controversy*, (IEA, London, 1981), p. 11.

2 A distinction made by J. A. Schumpeter *History of Economic Analysis* (Allen and Unwin, London, 1954). For other definitions of political economy see R. J. Barry Jones (ed.) *Perspectives on Political Economy* (Frances Pinter, London, 1983).

3 See R. D. Collison Black et al. (eds), *The Marginal Revolution in Economics* (Duke University Press, North Carolina, 1973), esp. the chapter by Donald Winch.

4 L. Robbins, *The Nature and Limits of Economic Science* (Macmillan, London, 1935), p. 16.

5 N. Bukharin, *The Economic Theory of the Leisure Class* (Monthly Review Press, New York, 1972).

6 See P. Clarke, *Liberals and Social Democrats* (Cambridge University Press, Cambridge, 1978).

7 This intellectual mood is well caught in A. Crosland, *The Future of Socialism* (Cape, London, 1956).

8 For instance, A. Pigou, *Socialism versus Capitalism* (Macmillan, London, 1937).

9 See the important argument by Jim Tomlinson, 'Why was there never a "Keynesian Revolution" in economic policy', *Economy and Society*, 10: 1 (1981), pp. 72-87.

10 For the revival of liberal political economy as the guiding policy for the world system see Nixon Apple, 'The rise and fall of full employment capitalism', *Studies in Political Economy*, 4 (1980) pp. 5-39.

11 Herbert Spencer, *Man versus the State* (Williams and Norgate, London, 1907).

12 Robert Nozick, *Anarchy, State, and Utopia* (Blackwell, Oxford, 1975).
13 See F. A. Hayek (ed.), *Collectivist Economic Planning* (Routledge, London, 1935).
14 See Nick Bosanquet, *After the New Right* (Heinemann Educational Books, London 1983), ch. 3.
15 M. Friedman and A. Schwarz, *A Monetary History of the United States* (Princeton University Press, Princeton, N.J., 1963).
16 Especially by journalists such as Sam Brittan, Nigel Lawson, and Peter Jay.
17 See E. Brett *International Money and Capitalist Crisis* (Heinemann Educational Books, London, 1983).
18 F. A. Hayek, *A Tiger by the Tail* (IEA, London, 1972).
19 For an exposition and critique see Bosanquet, *After the New Right*.
20 See W. Rees-Mogg, *The Reigning Illusion* (Hamish Hamilton, London, 1974).
21 M. Friedman, *Monetary Correction* (IEA, London, 1974).
22 M. Friedman, *The Counter-Revolution in Monetary Theory* (IEA, London, 1970), p. 24.
23 M. Friedman, *Inflation and Unemployment* (IEA, London, 1977).
24 Hayek, *A Tiger by the Tail*.
25 F. A. Hayek, *The Constitution of Liberty* (Routledge and Kegan Paul, London, 1961), p. 267.
26 Hayek, *The Constitution of Liberty*, p. 270.
27 For example Keith Joseph, *Solving the Union Problem is the key to Britain's Recovery* (CPS, London, 1974).
28 M. Friedman, *Free to Choose*, (Secker & Warburg, London, 1980).
29 Ludwig von Mises and F. A. Hayek are the two most important modern representatives of the school.
30 See L. von Mises, *Socialism* (Routledge and Kegan Paul, London, 1936).
31 F. A. Hayek, 'The use of knowledge in society', in *Individualism and Economic Order* (Routledge and Kegan Paul, London, 1949).
32 A typical text is George Gilder, *Wealth and Poverty* (Buchan and Enright, London, 1982).
33 For a survey see James Buchanan, *The Economics of Politics* (IEA, London 1978), and Nick Bosanquet, *After the New Right*.
34 See L. Harris, 'State and economy in the Second World War',

State and Society in Contemporary Britain G. McLennan et al. (eds.), (Polity Press, Cambridge, 1984), pp. 50-76.

35 F. A. Hayek, *Law, Legislation, and Liberty* (Routledge and Kegan Paul, London, 1976).

36 See Peter Singer, Bernard Williams, Robert Wolff and others in *Reading Nozick*, ed. J. Paul (Blackwell, Oxford, 1982).

37 M. N. Rothbard in I. M. Kirzner (ed.), *Method, Process, and Austrian Economics* (Lexington Books, Lexington (Mass), 1982), p. 186.

38 Sam Brittan is one.

39 For surveys see William Keegan, *Mrs. Thatcher's Economic Experiment* (Allen Lane, London, 1984); and Robert Behrens, *The Conservative Party from Heath to Thatcher* (Saxon House, London, 1980).

40 See N. Wapshott and G. Brock, *Thatcher* (Futura, London, 1983).

41 K. Joseph, *Stranded on the Middle Ground* (CPS, London, 1976).

42 See D. Schoen, *Powell and the Powellites* (Macmillan, London, 1977).

43 One of the most articulate was Ian Gilmour. See his *Britain Can Work* (Martin Robertson, Oxford, 1983).

44 See Andrew Gamble, 'The free economy and the strong state' in R. Miliband and J. Saville (eds), *Socialist Register 1979* (Merlin, London, 1979).

45 See *Why Britain needs a Social Market Economy* (CPS, London, 1975).

46 David Owen, *A Future that will work* (Penguin, Harmondsworth, 1984).

47 Peter Riddell, *The Thatcher Government* (Martin Robertson, Oxford, 1983).

48 Arthur Seldon, *Agenda for Social Democracy* (IEA, London, 1983).

Chapter Two

The Free or the Good

DAVID EDGAR

The Assault on the Sixties

In the month immediately preceding the Argentinian invasion of the Falkland Islands (March 1982), a number of British ministers made speeches about the declining moral fabric of the nation. The context of these speeches was the continuing debate on the causes of, and responsibility for, the urban riots of the summer before − a debate that was revitalized by the publication of police figures purporting to expose the extent of the involvement of young blacks in London in violent street crime.[1]

On 17 March, for example, junior Home Office minister Timothy Raison laid the blame for 'crime and hooliganism' on a pot-pourri of environmental factors: from inadequate schools and broken homes to a lack of 'meaningful work' and 'sour media and mores which may set the tone'.[2] While ten days later, the Prime Minister herself placed responsibility for the breakdown firmly on ideas sown some years before: 'We are reaping what was sown in the sixties', she announced: 'The fashionable theories and permissive claptrap set the scene for a society in which the old virtues of discipline and self-restraint were denigrated'.[3]

In blaming the sins of the eighties on the whims of the sixties, Mrs Thatcher was echoing an earlier speech made by another junior minister, Dr Rhodes Boyson of the Department of Education. On 5 February, Dr Boyson had told Conservatives in Loughborough that:

> The permissive age, which blossomed in the late 1960s, bringing in its wake such intense suffering, has created a pathless desert for many of our young people . . . Tradition − the cement which helps to hold society together − has been scorned as restrictive and replaced in most cases by a destructive, naive arrogance . . . We have created our own

plagues by the break-up of stable families, with a malignant effect on many of our children, while many of our city streets and entertainments flaunt debased morals and false values. We have undermined the authority of parents and have had to take more children into care as a result. Similarly, the authority of head teachers and their staffs has often been attacked and society has reaped dragons' teeth in the form of juvenile revolt.[4]

The demonization of the sixties has been a characteristic of the New Right on both sides of the Atlantic. Indeed, the New Right phenomenon itself can be seen as a backlash against the social radicalism of the decade, as well, of course, as a reaction against the economic reformism of the thirties and forties. If, in their first terms of office, Margaret Thatcher and Ronald Reagan set out to demolish the extant works of the New Deal and the welfare state, then it is fair to say that they are now being encouraged to confront the social libertarianism that characterized public policy and attitudes in the sixties, from anti-militarism to anti-racism, from the liberalization of sexual life and the liberation of women to the protection of the environment and the privacy of the individual.

For many New Rightists — and for most commentators as well — the manifest inadequacies of John Maynard Keynes were on a natural continuum with the manifold iniquities of John Winston Lennon. But the contradiction between the libertarian rhetoric of those mainly concerned with the roll-back of the welfare state, and the growing authoritarianism of those primarily interested in the reimposition of traditional social values, has become increasingly obvious. Conflict between the economic liberals and the social authoritarians is a relatively new phenomenon in Britain, where long draughts of refreshing power have slaked the Conservative thirst for theory. In the USA on the other hand, the Right's long dark years of intellectual opposition tended to encourage ideological introspection, and led both factions to nail their colours firmly to the mast.

One of the most succinct statements of the social authoritarian position was made in 1962 by Brent Bozell, speech writer to Republican Senators Joseph McCarthy and (later) Barry Goldwater. For Bozell, 'the chief purpose of politics' was not to succour freedom but 'to aid the quest for virtue'. Indeed, he went on, 'the story of how the free society has come to take priority over the good society is the story of the decline of the West'.[5] It is in the arena of that dichotomy that the real battle within contemporary conservatism is being joined.

Libertarians against Traditionalists

As George H. Nash points out in his monumental history of *The Conservative Intellectual Movement in America since 1945*, the years after Pearl Harbor were not encouraging for the American Right. Not only had traditional conservative isolationism been routed, but the consequence of Roosevelt's interventionism was that America was fighting in alliance with Communism against a regime universally regarded as being on the extreme Right (the barbarity of whose practices were becoming daily more apparent), and was doing so, furthermore, on the back of an economy rescued from near-collapse by governmental action on a hitherto unprecented scale.

Strangely, it was the publication of a short book by a mid-European economist, then living in London, which gave the American Right new heart. From its first appearance in 1944, Friedrich A. Hayek's *The Road to Serfdom* had an extraordinary impact on an American Right, which had hitherto seen itself, half-proudly but half-despairingly, as a kind of Calvinist 'remnant', a tiny group aware that history and the masses had passed it by. With the publication of *Serfdom* however, it could take new heart, and by 1947 the 'remnant' was able to mount a major international conference, at Mont Pelerin in Switzerland, to promote its ideas. In the words of a young Chicago economist, Milton Friedman, 'the importance of that meeting was that it showed us that we were not alone'.[6]

But although indeed no longer alone, the 'we' referred to represented only part of the American Right. The significant characteristic of the political philosophy of both Hayek and Friedman was, and is, not so much their advocacy of laissez-faire economics *per se*, as the belief that the free market is a necessary *and sufficient* condition for the just society. As *Serfdom* has it, 'we have progressively abandoned that freedom in economic affairs without which personal and political freedom has never existed in the past', a freedom which consists primarily in 'the respect for the individual man *qua* man, that is the recognition of his own views and tastes as supreme in his own sphere, however narrowly that may be circumscribed'.[7] Similarly, Friedman argues strongly in

Capitalism and Freedom that the major problem with governmental intervention in the economy is that it conflicts with 'one of the strongest and most creative forces known to man — the attempt by millions of individuals to promote their own interests, to live their lives by their own values'.[8]

It was on the question of values that the individualists parted company most dramatically with traditional conservatism. As Hayek himself put it in his essay *Why I am not a conservative*, it is only 'the coexistence of different sets of values that makes it possible to build a peaceful society with a minimum of force'. Indeed, for Hayek, 'the most conspicuous attribute of liberalism that distinguishes it as much from conservatism as from socialism is the view that moral beliefs concerning matters of conduct which do not directly interfere with the protected sphere of other persons do not justify coercion'.[9]

Such views were anathema to a significant group of American conservatives, most of them surrounding the journal *National Review* (the motto of which, according to its founder William F. Buckley, was that it 'stands athwart history yelling Stop').[10] As archtraditionalist Russel Kirk argued: 'Once supernatural and traditional sanctions are dissolved, economic self-interest is ridiculously inadequate to hold an economic system together, and even less adequate to preserve order'.[11] While for Richard Weaver — who saw the model of the virtuous society in the Old South — 'capitalism cannot be conservative in the true sense as long as its reliance is on industrialism, whose very nature it is to unsettle any establishment and initiate the endless innovation of technological "progress"'.[12]

As Michael W. Miles argues in *The Odyssey of the American Right*, the principal divisions between the economic liberals and the social traditionalists were religious as well as ideological, the 'libertarians' deriving from 'the old Protestant Right', the traditionalists, often Catholic, less concerned with individualism and freedom and more with 'God, family and order'.[13] What both factions had in common, in the forties and fifties, was an alienation from, and deep distrust of, the majority, a prejudice darkly expressed by German émigré Peter Viereck, who argued in 1949 that 'we don't need a "century of the common man"; we have it already, and it has only produced the commonest man, the impersonal and irresponsible and uprooted mass-man'.[14] The American Right, then, watched with some distaste as its post-war standard-bearers sought to court a plurality for their views. For most libertarians,

Senator Joseph McCarthy's anti-communist crusade of the early fifties represented a basic challenge to freedom of conscience (and few traditionalists were happy with his rabble-rousing style). But, conversely, Senator Barry Goldwater's subtle compromise between 'southern' traditionalism and 'western' individualism (in his 1964 Presidential platform) led merely to electoral ignominy.

It was not until the late 1960s that the 'revolting masses' of right-wing demonology were transmuted into the new 'silent majority' of Nixonian myth, a majority of whom were either southern traditionalists or northern workers, neither of which groups was particularly attracted by liberal economic theory, but both of which shared what one chronicler of the New Right described as a profound revulsion against the ideologues of the 1960s, particularly those promoting affirmative action, 'unilateral disarmers slashing Pentagon budgets' and 'radical feminists, students and homosexuals repudiating and assaulting traditional values', in association with 'a burgeoning "knowledge elite" turning increasingly hostile to capitalism'.[15] Thus, after all the debates and arguments in the post-war years, it was the social issues that finally came to dominate the Right's political agenda.

Powell and his Allies

Because of the slacker grip of party loyalties in the USA, American conservatives could cast themselves in an oppositional role during the Eisenhower, as well was the Truman and Johnson years. In Britain, the Tory Party's thirteen uninterrupted years of power kept its ideologues under firm control, while the leadership retained its commitment to the post-war settlement and its belief 'in Keynes, in the welfare state as we have come to know it, in high government spending, in government's ability to create full employment and encourage growth'.[16] It is true that even during the thirteen years there were flashes of what might now be called monetarist or Friedmanite strategy − in the first years of the peacetime Churchill government with its 'bonfire of controls', and during the early Macmillan period, when the then Chancellor of the Exchequer and two of his junior ministers resigned over their belief in a tighter fiscal and monetary policy. And there were groups − like Aims of Industry (founded in 1942) and the Institute of Economic Affairs (1957) − which advocated economic liberal ideas, and others (like the Monday Club, founded in 1960) which proselytized the more ancient and venerable conservative traditions of paternalism, imperialism and racism.

But the major change came, predictably, with the loss of power in 1964, and it was one of the two ministers who resigned with Peter Thorneycroft who came to represent the breaking of the consensus most powerfully. Enoch Powell was probably the most senior committed economic liberal in the Conservative Party. Echoing the libertarian rhetoric of Hayek and Friedman, he wrote in 1966 that 'when a society's economic life ceases to be shaped by the interaction of the free decisions of individuals, freedom is in a fair way to disappear from other sides of its existence as well'.[17] And, indeed, in the 1960s Powell clearly saw the advocacy of such ideas as the *primary* purpose of his political life:

> Whatever else the Conservative Party stands for, unless it is the party of free choice, free competition and free enterprise, unless − I am not afraid of the word − it is the party of capitalism, then it has no function in the contemporary world.[18]

The fact that Powell's commitment to market forces was always tempered by a fair deal of old-fashioned welfare paternalism (the National Health Service, for instance, being justified on the grounds that 'a civilized, compassionate nation can do no other',[19]) does not completely obviate the sense that his later views on race represent a significant disjuncture with his opinions on the economy. As Paul Foot exposes, Powell in his early days attested that he would always 'set my face like flint against making any difference between one citizen of this country and another on grounds of his origin'.[20] It is surely fair to see no little contradiction between Powell's oft-expressed belief that labour should be free, and indeed encouraged, to move between regions but not between countries; that freedom of movement should apply internationally only to capital. Powell himself, perhaps aware of the problem, has addressed himself to the relationship between his nationalism and his liberalism, and came up with an explanation that is really no more than a tautology:

> It is not for the sake of a dry-as-dust theory, or because of the academic beauty and precision of a market economy, or from materialist calculation . . . that we are called upon to commend the test of competition to the nation, and to submit our politics and actions to that test first. The demand comes passionate and direct from the heart of national pride itself. Britain today needs desperately for its own sake, for the sake of self-respect, to regain the confidence and the

conviction that it can hold up its head in competition with all comers in the world.[21]

The idea that nationalism can only exist when a nation is economically competitive, is not only dubious in the sense that nationhood is tested most strongly in times of war when such conditions cannot by definition apply. The concept of a people finding itself through equivalent facility in the market-place, contrasts starkly with Powell's own definition of national consciousness as 'a sense of difference from the rest of the world, of having something in common which is not shared beyond the limits of the nation'.[22]

Whether or not Powell's change of course in the late 1960s was a genuine conversion or an act of opportunism, change it was. The economics of Adam Smith might seem 'dry-as-dust' to Powell's electors in Wolverhampton: the issue of immigration was anything but. Laissez-faire economics has usually been a minority obsession. Powell's three major anti-immigration speeches of the late 1960s were a bid, over the heads of the flaccid consensualists of both parties, for a new majority. As Powell put it, with a typical combination of grandiosity and dry impishness, 'the greatest task of the statesman . . . is to offer his people good myths'.[23]

The importance of Powell's majoritarianism has been acknowledged both by commentators on, and adherents of, Thatcherism. In the wake of the 1979 election, Andrew Gamble noted that 'without "Powellism", "Thatcherism" would not have had the same opportunity',[24] a point echoed by the *Sunday Telegraph's* Peregrine Worsthorne, in the immediate aftermath of June 1983:

> It was Enoch Powell who first sowed the seeds whose harvest Margaret Thatcher reaped last Thursday . . . and to his great voice should credit go for shattering the Butskellite glacis, the dissolution of which led to the avalanche.[25]

But there is a huge irony contained within the career of Enoch Powell — an irony that goes beyond the fact that by the time his party embraced his philosophy, he was no longer a part of it. The paradox is that between 1974 and 1979 it was Powellism Mark I — economic rather than nationalist Powellism — which came to gain an increasing hold over the Conservative Party. Following Edward Heath's defeat at the February 1974 General Election, the Conservative Party fell increasingly under the influence of a mushrooming number of campaigns, organizations and groupings proselytizing free market economics — from academic study groups like an increasingly prestigious and influential Institute of Economic Affairs (joined in 1974 by Sir Keith Joseph's Centre for Policy Studies), to populist movements like the National Association of Ratepayers' Action Groups, the Association of Self-Employed People and the National Association for Freedom. Electoral failure is almost bound to increase ideological voltage: what was significant about the post-1974 upsurge was the singular magnetism of the libertarian pole of the Conservative Right.

There were both political and economic reasons for this phenomenon. Politically, the years following Powell's 1967-8 speeches had demonstrated the risks involved in playing the racist card. The growth of fascist groups like the National Front made any organization presenting a militant anti-immigration line vulnerable to infiltration — which was precisely what happened to the Monday Club during the two years following the Heath government's admittance of 30,000 Asian refugees from Uganda in 1972. As a number of people have pointed out, the ideology of the National Association for Freedom was in large part built around a political model that set it at the greatest possible distance from the National Front.[26] As NAFF founder Norris McWhirter argued:

> In the west the internal struggle is that between the libertarian elements and the corporatists. The nationalizers, the neo-Keynesians and the advocates of universal welfare with their cohorts of index-pensioned civil servants are ranged against the advocates of market economics.[27]

By placing the political fracture line between 'individualism' and 'collectivism', the NAFF was able to pit itself against both the Left and what it acknowledged to be the fascists of the National Front, frequently making the point that 'the abbreviation "Nazi" . . . actually stands, of course, for National *Socialist*'.[28]

Far from wishing to promote the communal oneness of the nation, then, the NAFF was careful to base its highly successful propaganda 'upon the presumption of the value of the human being as an individual, and not on the concept of men and women as mere units within the collectivist State'.[29] The NAFF was also aware of the increasing prestige of free market ideas in the intellectual and academic worlds (Milton Friedman and F. A. Hayek received Nobel Prizes for economics in the early seventies). But perhaps most important of all was the growing economic desperation of the Tory grass roots, faced with what they saw as an exponential increase in trade union power on the one hand, and an equally ratchet-like growth in the power of government to constrain, direct and regulate, on the other. It was the image of the self-employed small businessman, harassed by restrictive practices all day, dripping midnight oil on his VAT return, which inspired NAFF ideologues like David Kelly:

> I consider that history will see the period of the Heath government as one of the most crucial in cementing the acceptance of Socialism in Britain. It was at this time that the self-employed came to feel most abandoned . . . their so-called own kind turned on them.[30]

So on 3 May 1979 the Conservative Party, the party of order and government and rule, went to the country with a manifesto that committed the incoming government to redress a balance that 'had been increasingly tilted in favour of the state at the expense of individual liberty'. Four and a half years later on the other hand, at the Tory Conference following another crushing victory, a delegate from Bristol stated in the law and order debate: 'We are paying the price for too many years of free expression and freedom.' What had changed?

USA: Neo-Conservatives and the New Right

In March 1952, the American Jewish magazine *Commentary* ran a piece by a young intellectual called Irving Kristol, a graduate of City College New York, and, like many such, also a graduate from militant Trotskyism. 'There is one thing that the American people know about Senator McCarthy', Kristol wrote, 'he, like them, is unequivocally anti-communist. About the spokesmen for American liberalism, they feel they know no such thing.' Nine years later, *Commentary's* new editor, Norman Podhoretz, a well-known radical and accepted spokesman for the 'beat' generation of American novelists and poets in the fifties, wrote an article railing against 'all the white liberals who permit Negroes to blackmail them into adopting double standard of moral judgement, and lend themselves – again assuming a responsibility for crimes they never committed – to cunning and contemptuous exploitation by Negroes they employ or try to defend'.[31] While in October 1970, Podhoretz published an article by another former radical, Nathan Glazer of Harvard, which charted Glazer's progression from being 'a radical − a mild radical it is true, but still someone who felt closer to radical than to liberal writers and politicians in the 1950s' to that of believing that the position he formerly espoused was 'so beset with error and confusion that our main task . . . must be to argue with it and to strip it ultimately of the pretension that it understands the causes of our ills and how to set them right'.

The process of defection from Marxism to liberalism, followed by an equally stark shift from liberalism to conservatism, is a common trajectory for almost all the eastern intellectuals collectively dubbed 'neo-conservative' in the late 1970s, a group led by Kristol, Podhoretz and Glazer (and articulated by their journals *Commentary* and *The Public Interest*), and also including academics Daniel Bell, Samuel P. Huntingdon and Robert Nisbet, and politicians like Senator Daniel Patrick Moynihan and UN Ambassador Jeane Kirkpatrick. Following as said a remarkably common path of political defection (Kristol enjoys remarking that he has been 'moving consistently to the Right since 1942'), the present position − and, just as importantly, the tone − of American neo-conservatism was well defined by Adam Meyerson of the *American Spectator*:

> Neo-Conservatives are liberals with a sense of tragedy. We wish it were possible to live without defence budgets, but realize that it is not. We'd like to campaign for comprehensive national health insurance, but are afraid that its costs would interfere with other humanitarian ends . . . And Neo-Conservatives are conservatives with a liberal attachment to the common man. We think that, for all its many, many injustices, the United States has given more freedom and more opportunities both for self-rule and for economic advancement to more people over a longer period of time than has any other political system in the history of the world. So we think that our institutional traditions and constitutional heritage should be modified only with the greatest caution and deliberation.[32]

'Caution' and 'deliberation' are key neo-conservative words (another is 'prudence'), and in that way the neo-conservatives are considerably removed in style from the network of organizations and campaigns jointly defined as the 'New Right' in the run-up to the 1980 Presidential election, when it acted as a marriage-broker to a coalition of anti-abortionists, gun-owners, tax-reducers, John Birch Society stalwarts and Protestant preachers which was later to call itself the 'Moral Majority'. (In *Back to Basics*, Burton Yale Pines describes how leading New Right organizers Paul Weyrich and Howard Phillips assembled the components of the Moral Majority, in collaboration with its most public spokesman, the Reverend Jerry Falwell.)[33]

The strength of organizations like the National Political Action Committee, the Committee for the Survival of a Free Congress and the Conservative Caucus (all founded in the 1974 – 5 period), lies in their use of sophisticated direct mail technology. All three of the above organizations are closely linked with Richard A. Viguerie, the first executive director of the Young Americans for Freedom in the early 1960s, and fund-raiser for George Wallace's 1972 Presidential campaign. Viguerie's technique is to build up computerized mailing lists of supporters of single-issue right-wing campaigns, and either to lease them out to other conservative groups or to use them in his own campaigns. By 1980, Viguerie was reported to have ten million names on twenty-five lists, variously in receipt of letters and appeals like the following:

> Dear Friend, I think you will appreciate, more than most Americans, what I am sending you. I have enclosed two flags: the red, white and blue of Old Glory – and the white flag of surrender. I want to show you, by these two flags, what is at stake for America under the SALT II treaty with Russia . . . [34]

The luridness of the New Right's propaganda (a Viguerie letter signed by New Right Senator Jesse Helms stated unequivocally that 'your tax dollars are being used to pay for grade school courses that teach our children that cannibalism, wife-swapping and the murder of infants and the elderly are acceptable behaviour')[35], has perhaps obscured the similarities between its ideological bias and that of the neo-conservatives. For, despite what New Right biographer Burton Pines calls the neo-conservative discomfort with 'the direct, insistent and studiedly unsophisticated manner of the social issues crowd',[36] the two groups share an ideological commitment to the socially authoritarian rather than the economically liberal end of the spectrum when the two conflict. The New Right's house journal *Conservative Digest* admits that 'attention to so-called social issues – abortion, busing, gun rights, pornography, crime – has . . . become central to the growth of the New Right', because 'the New Right is looking for issues that people care about, and social issues, at least for the present, fit the bill'.[37] Richard Viguerie has admitted that 'I'm willing to make concessions to come to power . . . We're going to have to be willing to use the government to stimulate the economy more than I think we should in order to get the votes.'[38] And, for at least one mainstream Republican (George Bush's campaign manager David Keene), these compromises 'go right to the core of what we consider conservatism — our dedication to preserving the free enterprise system'.[39]

The neo-conservative case against economic liberalism is both more sophisticated and to a certain extent more opaque. Irving Kristol writes for *The Wall Street Journal* and he and many of his fellows are, or have been, employed by the American Enterprise Institute, which is as its name implies. But the theme of much of Kristol's writing — encapsulated in the title of his essay collection *Two Cheers for Capitalism* — is a serious questioning of 'the original liberal idea that it is possible for the individual, alone or in voluntary association with others, to cope with the eternal dilemmas of the human condition'. The reason why Kristol is unable 'to celebrate the unqualified virtues of individualism'[40] is that while Adam Smith's hidden hand 'has its uses in the market place, which is the domain of "economic men" rather than of citizens, and where the specter of bankruptcy does impose a kind of self-discipline', the results of the 'emancipation of the individual from social restraints' are disastrous when 'extended to the polity as a whole, which can go bankrupt only once, and whose destiny is finally determined by the capacity of its citizenry to govern its passions and thereby rightly understand its enduring common interests'.[41] And the paradox is that, by encouraging the pursuit of 'self-seeking, self-indulgence and just plain . . . selfishness',[42] the untrammelled free-marketeers like Friedman and Hayek might unwittingly promote the destruction of the economic system they so fervently espouse:

> The idea of bourgeois virtue has been eliminated from Friedman's conception of bourgeois society, and has been replaced by the idea of individual liberty . . . (But) what if the 'self' that is 'realized' under the conditions of liberal capitalism is a self that despises liberal capitalism, and uses its liberty to subvert and abolish a free society? To this question Hayek — like Friedman — has no answer. And yet this is *the* question we now confront, as our society relentlessly breeds more and more such selves, whose private vices in no way provide public benefits to the bourgeois order. Perhaps one can say that the secular, 'libertarian' tradition of capitalism — as distinct from the Protestant-bourgeois tradition — simply had too limited an imagination when it came to vice . . . It could refute Marx effectively,

but never thought it would be called upon to refute the Marquis de Sade.[43]

It is clear that in this key passage, Irving Kristol has a particular period of recent history in mind. As he told *Newsweek* (19 January 1976), 'if there is only one thing that Neo-Conservatives are unanimous about, it is their dislike of the "counter-culture" which has played so remarkable a role in American life in the last 15 years'. Or, as commentator Elizabeth Drew has written, the neo-conservatives 'are on common ground against what they see as the spoiled children and their indulgent elders of the late sixties and early seventies'.[44] Or, again, as neo-Conservative Robert Nisbet argued:

> I think it would be difficult to find a single decade in the history of Western culture when so much barbarism − so much calculated onslaught against culture and convention in any form . . . passed into print, into music, into art, and on to the American stage as the decade of the 1960s.[45]

Nisbet then proceeded to define the central, primary heresy of the 1960s as a massive 'revolt against authority' and 'consecration of disorder', an analysis echoed by Samuel P. Huntingdon in his article 'The Democratic Distemper', in which he described the sixties as a time in which:

> people no longer felt the same obligation to obey those whom they had previously considered superior to themselves in age, rank, status, expertise, character and talents . . . democratic principle was extended to many institutions where it can, in the long run, only frustrate the purpose of those institutions.[46]

For the problem was not merely confined to the behaviour of college students in the 1960s, because, of course, it was by no means certain that upon graduation they would grow out of what Kristol dubbed their 'phase of infantile regression'.[47] Indeed, perhaps the most important ideological construct developed by the neo-conservatives is the notion that a significant proportion of the 'Vietnam generation' of college students now forms the core of a 'New Class' of 'scientists, teachers and educational administrators, journalists and others in the communications industries, psychologists, social workers, those lawyers and doctors who make their careers in the expanding public sector, city planners, the staffs of the larger foundations, the upper levels of the government bureaucracy and so on', which, while 'not much interested in money' is 'keenly interested in power', a power which it wishes to transfer from business to government, where the new class itself will 'have a major say in how it is exercised'.[48]

And in a situation where, as Kristol argues, 'to see something on television is to feel entitled to it';[49] in a time, further, when (as Nathan Glazer sees it) 'our systems of communications are such that everyone is aware of the level of goods and services that prevails in some places, and the deficiencies that still obtain in others';[50] then, as Robert Nisbet claims, the uses of that power become the satisfaction of the appetites of the poor:

> Expectations cannot do other than increase exponentially. Envy . . . quickly takes command, and the lust for power with which to allay every fresh discontent, to assuage every social pain, and to gratify every fresh expectation soon becomes boundless.[51]

Or, as New Rightist William S. Rusher put it, in less elegant but more electorally practical terms:

> A new economic division pits the producers – businessmen, manufacturers, hard-hats, blue-collar workers, and farmers – against the new and powerful class of nonproducers comprised of a liberal verbalist elite (the dominant media, the major foundations and research institutions, the educational establishment, the federal and state bureaucracies) and a semipermanent welfare constituency, all coexisting happily in a state of mutually sustaining symbiosis.[52]

For Rusher, then, a 'vast segment of society' (the welfare class) is being 'carefully tended' and indeed 'forever subtly expanded' by the New Class 'as a justification for their own existence and growth'.[53] And thus the New Class becomes, as Burke wrote of the 'political men of letters' of the French Revolution, 'a link to unite, in favour of one object, obnoxious wealth to restless and desperate poverty'.[54]

In summary, then, the neo-conservative case is that liberal capitalism, unlimited by bourgeois constraints, encouraged the post-war generation in the belief that it has a right to the instant satisfaction of all appetites, regardless of effort. In the late 1960s, this conviction shifted from the purely economic into the political arena, with the consequence that a whole new class of people entered the distributive sectors of government, there encouraging its clients to believe in turn that they were entitled, as of right, to the full benefits of a consumer society, whether or not they could afford them. Thus liberal capitalism gave permission to the post-war boom generation to pursue its appetite for moral self-satisfaction regardless of the political consequences; allowing this new class in its turn to foster in a new underclass the notion that it had the right to satisfy its physical appetites without economic restraint, to the point where liberal capitalism itself is threatened by social violence on the one hand or financial collapse on the other.

Just as important as the bones of the argument, however, is the vocabulary chosen to express it. Drew's 'spoiled children', Kristol's 'infantile regression', Nisbet's 'revolt against authority': all speak of the neo-conservative belief that above all else they are the proselytizers of 'adulthood − the things you learn when you grow up'.[55] And the notion that the radicalism of the sixties was no more than a peculiarly virulent outbreak of juvenile dementia runs through neo-conservative polemics against the movements of the time: from the student movement itself ('what the dissatisfied students were looking for were adults − adults to confront, to oppose, to emulate');[56] to the demographic causes of crime (' "there is a perennial invasion of barbarians who must some how be civilized" . . . that "invasion" is the coming of age of a new generation of young people');[57] to feminism (the women's liberation movement demands on behalf of women 'a freedom demanded by children and enjoyed by no one: the freedom from all difficulty')[58] and, in the company of Norman Podhoretz, beyond:

> In the case of the white young, the contemptuous repudiation of everything American and middle-class was mistaken for a form of idealism when it really represented a refusal to be who they were and to assume responsibility for themselves by taking their place in a world of adults . . . But if the plague seems for the moment to have run its course among these groups, it rages as fiercely as ever among others: among the kind of women who do not wish to be women and among those men who do not wish to be men . . . there can be no more radical refusal of self-acceptance than the repudiation of one's own biological nature; and there can be no abdication of responsibility more fundamental that the refusal of a man to become, and to be, a father, or the refusal of a woman to become, and be, a mother.[59]

It is an extraordinary passage. From it, it is clear that, for Podhoretz at least, the enemy is no longer merely the infantile, or even just the barbarian: he wrestles with plague-carriers, he jousts with demons.

UK: The Peterhouse School

The main intellectual challenge to the hegemony of the economic
liberals in the Conservative Party in Britain in the 1970s has been
centred not round an organized faction so much as a loose grouping
of graduates from a particular Cambridge college. In 1978, Maurice
Cowling, fellow of Peterhouse, Cambridge, edited a selection of
Conservative Essays, in which the essayists included Peterhouse
graduates Roger Scruton, Peregrine Worsthorne and George Gale
and the college's present dean, Edward Norman. Other Peterhouse
men prominent in the advocacy of social-authoritarian positions
include John Vincent (like Scruton, a *Times* contributor), Colin
Welch (like Worsthorne, a regular writer for both the *Spectator* and
the *Telegraph* group), novelist Kingsley Amis and Patrick Cosgrove,
Mrs Thatcher's biographer.

The project of *Conservative Essays* was to attack the rhetoric of
freedom with which the economic liberals in the Conservative Party
sought to promote their aims. In his introduction, Cowling attacked
the economic liberals for 'lending themselves too readily to the idea
that in some exclusive way "freedom" is the ultimate value', arguing
instead that 'it is not freedom that Conservatives want: what they
want is the sort of freedom that will maintain existing inequalities
or restore lost ones'.[60] (In this view, he was to be echoed by fellow-
contributor Roger Scruton, who in his book *The Meaning of
Conservatism* claimed that liberalism, economic or otherwise, was
no less than 'the principal enemy of conservatism', adding that
democracy itself can be 'discarded without detriment to the civil well-
being as the conservative conceives it'.)[61] Indeed, the keynote essay
in many ways was that of the *Sunday Telegraph's* Peregrine
Worsthorne, who insisted that 'if one were to probe into the hearts
of many potential and actual Tory supporters − and others besides
− one might well discover that what worried them most about
contemporary Britain was not so much the lack of freedom as its
excessive abundance . . . The trouble about Labour on this view is
that it has set too many people far too free.'[62]

But perhaps the most striking thing about *Conservative Essays*
as a volume is its obsession with ideas of nationhood and race. Thus
T. E. Utley ('massed immigration has saddled [the nation] with a
"racial problem" to which it has still given no systematic
thought'),[63] John Biffen (the 'scale of immigration that has
transformed the heartland of many English cities . . . has not been

willed by the British people'),[64] and George Gale ('in rejecting Powell, the Conservative Party . . . ignored the instincts of the nation, and chose instead the modish hypocricies of Hampstead about immigration'),[65] joined Cowling himself in a call for a reassertion of national identity, and the manufacture thereby of 'a spiritual glue that would bind down the elite and force it to use a language that would bind it to everyone else'.[66]

It might be cynical to argue that it is the assumed electoral potency of the race issue that led not only Maurice Cowling's social authoritarians to evoke the mystic onenesses of nationhood, but also a number of key figures on the libertarian right. Despite the National Association for Freedom's strenuous (though not always totally successful) attempts to evade the issue in the late seventies, two fully-paid-up libertarians seemed perfectly content with the Powellite position that it is perfectly possible to argue for the full play of market forces on the capital side of the equation, while strenuously resisting the free flow of labour.

On 8 September 1976, the Director of the Centre for Policy Studies, Alfred Sherman, wrote in *The Daily Telegraph* that 'nationhood can neither be ignored or wished away' as 'man's main focus of identity', quoting in support Edmund Burke's 'partnership between those who are living, those who are dead, and those who are to be born'. Less loftily, in the same paper the following day, he wrote that 'the imposition of mass immigration from backward alien cultures' was just one symptom of a generalized attack by person or persons unknown on 'patriotism, the family, and . . . all that is English and wholesome'. While four months later, no less a person than Hayek himself, who in *The Constitution of Liberty* had bitterly criticized the Conservative 'hostility to internationalism and its proneness to a strident nationalism',[67] wrote to *The Times* in support of strict immigration control, on the grounds that the

> ordinary man only slowly reconciles himself to a large increase in foreigners among his neighbours, even if they differ only in language and manners, and that therefore the wise statesman, to prevent an unpleasant reawakening of primitive instincts, ought to aim at keeping the rate of influx low.[68]

Such instincts were rudely shaken from slumber by events in the early 1980s, which effectively concluded the pure libertarian phase of Thatcherism, and substituted a new authoritarianism that owed much more to Peterhouse than to the Institute of Economic Affairs.

There was more than a hint of 'I told you so' in Peregrine Worsthorne's immediate response to the riots of the summer of 1981:

> More violence there is certain to be. If it is not in the inner cities, then it will be on the picket lines. It was always Utopian to expect the body politic to suffer the pains of economic retraction without violent convulsions. One suspects that those who voted Mrs Thatcher into office did so in the belief that a Tory Government would know best how to control them; that having willed the economic ends it would have the courage and determination not to shirk the necessary social means.[69]

What was particularly instructive about the instant analysis that proceeded from the pens of conservative commentators in the wake of the riots, was how closely it was modelled on the constructs developed by the neo-conservatives in the USA. On the very morrow of Toxteth, George Gale blamed the riots on a 'revulsion from authority and discipline' which reached its zenith during the 'permissive revolution' of the sixties;[70] not long after, Edward Norman argued that the rioters had been 'nurtured in a society which offered them seemingly endless expectations to personal and social satisfaction',[71] a society furthermore in which (according to Colin Welch) 'all fidelity, restraint, thrift, sobriety, taste and discipline, all the virtues associated with work, with the painful acquisition of knowledge, skill and qualifications' have been undermined.[72]

Present too was the concept of the New Class — albeit described as the 'liberal establishment' (by Peregrine Worsthorne, commenting on the 'sheltered lives' that had been led by 'the likes of Lord Scarman' before the Brixton riots confronted them with the reality of 'Enoch Powell's increasingly urgent reiterated warnings about the inevitability of racial violence'),[73] or indeed as the 'radical establishment, founded in the 1960s' (by Ronald Butt of *The Times*).[74] Like their American counterparts, the British conservatives see the New Class as a potent tool for the mass-brainwashing of the public, by which technique, according to Powell himself as early as 1970 'the majority are reduced to a condition in which they finally distrust their own senses . . . and surrender their will to the manipulator'.[75] And, like the American new class, the British version is accused of inspiring, if not creating, an underclass. Thus, Paul Johnson, with characteristic lightness of touch, writes of a 'mercenary army' consisting of 'the burgeoning bureaucrats of expanded local and central government; the new breed of "administrators" who control schools and hospitals and even the arts; sociology lecturers and others on the fringe of the higher education afflatus; so-called social workers with their glib pseudo-solutions to non-problems',[76] who have in common 'an interest in exciting public demands, real or imaginary'.[77] While for the *Spectator's* Richard West, writing after the first Brixton riots of April 1981, the conspiracy theory applied directly to the question of the urban uprisings:

> Here, as formerly in the United States, the champions of the black cause are middle-class, well-meaning or radical whites . . . They see in the grievances of the blacks a weapon for use against all bourgeois society.[78]

So thus, as US neo-conservative Midge Decter continued, in an article glowingly quoted in *The Daily Telegraph* days after Toxteth,[79] the purveyors of 'enlightened liberal attitudes' had 'given permission' to the rioters to 'go on their spree of looting', by promoting the idea among young blacks that 'race and poverty were sufficient excuses for lawlessness'.

And, like their American counterparts also, British conservatives are concerned to point the finger of blame for urban disorder at a cult of youth and youthfulness, initially promoted and developed in the 1960s, but now being transferred by that decade's graduates to a new generation. As Colin Welch writes:

> The decade of the 1960s (or perhaps more precisely of '65-'75) is often remembered . . . as a horrendous episode which ended in tears, after which reason resumed her sway and wiser counsels prevailed. This is but a comforting illusion. The poisons then injected into our system, though doubtless diluted, course still through its veins . . . The revolting students of the 1960s are the revolting teachers of today, reproducing themselves by teaching as received wisdom what they furiously asserted against the wisdom received from their own teachers.[80]

Welch goes on to name the received wisdom in question as a form of 'puerilism' or 'adolescent barbarism', having earlier defined it as a variety of 'poison'. In this of course, he echoes Norman Podhoeretz's definition of feminism and homosexuality as a form of plague. And he is not alone: the language of demonology is now *de rigeur* for the discussion of the social reforms of the last twenty years, as Christopher Booker demonstrates:

Looking back over what has happened we may be put in mind of one of those fairy stories or myths where someone is told that a certain box or bottle or door must not be opened, because they will regret the consequences . . . And the point of the story is always that once the demons are unleashed they can never be put back again. Many people must feel the same about what has happened in our society over the past 25 years — that . . .the demons of drugs, pornography, violence and permissiveness in all its forms, are now raging out of control.[81]

No wonder, then, that the Tory libertarians have fallen silent. No wonder that even the National Association for Freedom (renamed the Freedom Association), heralded 1983 by announcing that it was no longer primarily concerned with 'the political forces currently threatening our freedom', but rather with 'rising crime, sexual permissiveness and family breakdown'.[82] How could they not be, with the devil himself stalking the land?

Family and State

In all crucial aspects, then, the New Class model has been recast in British terms, and in terms, furthermore, that have united an extraordinarily wide variety of British conservative, from self-styled libertarians like Alfred Sherman and Paul Johnson, via reluctant wets like Ronald Butt, to High Tory traditionalists like the Peterhouse trio of Norman, Worsthorne and Welch. One reason for the attractiveness of the model may well be that it goes some significant way towards squaring the circle between an intellectual adherence to the free market and the emotional attachment to authority and imposed tradition. To talk of the new class as the donor not just of welfare payments but of 'permission' — indeed to attest that a state that cannot of course be 'compassionate' can nonetheless be 'permissive' or otherwise — is to speak the language of parenthood. And it is worth noting that, in the British context, the metaphor of the disadvantaged as children demanding rights of the beneficent state, has wider application than it does in the USA, by virtue of the greater size of the public sector. As Powell himself argued, the 'translation of a want or need into a right is one of the most widespread and dangerous of modern heresies',[83] a concern reiterated by Alfred Sherman when he berates 'armies of social workers' not only for 'recruiting armies of welfare claimants', but

also for 'encouraging them to press for what they call "rights" ' .[84]
While for Kenneth Minogue, LSE political scientist and *Conservative Essays* contributor, the 'politics of compassion' have turned not just the poor and the recipients of welfare, but the entire British population, into 'a collection of noisy corporate children crying "it's not fair" as they roll up their sleeves, not to do something for themselves, but to display their sores and scars' — encouraged, naturally, by 'a sizeable army of bureaucrats, counsellors and managers of the lives of the needy who constitute a major corporate interest in our political life'.[85]

In this context, the contradiction between the anti-statism of free market ideology, and the authoritarianism of the traditionalists, suddenly appears less acute. Indeed, in this sense, it's possible to see Thatcherism not as a libertarian ideology, calling for the dismantling of the state, but as the articulation of demands for the reassertion of the paternal authority of the state over its pampered and infantilized subjects, for the firing of the indulgent nanny and the hiring of the no-nonsense martinet. From this perspective, the crucial role of the free market is not to emancipate the entrepreneur but to chastise the feckless, an instrument not of liberation but of discipline. Hence, perhaps, the extraordinary recommendations of the Government's 'Family Policy Group' (leaked to *The Guardian* on 18 February 1983), which sought to transmit free market values to the young via the family, not least by 'training children to manage their pocket money'. And hence also, some more recent pronouncements by Mrs Thatcher herself, including an interview in which she compared governing the country to bringing up a chid ('you don't get the best out of them unless you are really rather firm'),[86] and a speech in which she sought to reduce a whole series of social conflicts and tensions to the ethical scale of the nursery moralism:

> Young people are impressionable. How we behave — whether as parents, teachers, sportsmen, politicians — is bound to influence how our children behave. When teachers strike and cause disruption — that's a bad example. When football idols play foul — that's a bad example. When local councils refuse to set a legal rate — that's a bad example. And when some Trade Union leaders, yes, and some politicians, scorn the law and the courts and the police — these are bad examples. So too is picket-line violence. And who can help but worry about some of the violence we see on our television screens? The standards of society are set by what we tolerate, by the discipline and conventions we set.[87]

Or, as Paul Johnson put it, in a hostile review of former Thatcher aide Ferdinand Mount's book *The Subversive Family*,[88] 'civilized societies require institutions which restrain our passions and supplement our shortcomings. The three principle ones are the family, organized religion and the state . . . In my view, family, church and state are complementary institutions, both of control and charity'.[89]

'Control and charity'. What more suitable slogan could there be for an ideology that seeks to reimpose the values of the soup-kitchen and the workhouse?

Squaring the Circle

In the search for that elusively silent majority that would transform the American Right from a remnant into the trumpet of the age, a Nixon aide is reputed to have pointed out that the majority of the American people were 'unyoung, unblack and unpoor'. The achievement of both Reaganism and Thatcherism has been to weld together the instincts of individual greed and collective self-righteousness into a coherent model of the world, in which the rhetoric of freedom can co-exist with the reassertion of virtue. Put crudely, the new authoritarianism allows people to vote in their own, narrow self-interest, but yet to feel good about doing so. One might say, it gives them permission.

Notes

1 The Metropolitan Police's 'racial' crime statistics were published on 10 Mar. 1982.
2 Quoted in *The Daily Telegraph*, 18 Mar. 1982.
3 Quoted in *The Guardian*, 28 Mar. 1982.
4 Dr Rhodes Boyson, speaking to the Loughborough Conservative Association, 5 Feb. 1982.
5 L. Brent Bozell, 'Freedom or virtue?', *National Review*, 11 Sept. 1962, quoted in George H. Nash, *The Conservative Intellectual Movement in America since 1945* (Basic Books, New York, 1976), pp. 176-7.
6 Nash, *Conservative Intellectual Movement*, p. 26.

7 F. A. Hayek, *The Road to Serfdom* (Routledge, London, 1976), pp. 10-11.

8 Milton Friedman, *Capitalism and Freedom* (University of Chicago, Chicago, 1962), p. 200.

9 F. A. Hayek, *The Constitution of Liberty* (Routledge, London, 1976), p. 402.

10 Nash, *Conservative Intellectual Movement*, p. 151.

11 Ibid., p. 81.

12 Ibid., p. 204.

13 Michael W. Miles, *The Odyssey of the American Right* (Oxford University Press, New York, 1980), p. 254.

14 Nash, *Conservative Intellectual Movement*, p. 65.

15 Burton Yale Pines, *Back to Basics* (William Morrow and Co., New York, 1982), p. 268.

16 David Howell, *The Conservative Tradition and the 1980s* (Centre for Policy Studies, London, 1980).

17 Quoted in Neill Nugent and Roger King, *The British Right* (Saxon House, Farnborough, 1977), pp. 107-8.

18 Quoted in Andrew Gamble, *The Conservative Nation* (Routledge and Kegan Paul, London, 1974), p. 116.

19 Nugent and King, *The British Right*, p. 105.

20 Quoted in Paul Foot, *The Rise of Enoch Powell* (Penguin, London, 1969), p. 66.

21 Nugent and King, *The British Right*, p. 117.

22 Ibid., p. 111.

23 Gamble, *The Conservative Nation*, p. 115.

24 Andrew Gamble, 'The decline of the Conservative Party', *Marxism Today*, Nov. 1979.

25 *The Sunday Telegraph*, 12 Jun. 1983.

26 R. King and N. Nugent, *Respectable Rebels* (Hodder and Stoughton, London, 1979), pp. 186-7.

27 Norris McWhirter in *In Defence of Freedom* ed. K. W. Watkins (Cassell, London, 1978), p. 61.

28 *Free Nation*, 5 Aug. 1977.

29 Lord de l'Isle in Watkins (ed.), *Defence of Freedom*, p. 17.

30 Quoted in King and Nugent, *Respectable Rebels*, p. 56.

31 *Commentary*, Feb. 1963.

32 Quoted in *The Listener*, 17 Jul. 1980.

33 Pines, *Back to Basics*, p. 294-5.

34 *The Conservative Caucus*, direct mail leaflet, c 1979.

35 Quoted in *The Guardian*, 14 Nov. 1978.

36 Pines, *Back to Basics*, p. 329.
37 *Conservative Digest*, Jun. 1979.
38 Quoted in *The Nation*, 29 Jan. 1977.
39 *The Nation*, 29 Jan. 1977.
40 Quoted in Nash, *Conservative Intellectual Movement*, p. 340.
41 Irving Kristol, *On the Democratic Idea in America*, (Harper and Row, New York, 1973), pp. vii-xiii.
42 Kristol, *Democratic Idea*, p. 27.
43 Irving Kristol, *Two Cheers for Capitalism*, (Basic Books, New York, 1978), pp. 67-8.
44 Quoted in Peter Steinfels, *The Neo-Conservatives*, (Simon and Schuster, New York, 1979), p. 10.
45 *Encounter*, Aug. 1972.
46 *Public Interest*, Feb. 1975.
47 Kristol, *Democratic Idea*, p. 104.
48 Kristol, *Two Cheers*, pp. 27-8.
49 Kristol, *Democratic Idea*, p. 26.
50 *Commentary*, Oct. 1970.
51 Steinfels, *The Neo-Conservatives*, pp. 243-4.
52 William S. Rusher, *The Making of the New Majority Party* (Green Hill, Illinois, 1975), p. 14.
53 Ibid., p. 33.
54 Edmund Burke, *Reflections on the Revolution in France* (Doubleday, New York, 1961), pp. 124-5.
55 *Esquire*, 13 Feb. 1979.
56 Kristol, *Democratic Idea*, p. 125.
57 Norman B. Ryder, quoted by James Q. Wilson, *Thinking About Crime* (Basic Books, New York, 1975), p. 12.
58 Midge Dector, 'The liberated woman', *Commentary*, Oct. 1970.
59 Norman Podhoretz, *Breaking Ranks* (Harper and Row, New York, 1979), pp. 362-3.
60 Maurice Cowling (ed.), *Conservative Essays* (Cassell, London, 1978), p. 9.
61 Roger Scruton, *The Meaning of Conservatism* (Penguin, London, 1980), p. 16.
62 In Cowling (ed.), *Conservative Essays*, pp. 147-8.
63 Ibid., p. 49.
64 Ibid., p. 156.
65 Ibid., p. 183.
66 Ibid., p. 19.
67 Hayek, *Constitution of Liberty*, p. 405.

68 *The Times*, 1 Mar. 1978.
69 *Sunday Telegraph*, 12 Jul. 1981.
70 *Daily Express*, 7 Jul. 1981.
71 *Sunday Telegraph*, 19 Jul. 1981.
72 *Spectator*, 17 Dec. 1983.
73 *Sunday Telegraph*, 29 Nov. 1981.
74 *The Times*, 2 Jun. 1983.
75 Enoch Powell, *Powell in the 1970 Election* (Elliot Rightway, London, 1970), p. 108.
76 Paul Johnson, *The Recovery of Freedom* (Blackwell, Oxford, 1980), p. 72.
77 Ibid., p. 8.
78 *Spectator*, 18 Apr. 1981.
79 *The Daily Telegraph*, 27 Jul. 1981.
80 *Spectator*, 20 Oct. 1983.
81 *Daily Mail*, 10 Nov. 1983.
82 *Free Nation*, Jan. 1983.
83 Enoch Powell, *Still to Decide* (Batsford, London, 1972), p. 13.
84 *The Daily Telegraph*, 30 May 1977.
85 *The Daily Telegraph*, 8 Feb. 1977.
86 *London Standard*, 11 Apr. 1985.
87 Speech to Conservative Central Council, Newcastle-upon-Tyne, 23 Mar. 1985.
88 Ferdinand Mount, *The Subversive Family* (Jonathan Cape, London, 1982).
89 *The Observer*, 10 Oct. 1982.

Chapter Three

Competition and Compliance
The Utopias of the New Right

RUTH LEVITAS

Conflicting Utopias

The two dominant strands of thought within the New Right — neo-liberal economics and social authoritarianism — stand in a much more problematic relationship to one another than some commentators have supposed. One method of exploring their compatibility at the levels of both policy and ideology is to examine the kinds of society implied by the different strands — that is, the utopias which can be extrapolated from them — and the forms of legitimation involved. This way of considering the kind of society to which people aspire is, of course, problematic. In the first place, used maliciously, it can impute to people aspirations with which they genuinely would not wish to be associated, as well as those to which they would not wish to admit. Secondly, extrapolation may impute a coherence of vision greater than that which actually exists; it may thus both underestimate the role of pragmatism in influencing both policy and justifications of policy, and in so doing overstate the degree of divergence between factions of the New Right.

Although some caution is therefore in order, an examination of the New Right's utopias is possible and justifiable because it is not in fact necessary to extrapolate very far. A characteristic of both strands of New Right thought has been the confident assertion of the nature of the good society. Although Utley has argued that the contrasting utopias are fantasies, not of their proponents, but of their *opponents* within the Conservative Party, and do not exist as divergent aspirations at all,[1] this is demonstrably false. In 1959, Hayek claimed that 'what we lack is a liberal Utopia',[2] and spent much of the intervening years constructing one; and the Adam Smith

Institute has produced *The Omega File*, a series of reports which amounts to a detailed set of policy proposals to establish just such a utopia.[3] The volume of conservative essays to which Utley was contributing contained the skeleton of an alternative conservative utopia expressed more clearly in Scruton's *The Meaning of Conservatism*, albeit still in a less explicitly programmatic mode than the neo-liberal version.[4]

This illuminates both Utley's denial of the existence of these contrasting utopias and an important difference between them. Whereas the *Omega File* can be regarded as a utopian proposal, corresponding to that utopia deriving from the systematic application of the idea of free economic competition, conservatism finds it more difficult to appeal to a utopian future. Casey argues that 'it is characteristic of conservatism that unlike liberalism it does not aim to transcend history'.[5] Mannheim, who pointed to the tendency of conservatives to utopianize the past as manifested in the present, rather than the future,[6] would doubtless endorse Scruton's typification:

> The conservative, unable as he is to appeal to a utopian future, or to any future that is not, as it were, already contained in the present and past, must avail himself of conceptions which are both directly applicable to things as they are and at the same time indicative of a motivating force in men. And this force must be as great as the desire for 'freedom' and 'social justice' offered by his rivals.[7]

Thus 'no utopian vision will have force for him compared to the force of present practice'.[8]

The authoritarian conservative utopia is, therefore, always an immanent utopia, revealed in present practice, rather than a plan for a society to be constructed in the future. And, as Mannheim observes, the motive behind its articulation is to counter the utopias of liberalism and socialism. This means that it can only be understood in terms of its opposition to its rivals; so we will turn first to the neo-liberal utopia.

The Market Delivers the Good

The main contemporary exponent of what Bosanquet describes as the 'thesis' (the virtues of the market) is Friedman, while the 'antithesis' (the evils of intervention) is stressed by Hayek.[9] Both writers are generally opposed to government intervention; both are opponents of the welfare state, although both recognize the need for some relief of poverty. Friedman's main objection to intervention is that it limits economic growth; Hayek fears that any such intervention, including attempts to redistribute wealth through progressive income tax, will lead not just to less growth, but to increasing public expenditure, politicization and totalitarianism. Both essentially espouse (their own interpretations of) Adam Smith's view of the role of government.

The themes elaborated by Hayek and Friedman are also the central themes in the work of the Institute of Economic Affairs (IEA), the Centre for Policy Studies, the Social Affairs Unit and the Adam Smith Institute (ASI). The ASI's 'Omega project' is the most ambitious attempt to spell out the implications of neo-liberalism for social policy, and thus is the main articulation of the liberal New Right's utopia:

> The ASI's Omega project was conceived to fill a significant gap in the field of public policy research. Administrations entering office in democratic societies are often aware of the problems . . . they face, but lack a well-developed range of policy options . . . The Omega project represents the most complete review of the activity of government ever undertaken in Britain. It presents the most comprehensive range of policy initiative which has ever been researched under one programme.[10]

It should not be supposed that the proposals contained in the Omega reports are unlikely to be implemented, since there are connections between the ASI's organizers, the projects' authors, and government. The working parties included a number of MPs (several of whom were newly elected in June 1983); and many of the proposals have already found their way into policy. The *New Statesman* claimed early in 1984 that 'the Conservative Research Department . . . received Omega progress reports at every stage in the last year' and that the report on transport was very favourably received by the appropriate minister.[11] It is however very difficult to attribute the proposals in the reports to particular individuals, or indeed to the ASI as a whole, since most contain a list of contributors accompanied by two separate caveats:

> The views expressed in this publication are those of the author and do not necessarily reflect those of the publisher or copyright owner.

> All Omega Project reports are the edited summaries of the work of
> many different individuals, who have made contributions of various
> sizes over a lengthy period, and as such their contents should not be
> regarded as the definitive views of any one author.[12]

Nevertheless, the ASI seems, with these reports, to have established
itself as precisely the kind of advisory body to government that it
set out to be. However much it may pay lip-service to the idea of
policy options, it is clearly committed to removing restrictions on
the market economy, and, of course, to privatization.

Major themes throughout the reports are deregulation and
privatization. Specific policy proposals are supported by appeals to
accountability, efficiency and freedom, although several in fact
involve a greater centralization of control as a result of removing
powers from local government.

It is assumed that greater accountability will always be achieved
by limiting the role of government and increasing the role of the
market:

> It must be remembered that independent providers . . . are nearer
> to public demand than local authorities can ever be . . . their perpetual
> search for profitability . . . stimulates them to discover and produce
> what the consumer wants . . . In this sense the market sector is more
> genuinely democratic than the public sector, involving the decisions
> of far more individuals and at much more frequent intervals.[13]

The key question, of accountability to whom, is never directly
addressed, but some proposals seem likely to lead to limits on existing
democratic rights. It is argued that local and national government
employees should be debarred from organizing and standing in public
elections, as they have a vested interest in the outcome. In addition,
a distinction is introduced between ratepayers (who finance services)
and beneficiaries of services; the general tenor of this argument casts
doubt on the ASI's commitment to the existing franchise.

Those who benefit from local government services campaign for
their extension; ratepayers 'vote only for a package of policies and
services every few years, and can do little to express their views on
the level or quality of particular services'.[14] The concern about
'ratepayers' turns out to be primarily a concern about businesses,
rather than individuals.

It is argued that domestic rates should be replaced by a simple
per capita tax on all adults consuming local authority services (not
just rateable occupiers); and that this local tax on adults could be

'routinely lumped together and paid by the head of household',[15] which begs a number of questions about the nature of households and the reciprocal responsibilities of their members. Elsewhere, a tax on all electors is recommended. In addition, the abolition of the Rate Support Grant, the simultaneous transfer of responsibility for the finance of policing and education to central government, and a general increase in local government rents and charges to 'economic' levels, would generate surplus funds. These would be used to reduce commercial (not domestic) rates. Commercial rates are described as taxation without representation; it is therefore proposed that a business vote, based on rateable value, be introduced to represent the interests of commercial ratepayers. Clearly, this is a step towards representation in proportion to taxation, whose logical outcome is the disenfranchisement of those unable to pay rates or taxes. Reference elsewhere to ballots of ratepayers, and to rights of ratepayers to petition through the courts for the compulsory sale of council property, reinforce the impression that accountability is to those who pay.

Accountability is also a central theme in the Omega report on education policy. State schools are to be financed through a per capita grant to each school from its Local Education Authority; parents are to be encouraged to move to the private sector by means of tax rebates, since education vouchers seem to be politically unacceptable; and the system's responsiveness to consumer demand is to be increased by a system of school boards, chosen by and from parents, who would determine the school's policy and allocation of funds (including teachers' salaries). Parents would also be free to start new schools if they wished. A central inspectorate would be maintained to ensure adequate standards and lack of bias within a core curriculum, but beyond this there would be little control save that of market pressures. The purpose of this is to facilitate innovations, such as shift systems (which require fewer teachers), charging for non-essential subjects, and the use of teachers and parents to perform ancillary tasks on a voluntary basis. Both for existing and new schools, a system of matching funds is suggested, whereby funds raised by parents will be supplemented by an equal amount from state funds. In addition, local businesses may be allowed to allocate state funds to schools of their choice, or to make donations to schools tax-deductible. These proposals would, of course, lead to far greater inequalities of opportunity within the education system. And proposals for the reform of teacher-training amount to the destruction of the professional status of teaching. However, the issue of who constitutes 'the consumer' is never explicitly confronted. In the case of higher education, it is made quite clear that the student is the consumer, notwithstanding the recognition of the research role of universities. In the case of schools, accountability to the consumer means primarily parents, and secondarily employers. The interests of pupils are subsumed under those of their parents, in a footnote of most doubtful validity:

> It is worth emphasizing that parental choice effectively means family choice. The family, including the children, normally discuss and decide on educational matters, though the parents as legal guardians make the actual decision.[16]

Non-parents are not 'consumers' of education and 'it is remarkable that a single person or childless couple should pay higher taxes in order to educate other people's children, when their interest in doing so is marginal'.[17] Accountability, then, is to parents (who also constitute a source of free or cheap labour); to employers; and to the state inspectorate.

If s/he who pays the piper calls the tune, what is to become of those unable to compete in the market? The principle of income support is affirmed, and it is argued that 'such help should be, as far as possible, in the form of financial support such as to enable the recipient to maintain a basic standard of living for himself and his [sic] family' while retaining choice over the allocation of these resources.[18] The principle of subsidizing individuals rather than services recurs throughout the Omega reports.

The level of this support is addressed in general terms. The purpose, as with existing supplementary benefit provision, remains to ensure that 'no-one falls below an agreed standard of living'.[19] However, while at present minimum income levels are set for different categories of individuals and families, the new system will also introduce 'local and even seasonal variations in housing, food, transport and so on'.[20] An 'independent panel' would be responsible for establishing and updating the figures, and benefits would be indexed to prices of relevant goods. The purpose of a minimum standard of living would in practice not be achieved, since cost-based benefits (housing benefit, rate rebates, special payments) would be replaced by a (regionally assessed) *average* sum; where rates are concerned, it is argued that 'cost-based rebates . . . encourage political irresponsibility',[21] but presumably different regional rates would necessarily be reflected in the housing component of the cash benefit.

Financial help, of course, should go only to those in need, and universal benefits are to be abolished, especially child benefit. It is argued that the 'level and method of payment' of this benefit 'owes more to well-organized pressure in the past that aimed at providing women with some income of their own, than it does to any seriously thought-out plan to help families in need'.[22] The principle of helping only those whose income falls below a certain level conflicts with the report's third principle, that there should be an incentive to work, and that the poverty trap must therefore be abolished. It recommends that increases in income will only result in deductions of benefit of ninety pence in the pound!

The general argument that welfare payments should be in cash conflicts with Thatcher's suggestions in 1985 that an increasing range of payments should be made by voucher (presumably to limit individual choice).[23] However, it also conflicts with suggestions in the ASI's own reports. Ultimately, the welfare state is to be largely replaced by a system of compulsory private insurance, with the state paying, by cash or voucher, minimum contributions for those in receipt of welfare benefits. There are references to 'vouchers and grants' to needy individuals to enable them to buy services in the market-place, and to transport tokens. And pending comprehensive private insurance, the poor are to be issued with a 'medicard' which would entitle them to free basic health care; non-essential treatment would have to be paid for.

The crucial question, of course, is what is essential. The general proposals for reform of the National Health Service include the abolition of Regional Health Authorities; the contracting out of services; and charging for non-essential ambulance journeys (medicard holders can use public transport), non-essential drugs (including tranquillizers and appetite suppressants, free to nobody), visits to GPs, 'hotel and general' services in hospitals (amounting to £5 per day for such 'inessentials' as cleaning, laundry and food) and treatment for injures sustained while engaging in dangerous sports.

The main arguments for transforming the health service are an increase in public choice and efficiency, but also (more surprisingly) demand limitation; it is argued that free health care (which is substantially life-enhancing rather than life-saving) creates an infinite demand. It is suggested that charging would limit demand to what people are prepared to pay for — although it is also surmised that without the NHS 'people in the UK would probably have devoted more resources to health care, as they have in other countries'.[24]

The question is raised in the Omega report on health policy of how the welfare state can be reconstructed on market principles without some of the most needy slipping through the net. But,

> We must not underestimate our ability to deal with it at the time . . . It was rhetoric, not the details, of the new social security regime which first persuaded people that a welfare state was both moral and highly desirable. It is the desirability and superior morality of better health systems which should commend them . . . [25]

Such problems, are, therefore, reduced to a matter of detail.

Although privatization is deemed to increase accountability, the main justification is that it is more efficient. If it does not always seem so, this can be blamed on accounting practices, or on the failure to choose the right contractor. A vast list of local government services are candidates for contracting out, from refuse collection to cemeteries. One report even advocates privatizing prisons. The virtual abolition of local government involves centralization of power, since standards and guidelines for tendering would be laid down by the Audit Commission, and the Secretary of State is to specify the rate at which local government services are to go out to tender. Local authorities would also be required to withdraw from the provision of non-essential services, and any organization which believes it can undertake an existing service at lower cost than the local authority will have the right of appeal to the Secretary of State, the object being to help 'local tradesmen who feel that they are being unfairly crowded out by local authorities'.[26] The picture that is implied here of small local firms being 'crowded out' by the monopolistic power of large authorities is of course misleading; organizations such as Pritchards who have benefited from the privatization programme are neither small nor local.

Given the general emphasis on privatization, which extends to a recommendation to denationalize money, it is no surprise to turn to the Omega report on energy policy, and encounter proposals to privatize the coal industry. The arguments used in support of this are perhaps more revealing than the proposal itself.

It was widely suspected during the 1984-5 miners' strike that the dispute was not primarily about 'uneconomic pits', but about the government's 'determination to gain total control over the industry in order to force down real wages and to "reorganize" it, a euphemism that almost certainly implies privatization'.[27] Running down (and selling off) the coal industry, and breaking the power of the National Union of Mineworkers, were seen as linked to a strategy to increase control over energy supplies by decreasing reliance on coal and increasing reliance on nuclear energy. The pattern of investment in the coalfields (determining which pits are 'economic' or 'uneconomic') has been consistent with producing a coal industry suitable for privatization, as it has concentrated on the development of new technology in the central coalfields. The view that the Government planned for and engineered the strike was given credence by the wide circulation of an article first published in *The Economist* in May 1978, which leaked details of a strategy drawn up by Nicholas Ridley.[28] This strategy included building up coal stocks, recruiting non-union lorry-drivers, cutting off state benefits to strikers' families, and the development of new police tactics – all of which took place in the years leading up to the strike.

The Omega report on energy policy blames the 'problems' of the coal industry on nationalization and on the miners themselves. The *Plan for Coal* and subsequent developments show how 'powerful and well-organized . . . employees . . . can gain tremendous advantages while the taxpayer foots the bill'.[29] Even the current threat to mining communities is blamed on the failure to close pits over the last ten years, for had this been done, 'new industries would have developed to soak up the labour that was . . . gradually shed' and 'the transition would have been almost imperceptible'.[30] The solution is not to continue subsidies to existing pits. Rather,

> The correct approach must be to promote the generation of completely new businesses by making employment and trading conditions easier inside the designated area, including: the removal of wage restrictions and most planning regulations; the reduction, simplification, or removal of taxes such as national insurance payments, local authority rates, and corporation tax; more flexible employment regulations.[31]

Alternatively (or additionally) one can accept the decline of communities as inevitable, and give away council houses to tenants in the area; and/or 'improve the world competitiveness of British coal'.[32] This latter end is to be achieved by lowering the costs of coal extraction, for 'a mine that is . . . uneconomic under present practices might still be a viable proposition for a number of years if managed by a new private company or a co-operative of existing workers'.[33] For the restrictions which currently apply to private mines licensed by the National Coal Board, notably the 'obligation to provide the same wages and employment conditions as the NCB' are deemed to have 'no basis in common sense, and . . . should be swept away as a matter of priority'.[34] Eventually, even the large operations of Selby and Belvoir could be privatized.

As the strike drew to an end, the issue of privatization became more prominent. *Diverse Reports* suggested that Selby would fit well into the operations of a large multinational company (thus diverting one billion pounds of public investment into private hands);[35] and six MPs, including Harvey Proctor, signed a Commons motion calling for the privatization of the pits.[36]

It is plain from the Omega report on energy policy that the solution to unemployment lies in the deregulation of the labour market, and this is confirmed in the report on employment policy. Here the Manpower Services Commission is argued to be redundant. Its payment of interview and relocation expenses to the unemployed is argued to apply only at the lower end of the market (since most companies pay such expenses themselves), and is likely to become decreasingly necessary as the housing market and transport systems are themselves deregulated. The training functions of the MSC would be replaced temporarily by training vouchers, which could be phased out 'as the economy picks up and the quality of schooling improves'.[37] The problem of unemployment is blamed upon the reduction in mobility brought about by regulation of the housing market, and on government controls on working conditions, especially compulsory redundancy payments and minimum wage legislation. Almost all employment protection provisions should therefore be removed from firms with less than a hundred employees. Again, these suggestions are reflected in policies announced in the 1985 budget, which aim to reduce employment protection and limit the role of wages councils if not abolish them altogether.

According to the report on employment policy, jobs are scarce because wages are too high. Another reason for this is that wages 'cannot drop below the level of the benefit floor plus the premium necessary to induce people to work'[38] − so we should perhaps infer that the levels of income support guaranteed under the benefit system will not be very high. But the main culprit in the plot is held to be organized labour; trade union activities 'artificially' raise wage levels, especially those of the young. So it is logical that much of the report is in fact concerned with limiting the powers of trade unions, including removing the right to strike from public employees.

That the current role of local authorities in the provision of housing limits the mobility of labour is only one of the report's objections. In an ideal world, the allocation of housing, like any other commodity, would be subject to the interaction of supply and demand; the problem is that in the public sector 'individual choice is arbitrarily limited by the imposition of politically inspired notions of "need" ',[39] and the subsidy on council housing causes demand to exceed supply. Discounts on the sale of council housing would therefore be increased, and the rent structure on any remaining housing stock adjusted to reflect the demand for different types of housing. Local authorities would only be permitted to undertake new building or renovation of old property for the provision of sheltered housing, and then only if they could demonstrate that this could not be contracted out. In the private sector, two sets of changes are proposed. Firstly, an *increase* of subsidy by the abolition of stamp duty and the removal of the upper limits on mortgage tax relief, and secondly, the removal of rent control and the abolition of security of tenure for all new tenancies. This is not merely a device for increasing the supply of privately rented accommodation (which might well occur), but for giving the tenant greater choice – 'those current and future tenants who wish to avoid the economic and other costs of the restrictions should be allowed to do so if they choose'.[40] Even building regulations would be abolished since it is 'not necessary to prohibit private buildings of lower standard so that cheaper housing is available for those who need it';[41] adequate control can be exerted through compulsory public liability insurance. There is no attempt to disguise the fact that deregulation will lead to lower wages, worse conditions of employment, lower benefits and worse housing.

The economic arguments are not limited to the ASI. In February 1985, John Hoskyns published articles in *The Times* with the central theme that to get out of the recession we need more investment; to have more investment we must cut taxes; to cut taxes we must cut public spending; to cut public spending we must cut unemployment; to cut unemployment we must cut wages; and to cut wages we must devise a new poverty line based on real needs, or, in other words, cut benefits.[42] The ASI however appeals to libertarian policies which would adversely affect not only those less successful in the market, but the environment we all inhabit, through the removal of planning restrictions. It is argued that the whole philosophy of planning rests on the principle that owners do not have the right to do what they like with their own property without the permission of the community; that this is not a just principle for a free society; and that it does not work, that planning is ineffective. Controls would be retained for conservation areas and green belt land, but otherwise their role would be better carried out by a combination of economic forces acting to locate processes in the most appropriate areas, private institutions which would spring into being, and the law of nuisance (argued to be more effective than attempts at prior restraint). Except in restricted zones which would be under direct ministerial protection, individuals would be specifically permitted to use residential or other property for any new purpose, unless and until a complaint was upheld that this use created a nuisance; otherwise, the only restrictions would be minimum standards (not specified) for safety and public health. Restrictive covenants might be used to enable property owners, individually and collectively, to control the use of their own and adjoining property.

The three themes of accountability, efficiency and freedom which are used to legitimate the proposals in the reports involve very specific interpretations of these appealing ideals. Accountability means accountability to those who pay, particularly business interests, although they are at times deemed to deserve influence as 'consumers' of education even when they are not paying. Efficiency is conceived of as meeting effective demand, not in terms of effectiveness in meeting needs; indeed, needs which are not translated into effective demands can only be politically defined, and are thus generally regarded as inadmissible. Freedom is entirely negative freedom, the absence of restraint, deregulation; although ironically many proposals involve an increase in centralized power and an increasing reliance on legal procedures for those who can afford them. Freedom is also seen in entirely economic terms, as 'economic freedom is the essence of personal freedom'.[43] Criticism of the proposals needs to concentrate not just on the practical outcomes of such measures, but on the interpretation of these legitimating formulae.

Virtue against Freedom

Accountability and efficiency, however, are key words only for the neo-liberal New Right. The immanent utopia outlined in *Conservative Essays* and in the work of Scruton is quite different.

It is not particularly concerned with accountability or efficiency and is at times explicitly opposed to economic liberalism. And notwithstanding Thatcher's claim in her 1985 New Year message that what unites the vast majority of Britons is 'our unswerving belief in personal freedom',[44] the conservative New Right attaches a completely different meaning to the word 'freedom'.

The problems caused by the term freedom are recognized by at least some of the New Right themselves, and were discussed in an article in *The Salisbury Review*. Here it is argued that 'the individualism which reached its apogee in the sixties . . . could prove as inimical to Mrs Thatcher's purposes . . . as the collectivism she so strenuously opposes'.[45] The idea that the pursuit of individual freedom leads to the general good was never very plausible, and more importantly, it is quite antithetical to Mrs Thatcher's views. Referring in particular to the family policy documents leaked to *The Guardian* in February 1983, the author points out that Thatcher has no taste for the freedom from social bonds implied in individualism, but rather seeks for 'a mode of freedom that is compatible with virtue'.[46] Freedom is redefined to coincide with a view of the good (i.e. virtuous) society, in sharp contrast to the concept of freedom inherent in neo-liberalism and free market economics. It resembles closely the notion of true freedom being willing subordination to God (or in this case, the nation) which has traditionally been preached by the established Church.

The attack upon individual liberty is much more central and explicit than that upon the free market; although the latter is not regarded as the lynchpin of the good society, it is not necessarily seen as antithetical to social virtue in the way that claims for individual liberty are. Scruton claims that 'the value of individual liberty is not absolute, but stands subject to another and higher value, the authority of established government',[47] while Worsthorne argues that 'social discipline . . . is a much more fruitful . . . theme for contemporary conservatism than individual freedom'.[48] Indeed, Worsthorne goes so far as to say that 'the urgent need today is for the State to regain control over "the people", to re-exert its authority, and it is useless to imagine that this will be helped by some libertarian mish-mash drawn from the writings of Adam Smith, John Stuart Mill, and the warmed-up milk of nineteenth-century liberalism'.[49] Society is regarded as an organism, and power is an acceptable means, not to achieve justice, equality or freedom, but to 'maintain existing inequalities or restore lost ones',[50] or even 'to command

and coerce those who would otherwise reform or destroy'.[51]

The concepts which are appealed to in relation to this utopia are authority, allegiance and tradition (Scruton);[52] authority and tradition (Casey);[53] national identity and national security (Cowling);[54] and, overwhelmingly, nature. Scruton explicitly rejects support for liberal ideals or the minimal state, and, far from supporting the view that individual freedom should be curtailed only if this can be shown to be for the general good, argues that there should be constraint unless it can be shown that its removal will do no harm, thus reversing the burden of proof. In contrast to Hayek, who posits the existence of a protected domain of private life into which governmental authority should not intrude, a view apparently shared by Mount,[55] he argues that it is legitimate for the law to intrude into 'any area of social life which is vital . . . to the strength of the social bond'. This makes it inevitable that there should be 'family law, planning laws, laws which regulate the days and times when men may work, drink, or seek recreation, even laws which control the nature of permitted intoxicants'.[56] This is in tension with the ASI's proposals to deregulate the labour market and abolish planning constraints, and also with Scruton's own statement that 'sections of local government must be simply eliminated – including most social service, planning, advisory, cultural and para-educational departments'.[57]

The priority of maintaining the social (i.e. national) bond is paramount. Cowling argues that 'the only permanent claims [on loyalty or attention] are those which arise from the national interest defined in terms of sovereignty, historic continuity and national identity, and beyond these no other focus of loyalty is either necessary or desirable'.[58] He stresses the threat from within to national security; this is repeated in Scruton's claim that it is not an 'insuperable defect' for a law of sedition to allow for 'imprisonment without a trial, a reduced judicial process, or summary execution'.[59] (Just as Utley's main anxiety is about industrial unrest, Scruton has argued that Scargill is guilty of sedition.)[60] For Scruton, the allegiance of citizen to state takes the form of a transcendent bond, akin to that between parent and child, thus giving the state the authority, responsibility and 'despotism' of parenthood.[61] A corollary of this is that the family is central to maintaining the state, since it is the main social institution in which the habits of allegiance are acquired. In the same way, Burke argued that:

> To be attached to the subdivision, to love the little platoon we belong
> to in society, is the first principle, the germ as it were, of public
> affections. It is the first link in the series by which we proceed towards
> a love to our country and to mankind.[62]

Casey argues that the state must not merely attract, but claim
allegiance. He refers to Aquinas' concept of *pietas*, which he
describes as 'forms of respect that arise from the individual's sense
of his relation to something which comprehensively sustains and
supports him',[63] including parents, country and state. *Pietas*
combines with tradition to produce loyalty, since an individual's sense
of self is dependent upon the objectification of that self in the existing
social institutions.

The emphasis upon tradition has implications beyond the
immediately political. In Scruton's case, it has produced a eulogy
on the symbolic value of red telephone boxes, as well as a more
serious attack on modernism.[64] It has also given rise to the rather
more widespread phenomenon of 'young fogeydom' a fashion for
outdated upper-class modes of dress and behaviour.[65] Since many
of the neo-conservative New Right are not drawn from the section
of society they ape, young fogeys may be seen to be trying to create
a past that neither they nor the vast bulk of the population ever had;
it is the invention, rather than the perpetuation, of a tradition.

In relation to both the bond between child and parent and that
between citizen (or subject) and state, the principal legitimations are
appeals to nature and to intuition. Berry argues that a particular view
of nature is fundamental to the conservative positions:

> The family is . . . necessarily a hierarchic authority structure, and
> this, as a natural consequence of the dependence of the human infant,
> is an integral component of the conservative vision . . . Though the
> family is the prime source for authority and hierarchy, its very
> naturalness inclines conservatives to translate this mode into other
> institutions. Hierachy is the order of nature, and as such is
> ubiquitous.[66]

Or, as Scruton puts it:

> The family . . . shares with civil society the . . . quality of being non-
> contractual, of arising . . . out of natural necessity. And . . . it is
> obvious that the bond which ties the citizen to society is likewise not
> a voluntary but a kind of natural bond.[67]

The necessarily hierarchical structure of the family derives from
the natural dependence of the child, and is then extrapolated to

legitimate the hierarchical structure of society. The family envisaged here is not merely hierarchical but patriarchal. Implicitly, the parent-child relation referred to is that between *father* and child, not mother and child. The importance of inheritance (of property and privilege) can give an experience of continuity across generations, without which 'much of the motive for procreation is lost, and the child himself becomes . . . a reminder of one's isolation. The parent at rest with his child has a dominant desire, which is this: what I am and what I value, I here pass on.'[68] That this is not simply a use of the generic male is demonstrated by the contradiction between this statement, with the substitution of 'she' and 'her', and Scruton's own claim that 'a woman's body has a rhythm, a history and a fulfilment that are centred upon the bearing of children: this is what it means to be a woman'.[69]

The support and protection of the family is thus a central part of the conservative project, and any changes in law which tend to reduce rather than reinforce the obligations of life within this patriarchal family 'or which . . . facilitate the channelling of libidinal impulse away from that particular form of union' are highly undesirable.[70] Indeed, because it is through the channelling of libidinal impulse that society is formed, the right of the state to enforce family obligations refers not only to the parent-child relations, but to the 'bond' of marriage. Again, the libido to be channelled must be presumed to be male, since 'female desire aims to subdue, overcome and pacify the unbridled ambition of the phallus'; women naturally have the 'power to quieten what is most wild, and to confine what is most vagrant'; and in being so tamed, a man 'subjects himself to the kind of commitment which the women desires by nature, and he may desire only by art'.[71] Thus the natural necessity underlying the hierarchical structure of the family, and by analogy the state, is not merely the dependence of the human infant, but the biological basis of gender roles determining the confinement of women to nurturing roles within the (regulated) private sphere of the family, and the subordination of male heads of households to the state as citizens/subjects. The decline in 'traditional family life and sex roles' has also been held responsible for the unwholesome composition of the national diet. Snacks replace family meals (especially for the working class); lack of parental discipline is responsible for the consumption of sweets; and working mothers rely on processed convenience foods.[72]

Human nature, the foundation of conservative politics, also

underlies the relationship between family and property. Not only is inheritance necessary to men's motives to procreate at all, but private property is 'an absolute and ineradicable need'; the evidence adduced for this is 'intuition . . . which . . . lies at the very centre of the social sense of man'.[73] Prejudice is a natural counterpart of allegiance and of the desire for the company of one's own kind. Conservatism itself is natural, since 'instinct and self-interest coincide in the judgement that existing arrangements should be preserved'.[74] Or, more extremely:

> There is a natural instinct in the unthinking man . . . to accept and endorse through his actions the institutions and practices into which he is born. This instinct is rooted in human nature.[75]

This reliance on nature and instinct is antagonistic to reason. Berry argues that the location of the cohesiveness of the family 'in instinct, feeling or affection . . . means undercutting . . . claims . . . for the self-sufficiency of reason',[76] and Scruton certainly elevates intuition and instinct over thought. In a Channel Four television debate on capital punishment, he spoke in favour of its reintroduction. Most of the debate had centred on the issue of whether or not capital punishment is a deterrent to murder. He argued that the deterrent effect is irrelevant, as even if there is none, it remains the case that death is still the punishment which we all know to be the just and proper retribution; and he suggests elsewhere that in such matters, analysis and rational investigation are positively harmful:

> it is useful that we do not substitute analytical rigour . . . for the immediate perception of the horror of murder, for the prompt response to an insult, to an injustice, to an act of tyranny or violence. Mercifully most people do not go around thinking analytically about these responses. They arise out of our common human nature . . . [77]

The use of 'nature' as a legitimation of this conservatism is mystical rather than scientific; it is underpinned not by arguments of genetic causation and natural selection, but by a pseudo-religiosity. Thus it is

> one of the fundamental thoughts on which civilization depends, the thought that there is a profound, mysterious, and beneficial difference between women and men. The [alternative] thought that I exist as an individual independently of my sex, is one with the thought that my sex might have been chosen.[78]

Sexuality, he claims, is reduced to an attribute rather than an essence, and ceases to determine the relations between men and women, which thus lose their clarity. 'Much passes from the world when sexuality takes on this aspect.' This loss is part of the loss contained in secularization; a firm established Church is what is needed, and 'the restoration of the Church may well become a serious political cause'.[79]

Hayek also uses nature as a legitimation, but in a different way. He too relies on intuition in relation to our sense of justice, which derives from complex rules which we follow but are unable to express in words. True law, as opposed to legislation, involves the codification of these intuited truths. Nevertheless, these evolved rules seem to be socially learned rather than instinctive. His dismissal of socialism is partly on the grounds of its atavism: socialism 'is simply a reassertion of the tribal ethics' whose passing made modern society possible.[80] This morality was instinctive, but had to be restrained to make development possible, so that 'we often rebel against these new restraints and yearn for the easy socialism of the past'.[81] At least some of the time, Hayek's utopia is a triumph of culture over nature. It is, though, hardly a triumph of rationality, since he argues against institutional change because existing arrangements contribute to social order in a way that is beyond our understanding, so that 'the only guide we have is what has worked in the past';[82] the complexity of society is such that it is fundamentally unknowable and cannot be planned.[83]

Hayek, indeed, has argued explicitly that irrationality is essential to the preservation of social order, and against the pursuit of rationality or rational legitimations in social affairs. In contrast, the free market utopia is, at least ostensibly, based upon assumptions of rational choice, rational action, equal opportunities and formally free actors. Liberal economics assumes rationality (or at least economic rationality) on the part of the individual actor. This is why the ASI is able to claim as a regrettable 'fact' that wages 'cannot drop below the below the level of the benefit floor plus the premium necessary to induce people to work';[84] of course, this supposition of rationality is belied by the fact that in practice people *do* choose to work, even for wages lower than their benefit entitlement.

Minimalism versus Maximalism

At one level, then, it is clear that there are major divergences between the kinds of society implied by different sections of the New Right, in relation both to their key concepts and to the scope and nature of permissible state intervention. Crudely, this is a distinction between 'minimalists' and 'maximalists', and enough has been said to show that there is a logical inconsistency between the two strands and between their legitimating formulae. There are, however, areas where the divergences are more subtle.

The first of these is the question of rationality in relation to the supposed centrality of a particular form of the family. We have seen that the patriarchal family is fundamental to the conservative utopia, and that it is justified by appeal to its naturalness. No such model is invoked by the neo-liberals. However, the economistic model turns out, on close inspection, to be based upon a similar implied model of the family, and thus to be less gender-neutral than it at first appears. It has already been noted that references to heads of households, and the interests of parents and children in relation to the education system, beg questions about households and families. The patriarchal nature of the underlying model is revealed in such phrases as 'if a man's child has an accident . . .'; the mother is invisible![85] And in fact, one of the striking aspects of the Omega reports is the invisibility of women. Since they are dominated by the intention to remove constraints upon the free market, they focus solely upon that public sphere of the market place. Women are present here only as 'honorary men' (and thus to be deprived of most existing employment protection in relation to maternity rights). At the same time they are recognized as being a source of cheap labour, so that the report on defence policy can suggest that one possible economy is the substitution of women for men in support roles (although this is not translated into the policy proposals). Alternatively, women are present as 'shadow workers', occupying private spheres and economically dependent upon men active in the market. Above all, this position renders them available as volunteer workers in the health, education and social services, where the use of such volunteers is an integral part of the process of privatization and reduction of public spending. It is, of course, never specified in the Omega reports that these volunteers will be women. Greater clarity on the matter can be found in a document published by the IEA, which says that 'men will expect to specialize in market work and women will expect to specialize in household work'.[86]

The second and third areas of close congruence relate back to Adam Smith's statement of the proper functions of government — the maintenance of national defence and security, and of a judicial system resolving disputes and conflicts between (individual) interests. In this respect, the ASI's views on national defence are of particular interest.

There is an essential tension between minimalist demands for freedom and the limitation of government regulation and taxation, and the demand for strong national defences and increased defence spending. There is also a tension between the stress on nationhood, mobilized so effectively during the Falklands War and reflecting Cowling's themes, and the role of Britain as merely a strategic part of NATO's defences. Both these tensions are reflected in the *Omega File*, as is the contradiction between the pursuit of free trade and non-market considerations of the 'national interest'. This last point is touched on in the report on trade policy, in relation to the problem of the 'enemy' status of Eastern Europe:

> Trade with Eastern bloc countries raises questions that go beyond those of economic efficiency. Even from a myopic national point of view, it could be dangerous to become dependent on imports from a potential enemy or to supply it with goods that increase the threat.[87]

In defending market interests, it is necessary for the notion of national security to be extended beyond the threat of invasion by a foreign power specified by Adam Smith. National defence includes the protection of 'this country's pluralist democratic political system' against the imposition of another political order by force of arms. Clearly, this provides for the use of the armed forces against an external *or internal* threat of this kind. However, military action is permissible against 'any covert action or military intervention which put seriously at risk the livelihood and economic well-being of the British people'. Thus threats to 'British access to raw materials, energy supplies or overseas markets' may be deemed threats to national security, and may be legitimate grounds for military action, presumably whether such threats are external, or, in the case of the miners' strike, internal. In view of the economic and military interdependence of the Western nations, good relations with the USA must be fostered, including 'a better understanding of US security preoccupation outside the North Atlantic Treaty area, such as the spread of Cuban-trained and other guerilla movements in Central America'. It is stressed that the Western 'response' should not be geographically limited.[88]

The source of the threat is of course the Soviet bloc. It is argued that the essential inefficiency of centrally planned economies makes it inevitable that there will be an increasing disparity between the wealth of Western and Eastern blocs, leading the Soviet Union to seek to impede Western economic performance through a combination of economic, political and military means. The most immediate likelihood is of destabilization 'or even direct or proxy soviet aggression'[89] in the Middle East, although similar threats could arise elsewhere in Asia or Africa. But there is also a danger of direct military attack upon Western Europe, including Britain. It is further argued that the conventional armaments of the Warsaw Pact countries so far outstrip those of NATO that 'it is probable that a Warsaw Pact assault on Western Europe could be countered only by a rapid NATO escalation to the use of nuclear weapons . . . Nuclear retaliation from the USSR could be expected in such a situation.'[90]

The report therefore claims the legitimacy of military action for economic purposes, even where this involves a (conventional) first strike; and concedes the probability of a *nuclear* first strike by NATO forces. Further, it does not separate the interests of Britain, or, substantially, Europe, from those of the Western alliance as a whole, although it does note that an independent nuclear deterrent is the 'ultimate guarantee of British sovereignty and national independence',[91] and thus supports unequivocally the Trident programme. Elsewhere, it appears to concede the point that Britain has become little more than a NATO base, using more than once the phrase 'the United Kingdom base'.[92]

A somewhat less economistic conception of national and Western interests is evident in the Omega report on foreign policy; and the description of the Soviet threat even more extravagant. The polarized nature of world politics portrayed here leads the authors to mention with approval the military overthrow of the Allende government in Chile, and to describe the South West Africa People's Organization (SWAPO) as 'in effect an instrument of Soviet foreign policy'.[93] Even the United Nations is no longer a forum in which Britain can achieve its foreign policy objectives, so that an alternative league of democratic nations is recommended. There is much concern in this report with countering the ideological offensives of the Soviet bloc.

Thus in spite of the absence of rhetoric about the 'nation', there is little conflict between the views expressed by the ASI and a more overtly authoritarian view of national security. There is less mention of the 'enemy within' than in *Conservative Essays*. But there is no logical contradiction between the views expressed in the Omega reports and the extrapolation that military action is legitimate against *internal* activity which can be claimed to be a threat to the economic well-being of the British people, or a challenge to the democratic political system.

Such a hawkish stance sits uneasily alongside the market criteria and commitment to privatization which characterize the *Omega File* as a whole, and which are present elsewhere in the report on defence policy. In this context, the privatization of aspects of the work of the armed forces is proposed, such as maintenance of vehicles, buildings and weapons; catering; training of skilled manpower; construction; military hospitals; and research development. This process is also referred to as 'civilianization', and it is suggested that it is unnecessary for the armed forces to duplicate facilities already available (such as air transport) when existing facilities could be swiftly converted at times of need. Given that civilian transport systems are not to be national assets, but privately owned, this entails *either* putting the defence of the nation at the mercy of private enterprise, which could prove expensive in an emergency, *or* powers to commandeer civilian property in times of crisis. Such powers of course already exist: but the more the forces depend upon civilian provision, the greater the probability they will need to be invoked, constituting an interference with individual and market freedom. These problems are not seriously addressed.

'Civilianization' (which might be interpreted as 'militarization' of civilian society) also extends to the armed service personnel. The prime reason for this is cost, although it is noted that the cost of a regular volunteer force depends upon the demand for labour elsewhere in the economy; a secondary reason is that the involvement of more reservists and private companies increases the level of military readiness of the population as a whole. An increase in part-time volunteer reservists is sought, under the auspices of a national 'job sharing' scheme freeing people for periods of service; young people 'awaiting a first job' or those 'changing jobs' could undertake longer periods of service. Such volunteers would receive basic pay but none of the benefits (e.g. housing, pensions) of regular personnel, thus being cheaper. Those in full-time employment with (specified) appropriate skills would be encouraged to 'use their skills in the service of the country for a part of each year'[94] (implying that medical staff and coastguards, for example, are not so using their skills in civilian life). There is also a proposal that a Home Defence

Force of those too old or otherwise unable to be reservists should be set up.

There is no mention here of the word patriotism, yet the concept lurks below the suggestion that reservists should wish to serve their country, thus removing the need for paying the market price for the labour required to provide adequate armed forces. Nor is there any reliance on conscription as such: yet the reference to the young unemployed suggests this might in effect occur if no other work were available. (There are already some Youth Training Scheme places provided in the armed forces, and the proposal to remove the right to supplementary benefit of school leavers refusing YTS places does not increase their personal freedom and choice.) The move away from a regular volunteer force is inevitably a move towards conscription, although direct, rather than economic pressures, would conflict with the ASI's basic principles. It is also a move towards a concept of service to the nation through duty and allegiance, which is entirely compatible with the more conservative conception of society. There may however be conflicts. For those who are primarily concerned with the enemy within, the need is for a highly professional force, and the distancing of potential subversives from access to military information, equipment or training – so that the wide dissemination of such training through a 'volunteer' force could have its own drawbacks.

This concern of the authoritarian Right with internal subversion runs alongside a concern with law and order, and this too provides an ambiguous point of linkage with the neo-liberal position. Although this is not a dominant theme for free-marketeers except in relation to trade union activities, they do manifest a strong reliance upon the law – as enshrined in the judiciary and civil courts, rather than in overt policing. Adam Smith's second function of government, the duty of establishing the 'exact administration of justice' and thus protecting individuals from one another, is reflected in the ASI's emphasis on appeals to the courts in relation to the activities of local government, and the substitution of the law of nuisance for planning controls. Legal procedures become a substitute for political decisions – so that political decisions may in fact be disguised as judicial ones. The effect must necessarily be an increased recourse of law, and thus a removal of decisions from democratic control (and a decrease in accountability). Although this is not directly sought, it is entirely compatible with authoritarian government and the erosion of civil liberties. There is then little conflict between the two strands of New

Right thought in their policy implications for civil liberties. (This is discussed at greater length in chapter six). Further, the *Omega File* clearly involves a transfer of power to central government in order to establish and maintain a 'deregulated' market, in conflict with its own principles of accountability and freedom.

There are, clearly, marked contrasts in both rhetoric and ideology between the neo-liberal and neo-conservative views of the good society. These differences are underpinned by conflicting concepts of human nature and the relationship between individual and society; and they are obscured by a truly ideological use of language, particularly the word freedom, to mask the contradictions. However, the differences will only undermine the strength of the New Right if they are translated into conflicts over specific policies, and if these conflicts outweigh the common ground. That common ground is itself extensive, if sometimes unexpected, and repeatedly involves the neo-liberal position conceding to the neo-conservative as the strong state is required to preserve the 'freedom' of the market. There is no evidence of a consensus supporting either of the New Right's promised lands; but the forces of coercion are being progressively marshalled to prevent the formation and expression of a consensus against them.

Notes

1 T. E. Utley, 'The Significance of Mrs Thatcher', in *Conservative Essays,* ed. M. Cowling, (Cassell, London, 1978), p. 44.

2 *Cited in E. Butler, Hayek* (Temple Smith, London, 1983), p. 164.

3 *The Omega File* (Adam Smith Institute, London, 1983-4). The reports were published individually, and as a collection in 1985; page references are to the separate reports.

4 R. Scruton, *The Meaning of Conservatism* (Penguin, Harmondsworth, 1980).

5 J. Casey, 'Tradition and authority' in Cowling (ed.), *Conservative Essays*, p. 82.

6 K. Mannheim, 'The utopian mentality', *Ideology and Utopia* (Routledge and Kegan Paul, London, 1936), pp. 206-15.

7 Scruton, *Conservatism*, p. 27.

8 Ibid., p. 36.

9 N. Bosanquet, *After the New Right* (Heinemann, London, 1983), *passim*.

10 This passage appears at the beginning of the foreword to each report. See, for example, *OF: Trade policy*, p. iii.

11 D. Wade and J. Picardie, 'The Omega Project', *New Statesman*, 29 Jul. 1983, p. 8; 'Miscellany', *New Statesman*, 27 Jan. 1984, p. 5.

12 For example *OF: Communications policy*, p. ii-iv.

13 *OF: Local Government, planning and housing*, p. 13.

14 Ibid., p. 1.

15 Ibid., p. 25.

16 *OF: Education policy*, p. 5.

17 *OF: Local government*, p. 3.

18 *OF: Social security policy*, p. 5.

19 Ibid., p. 6.

20 Ibid.

21 Ibid., pp. 16-17.

22 Ibid., p. 2.

23 I. Aitken, 'Benefits may get US stamp', *The Guardian*, 5 Mar. 1985.

24 *OF: Health policy*, p. 14.

25 Ibid., p. 3.

26 *OF: Local government*, p. 11.

27 C. Sweet, 'Why coal is under attack', in *Digging Deeper*, ed. H. Beynon (Verso, London, 1985), p. 201.

28 'Appomattox or Civil War?', *The Economist*, 27 May 1978.

29 *OF: Energy policy*, p. 29.

30 Ibid., p. 32.

31 Ibid., p. 32.

32 Ibid., pp. 32-3.

33 Ibid., pp. 32-3.

34 Ibid., p. 35.

35 'Privatize the pits', *Diverse Reports*, Channel 4 television, 20 Feb. 1985; the figure of one billion pounds was put on the development costs of Selby in 'Facing the future of coal', *Panorama*, BBC 1 television, 4 Mar. 1985.

36 *The Guardian*, 7 Feb. 1985, p. 9.

37 *OF: Employment policy*, p. 12.

38 Ibid., p. 2.

39 *OF: Local government*, p. 52.

40 *OF: Scottish policy*, p. 22.

41 *OF: Local government*, p. 42.
42 J. Hoskyns, 'Overkill: the only answer', and 'An end to patchwork', *The Times*, 11 and 12 Feb. 1985.
43 *OF: Scottish policy*, p. 1.
44 Reported in *The Guardian*, 31 Dec. 1984.
45 I. Crowther, 'Mrs Thatcher's idea of the good society', *The Salisbury Review*, 3 (Spring 1984), p. 41.
46 Ibid., p. 42.
47 Scruton, *Conservatism*, p. 19.
48 P. Worsthorne, 'Too much freedom', in Cowling (ed.), *Conservative Essays*, p. 150.
49 Ibid., p. 149.
50 Cowling (ed.), *Conservative Essays*, p. 9.
51 Scruton, *Conservatism*, p. 25.
52 Ibid., p. 27.
53 Casey, 'Tradition and authority'.
54 Cowling (ed.), *Conservative Essays*, pp. 16-17.
55 F. Mount, *The Subversive Family* (Jonathan Cape, London, 1982).
56 Scruton, *Conservatism*, p. 80.
57 R. Scruton, 'Abolish council elections too', *The Times*, 18 Oct. 1983.
58 Cowling (ed.), *Conservative Essays*, p. 16.
59 Scruton, *Conservatism*, p. 91.
60 Utley, 'The significance of Mrs Thatcher', pp. 48-9: R. Scruton, 'King Arthur's real crime', *The Times*, 9. Oct. 1984.
61 Scruton, *Conservatism*, p. 111.
62 Cited in Mount, *Subversive Family*, p. 172.
63 Casey, 'Tradition and authority', p. 99.
64 R. Scruton, 'Putting heritage on the line', *The Times*, 29 Jan. 1985; R. Scruton, *The Aesthetic Understanding* (Carcanet, Manchester, 1983).
65 See P. Hillmore, 'Dead men's clothes', *The Observer*, 26 Aug. 1984.
66 C. Berry, 'Conservatism and human nature' in *Politics and Human Nature*, eds. I. Forbes and S. Smith (Frances Pinter, London, 1983), p. 61.
67 Scruton, *Conservatism*, p. 31.
68 Ibid., p. 145.
69 R. Scruton, 'The case against feminism', *The Observer*, 22 May 1983, p. 27.

70 Scruton, *Conservatism*, p. 144.
71 Scruton, 'Feminism'.
72 D. Anderson, 'Experts that are hard to stomach', *The Times*, 12 Mar. 1985. Dibgy Anderson is director of the Social Affairs Unit.
73 Scruton, *Conservatism*, p. 99.
74 Cowling (ed.), *Conservative Essays*, p. 11.
75 Scruton, *Conservatism*, p. 119.
76 Berry, 'Conservatism and human nature', p. 57.
77 R. Scruton, *The Politics of Culture and Other Essays* (Carcanet, Manchester, 1981), p. 167.
78 Scruton, *Conservatism*, p. 174.
79 Ibid., pp. 174-5.
80 Butler, *Hayek*, p. 22.
81 Ibid.
82 Ibid., p. 9.
83 F. A. Hayek, 'The moral tradition that reason must recognize', *The Guardian*, 17 Sep. 1984, p. 9.
84 *OF: Employment policy*, p. 2.
85 *OF: Health policy*, p. 12.
86 I. Papps, *For Love or Money*, Hobart Paper no. 86 (IEA, London, 1980), p. 29.
87 OF: *Trade policy*, p. 23.
88 OF: *Defence policy*, pp. 3-4.
89 Ibid., p. 3.
90 Ibid., p. 11.
91 Ibid., p. 14.
92 Ibid., pp. 23, 68.
93 OF: *Foreign policy*, p. 20.
94 OF: *Defence policy*, p. 24.

Chapter Four

Culture, Nation and 'Race' in the British and French New Right

GILL SEIDEL

Hegemony and the New Right

Unlikely as it may seem, the theoretical work of the Italian Marxist, Antonio Gramsci, particularly his concept of hegemony, has been appropriated by the New Right. For Gramsci there are two aspects of hegemony, or class domination. First, the bureaucratic, coercive apparatus of the state; second, a form of consensus in civil society where ideology is produced and diffused. This consensus is constructed by voluntary associations, and by schools, the media, churches, mass culture, architecture, and even the names of streets; these institutions of civil society are referred to as the hegemonic apparatus. Taken together, the two dimensions constitute the ideological structure of a dominant class. The movement towards socialism, Gramsci's objective, must pay particular attention to creating a counter-hegemony.

Central to this project is the cultural struggle. And what the British and French New Right have in common, despite their divergence, is that they both make interventions in culture. They are engaged in a cultural battle to unsettle and displace the dominant ideology which constructed the post-war liberal and social democratic consensus. Any project of this kind will seek to manipulate words and concepts as an integral part of cultural and political history. Language, particularly processes of renaming and redefinition, is a focus of struggle. The role of intellectuals, and particularly philosophers, is seen as primary in the creation of this counter-hegemony. This explains why the British and French New Right (and their counterparts in the Federal Republic of Germany and Italy) have fielded philosophers as their protagonists – Roger Scruton, amongst others, in Britain, and Alain de Benoist in France.

The French New Right, GRECE,[1] refers to this strategy quite explicitly as 'gramscisme de droite' ('right-wing Gramscism').[2] It was clearly defined in 1977 by Robert de Herte, pseudonym of Alain de Benoist, who emerged as GRECE's main theoretician:

> Every metapolitical strategy should be based on three clear definitions: the definition of the object (cultural power), the definition of the dominant ideas, and the definition of those which will take their place.[3]

For the strand of the British New Right grouped around *The Salisbury Review*, the main focus of this chapter, the project is comparable; the participants aim to reconstruct a new political language through which the concept of authority can be renewed. As with the French New Right, the stance is eminently anti-egalitarian.

> The main tasks for conservative rhetoric are to establish in the public mind the inseparability of market freedom and economic leadership, and to integrate the philosophy of the market into the underlying principle of order which both motivates conservative politics, and attracts the votes of a conservative electorate . . . Such a rhetoric . . . must . . . be taken from the broader realms of political ideology . . . Conservative rhetoric is, or ought to be . . . a rhetoric of order.[4]

These tasks are discussed in *The Salisbury Review*, in Cowling's earlier volume of *Conservative Essays*, [5] and in Scruton's more accessible writings in his Tuesday column in *The Times*. These texts rehearse a 'discursive ensemble',[6] that is, a network of meanings to be put into circulation which constitute the basis of a New Right conservative doctrine. In relation to these writings this chapter will address two related issues. Firstly, it will consider the construction of the concept of culture in the discourse (or social creation of meanings) of the British New Right. Secondly, it will explore the relationship between the concept of culture, and those of language, nation, national identity, and 'race'.[7] It will become clear that views of culture seen as the defining characteristic of national identity set the parameters for specific arguments about race. Hence ostensibly abstract disputes about the meanings of words have profound implications for public policy and people's lives. These discussions will illuminate particular verbal strategies and their centrality to the cultural struggle. Throughout, comparison will be made with the French New Right.

A pertinent starting point is Scruton's essay, 'The Politics of Culture', in that the different components constructed there are developed in subsequent essays in *The Salisbury Review*. Scruton is concerned with different forms of rationality, which are indistinguishable from 'society's . . . sense of history', 'historical continuity' and 'historical sense', the understanding of which is 'intuitive'.[8] The appeal to 'intuitive' understanding introduces an element of mysticism, and references to 'conservative instincts' which occur elsewhere in *The Salisbury Review* are of the same order. It could be argued that they are part of the register of irrationalism − or, alternatively, they could be part of a biological discourse. Scruton's appeal to 'nature' is discussed in chapter three. The overall construction of the relationship between society and history is politically suggestive, yet incomplete. It is complemented and clarified in his critique of E. P. Thompson in the first issue of *The Salisbury Review*, where Scruton argues in an unambiguously nationalist perspective that collective agents cannot include classes, as Thompson and Marxists contend; rather, it is 'national consciousness' which acts as 'a genuine agent in history'. For Scruton, the important social forces are 'language, religion, custom, associations and traditions of political order − in short, all those forces that generate nations'.[9] Clearly, 'nation' as an over-arching concept is a very particular and characteristic focus of the British New Right's ideological and discursive practice. It follows that the construction of 'nation', of 'we', in the discourse of the British New Right must be central to our enquiry.

In nationalist discourse in general the notion of 'we' which constructs 'the nation' does not necessarily cue racial identity. However, as constructed by the New Right, such a link can be shown to function in the slippage between race and culture. Enoch Powell, in a speech entitled 'The Spectre of a Britain that has Lost its Claim to be a Nation' has already rehearsed the main arguments:

> The presence of a common status where there was no common nationhood had produced in the cities of England a concentration of other nationals who asserted the contradictory claim to belong − and yet not to belong − to this nation . . . So far our response has been to attempt to force upon ourselves a non-identity and to assert that we have no unique distinguishing characteristics: the formula is 'a multiracial, multicultural society'. A nation which thus deliberately

denies its continuity with its past and its rootedness in its homeland
is on the way to repudiate its existence.[10]

Key phrases here are 'continuity with the past' and 'rootedness'. The
elision of nation, culture and race, and the emphasis on 'rootedness',
is fundamental to New Right discourse, and is repeated throughout
The Salisbury Review.

By January 1985, there had been eight issues of *The Salisbury
Review*. These contain six articles which specifically address the
question of nation and race, or racism, all within an implicit or
explicit vision of national culture. It is useful to examine these articles
chronologically to see how they build on one another to construct
a particular set of meanings with its own internal coherence. In
addition, a number of articles in the journal have been concerned
with Christian theology and liturgy, including one which explicitly
takes a position on racism. These can be seen as developing and
reinforcing the same discourse.

John Casey: 'One Nation: The Politics of Race'

This article,[11] in the first issue in 1982, begins with two quotations
from Burke, whose traditional and organicist view of society and
nation has enjoyed a resurgence on the Right. These are followed
by a quotation from T. S. Eliot on culture:

> It includes all the characteristic activities and interests of a people:
> Derby Day, Henley Regatta, Cowes, the twelfth of August, a cup final,
> the dog races, the pin table, the dart board, Wensleydale cheese, boiled
> cabbage cut into sections, beetroot in vinegar, nineteenth-century
> Gothic churches and the music of Elgar.

That 'culture' for Eliot subsumes a list of activites and interests
decidedly white and Christian, and frequently gender and class
specific into the bargain, is part of the fabric of our present analysis:
it reflects the ubiquity of ethnocentrism, racism and sexism in 'our'
dominant socio-cultural constructions. These initial quotations from
Burke and Eliot, hallowed, traditional conservative sources, prepare
the reader for the *Realpolitik*. They symbolize the shared political
and white (Christian) culture, the 'us'. The more clearly articulated
defence of that constructed 'us' is to follow. In the remainder of
the article, as the title suggests, nation is entirely predicated on race.

And, appropriately, with this new turn, the fourth quotation, not attributed in the body of the text, is from Enoch Powell.

> There is one problem when we come into contact with a lower culture for the first time . . . There is another problem where a native culture has already begun to disintegrate under foreign influence, and where a native population has already taken in more of the foreign culture than it can ever expel. There is a third problem where, as in some of the West Indies, several uprooted peoples have been haphazardly mixed. And these problems are insoluble.

Casey's article as a whole may be seen to reiterate three major speeches by Powell in 1968. The first, on 9 February, was an invitation to discuss immigration statistics and to play the numbers game; the second in Birmingham on 20 April, contained the 'rivers of blood' metaphor; and the third address at Eastbourne on 18 November linked black people with criminality and referred to 'dislodging' the indigenous population ('the people of England') and turning whole areas into 'alien territory'. These speeches construct different racist arguments which cue and feed on one another. These are further reproduced and exemplified by dominant media representations, and categories of 'common sense' which can be seen as a refracted, populist version of the dominant ideology.

An important fracturing of the racist consensus in the media was provided by the Campaign against Racism in the Media (CARM) in its television programme 'It ain't Half Racist, Mum'.[12] This illustrated the overall patterns of media discourse about the black community, and the ways in which these patterns contribute to the spiral of moral panic and racist logic in which: black = immigrant = too many = send them back. During the 1983 Conservative Party Conference, Harvey Proctor, Conservative MP and member of the Monday Club, put the case for repatriation by appealing to common sense. In a television interview for *Newsnight* on 11 October, he argued on the grounds of 'good sense'; in the debate on the repatriation motion on 13 October he argued 'it's not racism, it's realism'. Good, common or garden sense, importantly constructed by the media, thus claims the status of truth − a sort of circular argument, which, by its very nature, is unquestioning: it's true because it's common sense, and it's common sense because it's true.

Martin Barker has argued that the alleged invasion by foreign culture implies a particular theory of nation and of race. For the New Right, the nation is constituted by homogeneity of culture, and the problem of race lies in the fact of cultural difference. Alien cultures (not inferior, merely different) necessarily undermine social cohesion; this necessity derives from human nature. Such cultures must therefore be eliminated either by assimilation or by removal. What emerges, therefore, is a New Right theory of race and nation which focuses on culture and assimilation, on cultural alienness and difference.[13] This can be seen clearly in Casey's article, where he writes:

> There is no way of understanding British and English history that does not take seriously the sentiments of patriotism that go with a continuity of institutions, shared experiences, language, customs, kindship . . . English patriotism . . . has at its centre a feeling for persons of one's own kind.

In order to preserve the idea of 'our' culture, 'our' traditions and 'our' history as continuity, all coextensive with 'nation' and the 'sentiment' and 'fact of nationality', *defence* of this national culture must be seen as a 'principle', and as a 'moral idea'. Casey grounds nation in both authority and assumed common culture:

> If the account which I have given of the 'immemorial acceptance' of authority within the British state, and the immemorial loyalty that goes with it, be correct, then there must be at least a potential problem should a community exist in large numbers, which defines itself because of its numbers, culture and other observable characteristics, in separation from the rest of the community . . . do we not have the grave apprehension that the great English cities are now becoming alienated from national life . . . large . . . black and brown communities will turn Britain into a different sort of place.

The 'problem' of West Indians for Casey is that they are undisciplined and do not have a proper acceptance of authority. They are uneducated and have a different family structure; and in addition are prone to violence, drug abuse and criminality:

> the West Indian community is *structurally* likely to be at odds with English civilisation. There is an extraordinary resentment towards authority − police, teachers, Underground guards − *all* authority . . . Then there is the family structure which is markedly unlike our own: educational standards that are below those of all other racial groups . . . and the involvement of West Indians in a vastly disproportionate amount of violent crime . . . the West Indian life style . . . seems to include drugs and other unlawful activities.

Casey seeks to drive a wedge between West Indians and Asians. Asians are disciplined and have an identifiable (male) family head, at first sight making them more acceptable; but then there is a problem with 'them' too in that 'they' have a strong sense of their own culture, and therefore resist assimilation:

> What is finally at issue comes out more clearly with the Indian community or communities – industrious, peaceable people, with most of the domestic virtues. Nevertheless, by their large numbers, their *profound* difference in culture, they are most unlikely to wish to identify themselves with the traditions and loyalties of the host nation.

Casey has argued that black people are not like us. He is now ready to articulate the precise political project and policy recommendation which stems from this 'moral idea': compulsory repatriation or guest-worker status for black people.

> I believe that the only radical policy that would stand a chance of success is repatriation . . .
> The alternative . . . would be retrospectively to alter the legal status of the coloured immigrant community, so that its members become guest-workers . . .

The argument is reinforced by the vague but ominous claim that

> it does not . . . require much imagination to see what will happen if the present demographic trends in Britain continue.

The demographic argument evokes Powell's numbers game, but it also cues a whole range of xenophobic, racist and sexist discourses, including those of the National Front and British National Party, and of Le Pen's *Front National* in France. There is of course a difference in style. Casey's arguments are couched in restrained and seemingly detached academic language, which lends them legitimacy: Casey, after all, is a Cambridge don.

Other publications, including GRECE and John Tyndall's *Spearhead* seek to establish legitimacy and value freedom for their arguments by using similarly abstract language and cultural mystifications.[14] In marked contrast, the texts and speeches of the British National Party, the British Movement, and the *Front National* use a more populist, accessible language which manipulates common-sense categories. And beyond these differences of style, tone and modes of argument, with the National Front, the British Movement and the *Front National* we are dealing not only with racist discourse, but also with racist activism and violence. Despite these differences, the underlying message is the same: 'blacks out'. This desired aim may be achieved through voluntary repatriation (part of the 1970 Conservative Manifesto); or through compulsory repatriation, proposed by the National Front, by Harvey Proctor, and, here, by Casey.

Of course, the Conservative Party seeks to deny or to distance itself from the links alleged by the Young Conservatives to exist between the Monday Club and far right organizations like the National Front and WISE; and Mrs Thatcher's distaste for the National Front is on record. In addition, Proctor's motion on compulsory repatriation at the 1983 Conservative Party Conference was massively defeated.[15] The point here is not to allege an organizational connection, but rather to illustrate the discursive continuities and overlaps. These are far more significant and far-reaching in the social construction of meanings and 'common sense' than the intentions or affiliations of particular authors or politicians.

It is now customary for the Conservative Party and its individual members to seek to rebut charges of racism. Presumably Casey would do likewise, as did Powell in 1969. Interviewed by David Frost on 3 January, Powell successfully imposed the terms of the debate and was able to claim with conviction that he was not a racist:

> if by a racialist you mean a man who despises a human being because he belongs to another race, or a man who believes that one race is inherently superior to another in civilisation or capability for civilisation, then the answer is emphatically no.[16]

But, as Barker argues, the New Right's racism does not require the hypothesis of innate superiority, only that of cultural difference.

A number of complex processes are at work in these denials of racism. The move to the Right in Britain has meant that Mrs Thatcher can, in the same 1979 speech, both castigate the National Front and claim that Britain is being 'swamped by an alien culture'.[17] It could therefore be argued that she and her Party are explicitly anti-racist. Her argument, like Casey's, is constructed in a culturalist and demographic framework. 'We' have culture, 'they' have ethnicity, summarizes the culturalist stance. The other end of the argument (and this is rehearsed not only by Casey, but throughout *The Salisbury Review*) is that racism (or 'racialism') is an empty concept anyway. In this way, racism in its institutional forms, in ideology, and in its lived everyday material practices, is either trivialized or defined out of existence. Casey goes so far as to characterize 'racialism' as a 'vulgar, and above all *banal* catchphrase' and regards the concept itself as a sign of 'the decline of our political culture'.[18] The identification 'our' in this context is particularly illuminating in that it drives a clear (white) wedge between black people and anti-racists, and the rest of the community. Racism, therefore, is not merely trivial; the concept is also decadent.

The implied notion of decadence in Casey is not the same as the concept of decadence employed by the far Right, including the National Front. For the far Right decadence is the product of race-mixing, of miscegenation, so that black people and those who seek to form alliances with them are seen as responsible for biological and therefore social decline. Similarly, in Nazi doctrine, decadence, introduced initially by biological pollution — that is, intermarriage with 'Aryans' — is caused by Jews. In the case of Nazism, this familiar reversal blaming the victims in the framework of an efficient modern state generated a very particular set of material outcomes. Yet despite these differences, and irrespective of Casey's intentions, the repetition of the 'blaming the victim' syndrome, in holding blacks and anti-racists responsible for racism, is not without significance. These discursive parallels are important because 'they make it easier for the fascists to ride in on your coat-tails'.[19]

The general dismissal or trivialization of racism, including defining it out of existence, needs to be seen as part of a larger strategy of the New Right, both in and out of power, in Britain and elsewhere. Even repatriation would not then be racist, if the concept has no meaning. And the parameters are set for expelling 'foreign' cultures in order that 'ours' should live.

J. Enoch Powell: 'Our Loss of Sovereignty'

Powell's article follows immediately on Casey's, and though extremely succinct, shares the same presuppositions.[20] Powell, as a vociferous anti-marketeer, is arguing that the 'national instinct' has lost out in the subordination of Britain to the EEC. It is, however, the construction of the argument that is of interest, for it is only about foreign policy in so far as this is a mode of exemplification. He first evokes 'national . . . identity' in relation to the Falkland Islands; and contrasts the Foreign Office's inconsistent policy

towards sovereignty in relation to Northern Ireland. He praises
Thatcher for her 'swamping' speech, and her denial in April 1981
that the Brixton riots had anything to do with unemployment
(although there is cryptic criticism of her failure to carry these
statements through into action). Then, in the context of sovereignty
and the EEC, he raises the question of 'what sort of people we are'.
Like Casey's article, the argument turns out to be primarily about
'us', 'our' values and identity. Powell's text is, in a sense, a variant
of Casey's, and one which carries a particular ideological weight in
view of the cumulative and highly publicized speeches of its author
and their resonances. It is a rehearsal of networks of meanings, and
of possible alliances between ultra-conservative intellectuals, despite
their differences.

Ray Honeyford: 'Multi-Ethnic Intolerance'

A reading of this third article,[21] and an understanding of the
importance of Barker's concept of a new racism dependent upon
cultural difference, and concerned with assimilation, is assisted by
examination of an article by Scruton in *The Times* on 17 January
1984, 'Now they tell me: I'm actually black'. This exemplifies the
importance of redefinitions, and that of racism in particular, to the
whole cultural project of the New Right.[22]

Scruton purports to be providing an answer to readers' questions,
about where he stands on the issue of race: 'are you a member of
the white racist establishment, advocating policies of cultural
hegemony designed to deny the validity of black culture and black
experience . . .'? His reply is organized around a critique of an ILEA
publication, *Race, Sex and Class*, subtitled *multi-ethnic education
in schools*; although Scruton has quite explicit views on gender,
discussed in chapter three, in this instance the issue is completely
ignored. After taking issue with the ILEA's definitions, Scruton
reaches the remarkable conclusion that he is black − because he
belongs to an educated minority and is therefore excluded from these
particular power structures by the prejudice and hostility of the
uneducated (ILEA).

In the course of his argument, he questions the use of 'black' to
refer to groups who differ in 'culture and ancestry', and in particular
to the grouping together of Afro-Caribbeans and Asians, because
they differ in educational achievement. He takes issue (as do

Honeyford and Flew) with 'the extraordinary caricature of British history' which led the ILEA to the assertion that 'racism as an ideology had become institutionalized in British society'; and questions whether the black communities are implacably opposed to racism. He suggests, in fact, that membership of a minority culture could increase a person's 'natural xenophobia'. And, logically in terms of his own frame of reference, he challenges the validity of multiculturalism, mother-tongue teaching and equality, which are seen as the products of political enthusiasms. He makes out a defence of 'racism' (Scruton's quotation marks) in cultural terms:

> an educated person . . . would not assume that a teacher who endeavours to communicate the culture which is expressed in his language [invariably the masculine pronoun] – and who is aware that there is no greater mental discipline than to understand the achievements and institutions of the civilization into which one was born is a 'racist' actively seeking to exclude 'blacks' from privileges whose value he rightly seeks to explain to them . . . Such a person . . . will . . . meet with the most virulent hostility and prejudice from the uneducated.

It is Scruton, then, the 'educated person' defending educational values and 'the achievement and institutions of . . . civilization' who is cast aside and excluded. Here we have another reversal: in Casey's articles blacks were seen as indirectly responsible for racism; now the uneducated (the ILEA) exert power over the educated – a version of semantics which, like men's claim that feminism is sexist, ignores structural differences in power. In addition, Scruton is making claims about the quality of culture, and suggesting that British culture, particularly as exemplified in Shakespeare, is a universal norm. As it is both ennobling and civilizing it is an altogether appropriate British educational objective.

It is particularly significant in this article that the four terms in quotation marks to be redefined are 'black', 'multicultural', 'equality', and 'racist'. Yet Scruton would rebut any charge of racism. A few weeks later he declared his opposition to both racism and 'classism', arguing with impressive rhetorical flourish that class antagonisms are as repellent as anti-black or anti-Jewish prejudices or exclusions.[23]

The redefinitions engaged in by Scruton are important because they parallel the arguments of writers in *The Salisbury Review*, particularly those of Ray Honeyford, but also those of Antony Flew and Geoffrey Partington. All these articles, discussed below, may therefore be seen as variations of the same discourse. Honeyford's articles in particular have attracted public attention, because they have fuelled an educational controversy in Bradford, where Honeyford is a headmaster. The conflict which was initiated by the first of his articles in *The Salisbury Review* became so bitter that a majority of parents withdrew their children and for a week set up an alternative school in protest.[24]

In 'Multi-ethnic Intolerance', Honeyford argues that the irresponsible 'multi-ethnic brigade' have prompted a backlash and inflicted damage on the ethnic minorities. Firstly, this 'brigade' suggests that minority languages (that is, mother-tongue teaching) should be a medium of instruction, which Honeyford calls 'a prescription for linguistic chaos'. In addition, they create 'anti-British prejudice' and are attempting to 'purge' and 'sanitise' the school libraries, a 'literary censoriousness'. They cling to the absurd belief that black children suffer from a defective self-concept, and favour a notion of positive discrimination which implies the obligation to accept lower standards from young (West Indian) black people. This constitutes an insult and leads to the creation of a 'second-rate citizenry'. Generally, the 'multiculturalists' entertain 'two false and subversive notions': first, that we ought to 'sentimentalise and patronise ethnic minorities', and, secondly, that we should 'impose racial tolerance by government dictat'. Any challenge to these positions is dismissed by 'multiculturalists' as 'racist'. He concludes that these 'experts' who are 'hired by misguided authorities in order to prove their progressive intentions', represent an 'inverted McCarthyism' and are supported by 'an irrelevant if not positively malign quango', the Commission for Racial Equality (CRE), and 'a huge rag-bag of dubious voluntary organisations'. They combine to create an 'unhealthy colour consciousness in our schools' which is producing 'growing frustration and . . . despair'.

The enemy, the 'multiculturalists', are presented in purely negative terms as activists and agitators. They 'damage', prompt a 'backlash', 'purge', 'sanitise' and commit 'multiracialist assault'. They also argue (passionately), 'impede', 'assert', 'insist' and 'issue guidelines'. They are emotional, rather than reasonable, and deviant by association and by assumed political attitudes.

> I suspect that at the heart of this group . . . is the sort of extremism
> already well established in the feminist movement and in radical politics
> . . . The same people often welcome race riots . . .

Indeed, they are a lunatic fringe of 'Asian and West Indian intellectuals' and 'political extremists . . . with a background of polytechnic sociology'. We are not, of course, told that this 'multi-ethnic brigade' enjoys the support of the majority of parents.[25]

To sum up this first article by Honeyford, this 'movement', which is emotional, violent, anti-British and totalitarian, is damaging to both race relations and education. All these actions are being carried out against 'Afro-Asian settler children' who are seen as innocent, passive victims. The disproportionate presence of such children in schools is later argued to mean that the academic standards of white children are bound to suffer. Institutional racism is of course entirely absent: it does not enter Honeyford's political conceptualization. Hence the 'muticultural brigade' is seen to be lunging at, and destroying, not windmills but a hitherto tolerant and ordered society. In this way the 'multiculturalists' are presented as invaders, as outsiders. It is a familiar scenario. Central to this stategy are the two reversals: 'the inverted McCarthyism' and 'second-class citizenry'. Language and identity are clearly a site of struggle − in this case to re-establish traditional meanings and values, and hence order, as part of an organic view of education within a larger, untroubled, white vision of culture and tradition.

Antony Flew: 'The Race Relations Industry'

The main interest of this article is that (like Scruton and Honeyford), Flew denies the existence of institutional racism, and offers a critique of the concepts of racism and blackness used by the CRE.[26] There are also clear overlaps with Casey, in that Flew assumes that the only viable paths to good race relations are assimilation, (involving the elimination of black minority cultures), or repatriation:

> the object of the exercise . . . is . . . so to assimilate our immigrants that they become English or Scots or Welsh who just happen to have skins of a minority colour . . . Those who want to remain . . . Bangladeshi ought to be planning . . . to be returning to Bangladesh.

Flew claims that the CRE's use of the term 'black' is 'loose and confusing', but takes issue with its use to refer to both Afro-Caribbean and Asian people, arguing the superficially liberal-sounding case that they are not all the same: 'The point is to conceal relevant differences . . . while suggesting . . . that all equally are victims of (exclusively white) racism.'

His objection to the term 'black' is precisely that it 'emphasizes the common experience which both Afro-Caribbean and Asian people have of being victims of racism'. The evidence that it is unhelpful to think of 'all immigrants . . . as one homogeneous mass', and the proof that white racism cannot be to blame for black disadvantage, lies in the different levels of achievement reached by Asian and West Indian young people. These suggest that there may be among the latter 'deficiencies either of character or of education . . . which . . . should be . . . corrected by the efforts of the people themselves'. At the same time, if researchers 'were not so obsessed with race and racism', we might find out that there were 'significant differences in performance between those coming from different parts of the Caribbean'.

Apart from suggesting radical pruning of the CRE's budget, the main political and ideological effect of this argument is to polarize different sections of the black population. The struggle over the definition of 'black' is not merely semantic. In the same way, Flew takes issue with the definition of racism contained in *Education for Equality*, a document produced by Berkshire's Education Committee. The document describes racism as a 'combination of discriminatory practices; unequal relations and structures of power; and negative beliefs and attitudes'. Flew himself, like Powell, defines racism as 'the advantaging or disadvantaging of individuals for no other or better reason than that they happen to be members of this racial group rather than that'. Thus, the concept of institutional racism involves an 'outrageous redefinition' with 'ruinous implications'. In conclusion, he argues that to concede to such definitions, which rest on a concern for equality of outcomes (and thus on a Marxist analysis), rather than on the CRE's proper concern with equality of opportunity, is to open the door to purges, both of libraries and people − an issue raised by Honeyford, and, later, by Partington. Anti-racism, as often in the New Right, is implied to be Marxist in inspiration and totalitarian in practice. Such a view is supported by a closing reference to slogans of 'Sack Jensen', and even 'Kill Jensen' claimed to have been prevalent on US campuses; the general implication is that the 'often Marxist militants of race relations' condone and practice violence against their ideological opponents, and therefore constitute a direct threat to our civilization. This representation has already been cued by the language of Honeyford's article. The cumulative, linguistic construction of the Marxist-totalitarian 'other' is falling into place.

Ray Honeyford: 'Education and Race – An Alternative View'

Honeyford's second article[27] develops the same themes, expanding on the 'plight of those white children who constitute the "Ethnic minority" in a growing number of inner-city schools'. He again takes issue with the 'cant term' racism, and describes it as 'a slogan designed to suppress constructive thought'. Like Flew, he claims that 'the roots of black educational failure are, in reality, located in West Indian family structure and values'. Most of his vituperation is reserved for anti-racists, and also for Asian parents attending a meeting at Honeyford's school, at which 'the hysterical political temperament of the Indian subcontinent became evident', orchestrated by 'a Muslim leader' and 'a half-educated and volatile Sikh'. Despite this demonstration of parental involvement, Honeyford still claims that the real pressure for a multiracial curriculum comes from 'multi-racial zealots' (who subject him to 'libellous and mindless bombast') and the 'vehement, radical left of black organisations'. They have 'totalitarian' mentalities and 'aggressive' dispositions, and 'know little of the British traditions of understatement, civilized discourse and respect for reason'. Honeyford here makes an explicit claim of cultural superiority, echoing an earlier reference to the superiority of Shakespeare and Wordsworth over Linton Kwesi Johnson, and a claim that the English language is itself intrinsically superior:

> We in the schools are also enjoined to believe that creole, pidgin and other non-standard variants have the same power, subtlety and capacity for expressing fine shades of meaning, and for tolerating uncertainty, ambiguity and irony as standard English.

The suggestion that all languages are equally good is a 'mindless slogan' imposed on schools by cultural relativists.

Geoffrey Partington: 'Race, Sex and Class in Inner London'

This last of the six articles presents very similar arguments to those we have already encountered.[28] The title refers to the five booklets *Race, Sex and Class*, published by the ILEA in 1983 and criticized

E

by Scruton in the article discussed earlier. Partington offers a critique of their position which he sums up as 'a monstrous policy'.

Partington's representations match Honeyford's when he refers to the weakness of West Indian family structures. It is worth noting that West Indian family structures are presumed weak, or deviant, because a large number are female-headed households. As Miriam David argues in chapter five, this anxiety is discernible also in US family policies, which seek to bring such households into line with white middle-class norms.

Like Flew and Honeyford, Partington refuses to acknowledge the existence of institutional racism, and therefore cannot accept the rationale of curriculum change. Quoting (like Scruton) the second ILEA paper which stated that 'racism as an ideology had become institutionalised in British society', he questions the value for the life chances of black children in Britain, of mother-tongue teaching and proposed curriculum emphasis on Caribbean and world history. The proposed selection by librarians of 'books which do not contain racial stereotypes' is referred to as 'book burning', an emotive phrase which connotes both Chilean militarism and Nazism.

Partington remarks that Bernard Coard, author of *How the West Indian Child is made Educationally Subnormal in the British School System*, is no longer available to give advice 'whether on how to eliminate political colleagues or rivals such as Mr Maurice Bishop [of Grenada], or on how to eliminate racists or racist books in Britain'. This adds further semantic weight to the representation of the ILEA and of the 'multicultural zealots' (Honeyford's phrase) as thugs. If the ideologized picture is not yet clear, there is a further reference to 'purges ahead'. And Partington too takes issue with the use of 'black' which for the ILEA 'emphasises the common experience . . . of . . . victims of racism, and their common determination to oppose racism'. The ideological function of this critique in dividing the 'black' community has been discussed earlier with reference to Flew. Finally, Partington is outraged that the assimilation option is denounced as racist; and given that racism is again defined as advantaging or disadvantaging individuals because of their membership of a particular 'racial group' (Partington's terminology), he concludes that 'the policy of the ILEA is itself deeply racist in this strict and accurate sense of the term'.

This now-familiar reversal can also be found in the concept of 'anti-white racism'. This is an important semantic and mythic reversal which has been used extensively by the New Right. It is found in

France in the writings of Alain de Benoist as well as on the populist, proto-fascist Right, and in associated journals. The President of the *Front National*, Jean-Marie Le Pen, now a Euro-MP, sloganizes with 'à bas le racisme anti-français' ('down with anti-French racism') matched with the more ubiquitous and populist 'common sense' paraphrase, 'Les Français d'abord'('The French first'), which is also the title of his recent book prepared for the 1984 European elections. A theme of a series of articles in December 1983 in the ultra right-wing Catholic monthly, *Itinéraires*, was 'le soi-disant anti-racisme'('so-called anti-racism').[29] And, indeed, it can be found in *The Salisbury Review*, in an article by Biggs-Davison.

J. Biggs-Davison: 'A Theology of Politics'

At first glance, this article does not seem to have much bearing on the present discussion.[30] It is an argument about the proper role of the Church in, and the implications of Christianity for, secular society. It incorporates a strange patchwork of diatribes against the United Nations, the Campaign for Nuclear Disarmament, trade unions, the Kremlin, the World Council of Churches, and 'two Hebrew false prophets, Marx and Engels', reflecting a Manichean bile at work rather than a sophisticated set of arguments. Its relevance in the present context is its reference in the final section to 'anti-white racism', and its veiled antisemitism.

It is rare to find apparent antisemitism in *The Salisbury Review*; its contributors would distance themselves from this perhaps even more vehemently than from anti-black racism. The presence of prominent Jews in Thatcher's cabinet may well be a restraining influence.[31] It is doubly ironic in Biggs-Davison's case, given that he is chairman of the Conservative Friends of Israel. Arguably, his use of the word 'Hebrew' to characterize Marx and Engels sidesteps the more overtly antisemitic 'Jewish' in this context.[32] It could be read as a neutral descriptor; but it can also be read quite differently. For what is the effect of telling us (in Engels' case, wrongly) that they were Jewish? In the context of the arguments, in which Marxism is held to be incompatible with Christianity, a link is made between Jewishness, Marxism (and, incidentally, Soviet interests) which necessarily puts a negative construction on all three. Thus:

What music for Muscovite ears when 'Christian Marxists' − a clear contradiction in terms − attempted to synthesise the gospel with the dialectic, the eschatology of proletarian revolution with the Apocalypse, the Manifesto of those two Hebrew false prophets, Marx and Engels, with the *Magnificat!*[33]

It must also be pointed out that this verbal strategy cues traditional antisemitic writing. For national socialists, communism and capitalism were both seen as Jewish; and both are international. Elsewhere, in National Front texts, for example, 'internationalists' or 'cosmopolitans' are code words for Jews, though the lexical tradition is much older.[34] In using such a formulation, Biggs-Davison helps to put into circulation a set of meaning not obviously present in his text. The intentions of the author here are once again irrelevant — for this is how discursive meanings work.

It is interesting that, in addition, Biggs-Davison regards liberation theology and hence the World Council of Churches as serving Kremlin interests — for both are also targets for the religious Right in the USA, for the National Front, and for Odinist pagan cults associated with the far Right. Immediately following a reference to the massacre of missionaries, Biggs-Davison continues:

> If anything, Christianity now needs a programme to combat the World Council of Churches, its anti-white racism and its far more destructive 'classism', which causes it to look for, and to take the part of, only those whom it can see as 'oppressed'.

And in conclusion:

> We have heard enough of a religion that is 'horizontal' — reaching out fraternally to the world. A religion of love of neighbour that is not for the love of God is stunted and self-righteous. It is not Christian. At the same time, the 'horizontal' and the 'vertical', symbolised by those old spires that reached for Heaven, are not opposed: it took both to make the Cross.

The anti-classism is an echo of Scruton, who also discusses 'reverse discrimination' in an article on the American writer, Ronald Dworkin;[35] the 'anti-white racism' we have met before. The verticality that Biggs-Davison sees as so eminently desirable, that is, the hierarchical relationship in preference to the horizontal, loving, fraternal bond (while conceding to some necessary complementarily in order to complete the Christian symbol), also finds resonances in other New Right texts, in this case of the German New Right. The context here, however, is not Christian, as Christianity is not a cornerstone of the continental New Right. Rather it is anti-Judaeo-Christian and pagan, because the Judaeo-Christian tradition is seen as the origin of egalitarianism. There is a striking similarity in language and the reproduction of a similar authoritarian vision as part of an attack on egalitarianism:

> Our humanism is *vertical*: it places individuals into a *hierachical* structure which accounts for differences. Egalitarian humanism is horizontal: all individuals have the same place in the collective and are interchangeable.[36]

Thus what at first seems to be an article on a quite different subject turns out to have implications of direct relevance to the general characterization of culture, nation, and especially 'race' by the New Right.

How may these different strands be drawn together? First, the dominant British culture and its institutions deemed to be under threat are seen explicitly as non-secular and Christian; and, furthermore, the traditional form of worship is bound up with

> an experience of continuity and association; of community, family, group or church . . . The ritual involvement of the Church of England in State Functions . . . witnesses to the explicitly Christian basis of our institutions.[37]

And again: 'National consciousness provides . . . one of the strongest experiences of the immanence of God'.[38]

It is a culture in which nationality, religion and state institutions necessarily inform each other and are interdependent. Despite a rhetoric of tolerance, the religious message is, however, anti-ecumenical.

> Society is pluriform; there are many religions represented and followed. However, the United Kingdom remains, at least nominally, a Christian state. This should not be overlooked in our proper anxiety to give other faiths their place, and it may be questioned how far schools add to the confusion rather than the enlightenment of their pupils by teaching 'comparative religion' before the Christian faith has been properly understood.[39]

It is further argued that Christianity should be more hierarchical (Biggs-Davison's insistence on the 'vertical' relationship) and traditional, particularly in its liturgy. George Martelli argues against Vatican II, objecting to its decrees concerning the revision of the liturgy of the Mass and the use of the vernacular.[40]

Opposition to Vatican II, however, has wider implications. Martelli observes that its conclusion ran to over a thousand pages; and among the changes they contained, which he does not mention, was the dropping of the charge of deicide against the Jews, an issue which is of course the focus of Christian antisemitism. Opposition to Vatican II thus constitutes a link between traditional Catholics, and Catholics on the extreme Right, some of whose publications are overtly racist and antisemitic. This is especially the case in France.

Although the Christian component of the New Right in Britain has been less central than in America, it is significant in several ways. Apart from the fact that moral issues are becoming more important to the British Right, it can also be seen that anti-ecumenical arguments contribute to racist policies both directly and through their role in constructing 'the nation'.

Language and 'Rootedness'

The same pattern of parellels with the far Right is discernible in an important essay by Sally Shreir on the politics of language. This article shows an explicit awareness of the role of language in hegemonic and counter-hegemonic projects. National identity is claimed to be founded on 'natural emotions' and 'natural allegiances'; and there is a 'natural' relation between language and national identity, such that 'the affinity between national unity and linguistic conformity lies in the very nature of things.' In addition, intellectuals undermine this national unity, for 'when intellectuals cease to be patriots (as tends to happen) they become internationalists'.[41]

The resonances with French political writing of the anti-Dreyfusard camp in the late 1890s are striking, particularly with that of the nationalist deputy and prolific novelist, Maurice Barrès[42] and his long-term associate, Charles Maurras. Later, Maurras was to found the royalist and antisemitic *Action Française* whose central concept was that of integral nationalism,[43] and which, it has been argued, was a model for subsequent, more successful fascist movements.[44] At the same time, it was a focus of intellectual activity emphasizing national roots and national consciousness. Both Barrès and Maurras were repelled by the conventional notion of the intellectuals as an uprooted and therefore decadent class. 'Les déracinés', Barrès called them.

The notion of 'enracinement' ('rootedness') remains central to the French Right from Barrès onwards. The first cyclostyled issues of *Nouvelle Ecole* of GRECE, now a very lavish publication, carried the drawing of a tree on the back cover. The lexical variation for the members of the *Club de l'Horloge* (Clock Club), close to GRECE, is 'les racines du futur' ('the roots of the future'), which is also the title of the first collective work published by the *Club de l'Horloge* in 1977. These are Indo-European and pagan roots, translated into republican terms. The notion of rootedness is important in constructing a link between biological and cultural racism, and other examples can be found in the British New Right.[45] It is contrasted with the rootlessness of the left, the reason for its decadence and lack of identity.

The mystical affinity posited by Shreir between national unity and language calls for further discussion on ethnocentrism. In the light of this 'affinity', the arguments against mother-tongue teaching can be seen as patently ideological and part of the integral nationalist vision. Certainly, Gujarati or Caribbean Creoles in Britain are not part of 'the very nature of things'. They relate to the legacy of colonial history and a policy of labour recruitment and their human consequences. However, such explanations simply cannot be part of a 'naturalist' discourse because they construct a conflicting reality concerned with social processes, social agencies, and social movements. The rejection in *The Salisbury Review* of mother-tongue teaching (which is endorsed by an EEC, and hence international directive), in favour of schoolchildren achieving proficiency in 'standard English', is based on a number of assumptions. It implies that 'standard English', a variant which few people in Britain speak, is value-free; and any social or ideological representations either absent or intrinsically correct. It is part of any hegemonic project to portray its proponents' language and traditions as the norm, as taken for granted, as somehow natural, and part of a common-sense, unchanging view of the world. On the other hand, those of the dominated group, non-conformist by definition, are a legitimate object of scrutiny, and a potential threat to the existing order.

It is also part of that same untroubled ethnocentrism of this dominant Christian culture that it is traditionally monolingual, whereas globally people are commonly bilingual or trilingual. This attitude is embodied in a number of education reports of which the latest carries the telling title *A Language for Life*, emphasizing monoculturalism.[46] The Welsh and Gaelic languages are referred to as 'dialects'. French, by contrast, is seen as a high-status language spoken indigenously. But, as Roberts has pointed out,[47] French does not present the same problem for social control, as, say, Urdu, in the British context. Britain has never had an explicit language policy, because it has never considered that minority languages should be granted legitimacy by such recognition.

For the neo-conservative New Right in Britain, the politicization of education (by the ILEA in particular), the decline in educational standards, in respect for authority and in national consciousness (as a moral idea essentially linked to language, 'high' culture, and community), is not, as we have seen, accounted for in crudely biological terms as it is for the far Right. Although Ashworth, again writing in *The Salisbury Review*, claims that mystical concepts like 'mytho-genic zones' are 'indices of *real* national boundaries' as contrasted with 'fictitious communities', his overt argument is that nations are defined by a common consciousness.[48] Even here there is a tension, however. In spite of the fact that he says that nations are 'not *necessarily* consanguinous groupings',[49] so that assimilation, for example of Jews, is possible, the very emphasis suggests that nations are *usually* consanguinous; and the term 'mytho-genic' appears to mix culture and biology.

The criterion of consanguinity is, however, fundamental to the French New Right, who referred to '*les frontières*' and '*les patries charnelles*' and '*frontières du sang*' ('frontiers' and 'fatherlands of flesh and blood' and 'blood frontiers').[50] As recently as 1975, they have emphasised the racial dimensions of rootedness in a lexicon clearly reminiscent of '*Blut und Boden*' ('blood and soul') and '*Erlebnis*' (the phrase used by Hilter to denote authenticity and living experience).

GRECE published the following statements under the title '*Qu'est-ce que l'enracinement'* ('what is rootedness'):

> If France is merely a concept, totally removed from the realities of soul and blood, patriotism then becomes ideological and contains in itself all the germs of universalism: he who wishes to be French is French.[51]

> Our history needs to be demystified so that we may discover our sources of life, allow us to be penetrated once again by the great ethno-geographical currents which link France to Europe on the basis of common flesh.[52]

Since then it has updated its language and gained respectability. GRECE's position is of one differential racism: it favours 'ethnic diversity' and celebrates that diversity, but within a hierarchical framework. This allegedly pluralist stance has been popularized in the very ambiguous slogan 'le droit à la différence' ('the right to be different').

Conclusion

The racism of the neo-conservative New Right is cultural, and Casey's article is perhaps the clearest statement of the 'problem' of the massive presence of 'alien cultures'; Thatcher's 'swamping speech' is conceptually similar. Of course they argue that there is a difference between racism and nationalism. Sherman made such a distinction in the following terms:

> Racism is largely a New World phenomenon deriving from the aftermath of slavery . . . Nationhood and national consciousness are a positive force, providing a sense of belonging, social cohesiveness, patriotism and civic consciousness.[53]

But, as we have seen, this distinction depends upon a definition of racism in terms of individual attitudes, and a denial of the relevance of a concept of institutional racism.

Given the New Right's organic, hierarchical view of national culture and traditions and its insistence on its own 'authentic voice', it must wage ideological and semiotic guerilla warfare against all 'non-rooted', universal meanings in order to gain political space. Its discourse is therefore necessarily opposed to internationalisms of every kind and is, therefore, potentially antisemitic since historically Jews are the paradigm of rootlessness.[54] At the same time, it is anti-liberal, anti-socialist and anti-communist (and it is increasingly argued that communism equals fascism); opposed to radical feminism; and dismissive of Third World philosophies and aid programmes. These discourses are being circulated, transformed and reconstructed in the media and elsewhere.

Possible transformations are, in fact, being rehearsed in *The Salisbury Review*, particularly in relation to the concepts of race and nation. If the distinction between racism and nationalism is to be upheld, the phenomenon of institutional racism must be defined away. And it follows that 'black', which for anti-racists, as we have seen, derives some of its meaning from 'racism', and 'multiculturalism' must also be prime targets for redefinition or elimination.

This very process contains another reversal: it is precisely this activity of redefining and manipulating words and concepts out of existence that Shreir presents as a feature of communism and of communist, totalitarian discourse. The New Right is, of course, virulently anti-communist; but openly adopts the same strategy. It is an interesting paradox. In fact, of course, these verbal strategies are used by groups to both right and left, particularly by those unwilling to compromise; so that similar strategies may be employed by groups in very different structural positions, such as radical feminists. In a broader arena (including the Helsinki argreements), national and international 'freedom'/'freedoms' and 'right'/'rights' (to work, to strike) are a site of struggle between irreconcilable discursive and ideological frameworks.

But it is not merely a question of ideas, for this ignores the relationship between discourse and power. Foucault argues that different agencies, ideologically defined parties and professions have affiliations with particular discourses.[55] It is their capacity for circulation, exchange, and their possibilities of transformation, not their 'truth', that define the 'value'.[56] In other words, language and discourse create values and particular ways of thinking and speaking, and hence channels our political behaviour and actions in certain directions. And racist discourse, like any other system of exclusion, including sexist discourse, rests on institutional support.

Nationalism itself is not just an ideological, but an institutional phenomenon expressed, for example, in battles over the EEC budget, and in the Falklands War, as well as in the media representations of these. In some cases, nationalism is unambigously predicated on race, as in Casey's statement that 'the Falklanders were *British* by every conceivable test . . . by language, custom and race'.[57]

In other cases, the national or general interest invoked makes no such overt reference, as when Thatcher described working miners during the 1984-5 strike as 'working for Britain'. In both cases however, the possibilities of constructing national identity and national interest are linked to the existing power structures of society, to control of the hegemonic apparatus. Power helps to construct the concepts which can be used to consolidate and legitimate power, and the concept of nation, predicated on race, is one such concept.

In a comparable nationalist tradition, Maurras argued for the primacy of politics ('La politique d'abord' or 'politics first'). Gramsci, then the British and continental New Right, have modified this to 'culture first' in order to challenge the dominant consensus. But language is part of the history of culture, the source of meanings, and the political praxis of a given group. It is therefore central to this struggle.

Notes

1 Groupement de Recherche et d'Etude pour une Civilisation Europeénne (Research and Study Group for a European Civilization) was set up in January 1969. GRECE was a regrouping of a number of racist, ultra-nationalist and neo-fascist activists. Its principal journals are *Nouvelle Ecole* and *Eléments*. See P. Taguieff, 'La stratégie culturelle de la Nouvelle Droite en France 1968-1983', in *Vous avez dit fascismes?* (Arthaud/Montalba, Paris, 1984), pp. 13-152. On the Italian New Right, see *La Destra radicale*, ed. F. Ferraresi (Feltrinelli, Milan, 1984).

2 P. Taguieff, 'Le retournement de gramscisme', in *Politique d'aujourd'hui*, new series 1 Jul.-Sept. 1983), pp. 69-82. The Italian New Right, in its journal *Elementi*, is also concerned with 'Gramscismo di destra', or 'right-wing Gramscism'.

3 Robert de Herte, 'La révolution conservatrice', tr. G. Seidel, *Eléments*, 20 (Feb.-Apr. 1977), p. 7.

4 'Editorial', *The Salisbury Review* 1, (Autumn 1982), p. 38.

5 M. Cowling (ed.), *Conservative Essays* (Cassell, London, 1978).

6 M. Foucault, 'The order of discourse', in *Language and Politics*, ed. M. Shapiro (Basil Blackwell, Oxford, 1984), p. 122.

7 'Race', of course, is a social construct, which cannot be shown to have any basis in genetic discontinuities in the human population. It should therefore be understood as a purely social category throughout this chapter (and indeed elsewhere).

8 R. Scruton, *The Politics of Culture and Other Essays* (Carcanet, Manchester, 1981), p. 113.

9 R. Scruton, 'Thinkers of the Left: E. P. Thompson, *The Salisbury Review*, 1 (Autumn 1982), p. 14.

10 E. Powell, speech to Thurrock Conservative Association, 30 Oct. 1981 reported in *The Guardian*, 9 Nov. 1981, p. 14.

11 J. Casey, 'One nation: the politics of race', *The Salisbury Review*, 1 (Autumn 1982), pp. 23-8.
12 Screened by *Open Door* BBC 2, 1 Mar. 1979, repeated 4 Mar. 1979.
13 M. Barker, *The New Racism* (Junction Books, London, 1981).
14 See G. Seidel, 'Le fascisme dans les textes de la Nouvelle Droite', *MOTS*, 3, (Oct. 1981), pp. 49-59.
15 On the other hand, Professor Bikhu Parekh (Hull) stated in his submission to the European Parliament's Committee of Inquiry into the rise of racism and fascism that 90% of Conservative candidates in the 1983 general election favoured repatriation of 'immigrants'. In answer to a challenge from the Vice-chairperson (a British Conservative) that deportation and immigration controls were not racist measures, he quoted the Policy Studies Institute, whose survey showed that 83% of deportees are black. (European Parliament Socialist Group, re Committee of Inquiry into the Rise of Racism and Fascism, 12 Feb. 1985, Gtt/jc, PE/GS/52/85, p. 10).
16 Cited in Barker, *The New Racism*, p. 40.
17 Reported in *The Times*, 31 Jan. 1978.
18 Casey, 'One nation', p. 24.
19 Barker, *The New Racism*, p. 161.
20 J. Enoch Powell, 'Our loss of sovereignty', *The Salisbury Review*, 1 (Autumn 1982), pp. 28-9.
21 R. Honeyford, 'Multi-ethnic intolerance', *The Salisbury Review*, 4 (Summer 1983), pp. 12-13.
22 See, in addition, R. Scruton, 'Who are the real racists?', *The Times*, 30 Oct. 1984, where, in defence of Honeyford, Scruton argues that institutional racism is a myth.
23 R. Scruton, 'A socialist evil to rival racism', *The Times*, 28 Feb. 1984. It should perhaps be noted that 'multiracial', 'multicultural' and 'anti-racist' are by no means synonymous.
24 See, for example, B. Hugill, 'Multicultural row comes to a head', *New Statesman*, 15 Mar. 1985, pp. 14-15.
25 Out of 530 pupils in the school register, 250 parents signed a petition calling for Honeyford's dismissal. See *Drummond Parents' Action Committee Newsletter*, 1 (Oct. 1984).
26 A. Flew, 'The race relations industry', *The Salisbury Review*, 6 (Winter 1984), pp. 24-7.
27 R. Honeyford, 'Education and race – an alternative view', *The Salisbury Review*, 6 (Winter 1984), pp. 30-2.

28 G. Partington, 'Race, sex and class in inner London', *The Salisbury Review*, 7 (Spring 1984), pp. 33-7. Precisely the same themes were reiterated in a document which quoted Honeyford, issued by the Monday Club which Harvey Proctor MP chairs. See Simon Pearce, *Education and a Multiracial Society,* Monday Club Policy Paper, May 1985.

29 P. Taguieff, 'La nouvelle droite et ses stratégies', *Nouvelle Revue Socialiste*, (Jul.-Aug. 1984), pp. 29-37.

30 J. Biggs-Davison, 'A theology of politics', *The Salisbury Review*, 5 (Autumn 1983), pp. 31-3.

31 Their visibility as Jews is itself an issue. The fact that non-identifying assimilated Jews are being identified is significant. See, for example, A. Watkins, *Spectator*, 26 Nov. 1984, p. 9; a letter in *Spectator*, 8 Dec. 1984, p. 26; and R. Silver, 'Labour loses the Jews', *Spectator*, 15 Dec. 1984.

32 It is, however, less than surprising to find antisemitism surfacing in a Christian article. In S. Bruce, *One Nation under God?* (Queen's University, Belfast, 1983), Bruce demonstrates that a number of fundamentalist Christian supporters of the Moral Majority show hostility to Jews (although some supporters of the religious Right in the USA are committed to the 'Judaeo-Christian tradition'). The same activists will modify the discourse according to their audience. In one example, 'Zionist' is used as a codeword for 'Jewish' − a lexical slippage becoming common on the far Left as well as the far Right. Indeed, Silver ('Labour loses the Jews') points out that anti-Zionism, common in the Labour Party, is often a cover for antisemitism.

33 Biggs-Davison, 'A theology of politics', p. 33.

34 D. Edgar, 'Racism, fascism and the politics of the National Front', *Race and Class*, 19 (1977), pp. 111-31. M. Billig, *Fascists: A social-psychological view of the National Front*, (Academic Press, London, 1978).

35 R. Scruton, 'Thinkers of the Left: Ronald Dworkin', *The Salisbury Review*, 2 (Winter 1983), pp. 25-8.

36 P. Krebs in *Deutschland in Geschichte und Gegenwart* (*Germany past and present*), 1 (1981), pp. 31-2. This article is virtually a paraphrase of an interview given by Benoist, 'Contre tous les racismes' ('Against all racisms'), *Eléments*, 8-9 (Nov. 1974).

37 P. Moore, 'Tradition and worship', *The Salisbury Review*, 4 (Summer 1983), pp. 4-5.

38 'Peace on earth', *The Salisbury Review*, 2 (Winter 1983), p. 3.

39 Moore, 'Tradition and worship', p. 5.
40 G. Martelli, 'Neo-reformation and counter-reformation in the Roman Catholic Church', *The Salisbury Review*, vol. 2, 4 (Jul. 1984), pp. 32-6.
41 S. Shreir, 'The politics of language', *The Salisbury Review*, 4 (Summer 1983), pp. 6-10.
42 R. Soucy, *Fascism in France – The Case of Maurice Barrès* (University of California Press, Los Angeles, 1972).
43 C. Capitan-Peter, *Charles Maurras et l'idéologie d'Action Française* (Seuil, Paris, 1972).
44 E. Nolte, *Three Faces of Fascism*, (Holt, Rinehart and Winston, New York, 1966).
45 See Barker, *The New Racism, passim*.
46 *Language for Life*, otherwise known as *The Bullock Report* (Report of the Committee of Inquiry into Reading and the Use of English, 1975). This has now been superseded by *The Swann Report, Education for All* (Report of the Committee of Inquiry into the Education of Children from Ethnic Minority Groups, 1985).
47 C. Roberts, 'Language policy and the state: the "British" experience', International Colloquium on Orwell, Ecole Normale Supérieure, Paris, Oct. 1984.
48 C. Ashworth, 'Sociology and the nation', *The Salisbury Review*, 2 (Winter 1983), pp. 8-11.
49 Ibid., p. 9.
50 GRECE, *Qu'est-ce que l'enracinement?* (GRECE, Paris, 1975), p. 71.
51 J. C. Valla, 'La construction de l'unité française', tr. G. Seidel, *Qu'est ce que l'enracinement?* p. 32.
52 Ibid., p. 32.
53 A. Sherman, 'Britain is not Asia's fiance, *The Daily Telegraph*, 9 Nov. 1979, cited in Barker, *The New Racism*, p. 42.
54 Antisemitism has taken different forms since the foundation of the State of Israel. It is however worth recalling that Britain's first anti-immigration Act in 1905 was introduced to halt further Jewish arrivals and was called the Aliens Act. See S. Cohen, *That's Funny, You don't Look Anti-Semitic: An anti-racist analysis of Left antisemitism* (Beyond the Pale Collective, Leeds, 1984).
55 M. Foucault, *The Archaeology of Knowledge* (Pantheon, New York, 1977).

56 W. E. Connolly, 'The politics of discourse' in *Language and Politics,* ed. M. Shapiro (Basil Blackwell, Oxford, 1984).
57 Casey, 'One nation', p. 25.

Chapter Five

Moral and Maternal
The Family in the Right

MIRIAM DAVID

'Not only moral but right' is how Ronald Butt rebutted criticisms of the New Right's recent success in re-establishing family responsibility for young girls' sexual activity.[1] Victoria Gillick's campaign for parental consent over medical advice on sexual matters to under-sixteen year olds had prompted some critics to identify this as the rise of 'the Moral Right'.[2] Others argued that she had created Britain's 'Moral Minority', drawing a contrast with the now well-established and self-styled Moral Majority in the USA.[3]

In fact, the New Right in both Britain and the USA has long seen itself as developing a 'new' morality through its approach to sexual and family matters. Its particular emphasis has been on redefining women's place within the family, especially as mothers. This focus on the family is central to New Right ideology. It has developed as a response to the 'liberal' approach to women's social position which began to percolate into policy in the 1960s and 1970s. Indeed, in the USA, the New Right has presented itself clearly and deliberately as an 'anti-feminist backlash', opposing women's hard-won gains in the social and political arena.[4] The New Right has seized a political space opened up originally by feminists and transformed the agenda to its own interests. 'The personal is political' was, and is, a central tenet of the contemporary women's movement.[5] Personal matters such as sexual and social relationships are now centrally on the political agenda, but the aim of the New Right is to ensure that responsibility for such issues is returned to the so-called private family from the public sphere.

This chapter addresses the question of how much impact this approach to family morality has had on the policies and practices of New Right administrations. It argues that this New Right ideology about the family is intimately intertwined with economic and social policies and cannot easily be disentangled from them. Current economic policies assume a particular family form and a special place for the family in economic relationships: social policies are more explicitly about reconstructing particular family behaviour. It is the particular synthesis of economic and social policies, however, which makes the governments of both Thatcher and Reagan distinct from previous administrations. Both Thatcher and Reagan aim to transform economic and social life through a mix of policies which rely on a measure of so-called private family, rather than public and social, responsibility. As Worsthorne puts it:

> Thatcherism Mark 2 is going to be very much more deeply controversial than the Mark 1 variety . . . wanting to dismantle the socialist welfare state was controversial enough but the raw nerves touched by the ideal will be as nothing to those frayed to tatters by the attempt to build up what will amount to a Tory welfare state.[6]

Yet the question remains as to how far either of the two administrations has been able to put into practice the ideologies from which they derive their policies and, indeed, what the implications of their policies are. Do they, in fact, re-establish the privacy of the family and in what circumstances?

The New Right's ideas have developed specifically as an antidote to the policies and practices of the post-war politicial consensus obtaining in both Britain and the USA. Indeed, many have argued that the political successes of the New Right are directly accounted for by its blaming the liberal and social democratic administrations for policies which contributed to the growing economic recession of the 1970s. The New Right has claimed that its policies will lift the country out of the recession and return it to economic growth. Part of its attack is on the way the family has been transformed. The New Right has been critical of the pursuit of social welfare initiatives, especially the commitment to equal opportunities, whether between social classes, the sexes or the races.[7] It has argued that it is these policies that have contributed to both social change and economic decline. The main object of criticism is social, seen as familial, change.

It is indeed true that many Western capitalist societies have witnesses dramatic changes in their social and familial structure as well as the better-known economic decline in the post-war period. The shift has been from the predominance of traditional nuclear families (that is, families with a male breadwinner, female housewife/mother and dependent children) amongst households with dependent children, to a situation in which such households comprise either one-parent families (usually female-headed households) or families in which both parents are involved in paid employment. In other words, traditional nuclear families no longer typify family households and, in turn, family households with dependent children are not even any longer the predominant form of households. Petchesky goes so far as to claim that the traditional nuclear family is almost extinct.[8] A recent international report characterizes nicely these transformations in household structure:

> In modern advanced societies, the entourage in which children grow up has undergone profound changes over the course of the last few decades . . . The magnitude of certain social transformations . . . (for example . . . the . . . large-scale entry of women into active life) has given rise to the idea that major upheavals are affecting the organisation of family structure . . . between the generations within the family or the household.[9]

The report goes on to demonstrate the variety of changes:

> The family microcosm is extraordinarily differentiated and, even limiting the description to those families with children, the typology that can be constructed immediately becomes complex . . . there is an enormous number of different family worlds in which they [children] may grow up . . .It must also be remembered that households undergo changes over time. Of particular interest are the changes of environment for the child whose parents have divorced and remarried. Such families are often 'corporations' including a mixture of adults and children from two families. These observations are important because very often the variety of 'realities' is underestimated. Through stressing the role of the parents, one ends up forgetting about all the others, as if the majority of families consisted just of one couple and their children. Certainly this is the majority situation, in the sense that it applies to a great number of children, but a good number of other situations exist alongside it.[10]

The pressing issue, however, is not the recognition of these transformations but how their origins are understood and acted upon. The New Right blames the old Right, along with more social democratic administrations, for their creation.[11] It argues that social welfare policies have encouraged the shifts in 'family worlds'.[12] It seeks to reverse such family trends by policies aimed at reinstating and recreating the privacy of the traditional nuclear family.[13] It hopes to rescind or abandon policies and practices that legitimize and consolidate families either with a lone parent, especially those formed out-of-wedlock and where the parent is very young (a schoolgirl), or with two parents (one a working mother) involved in paid employment.[14] In other words, the conditions of contemporary motherhood have come under scrutiny by the New Right.

The New Right aims to recreate conditions which, it believes, obtained before the heyday of the social democratic political consensus. The argument is that such conditions ensure sufficient economic growth for society to thrive. The traditional nuclear family, in this view, was central to economic well-being, with the man as breadwinner and economic provider and the woman as economic dependent but consumer of goods and services in the market on behalf of her family. Motherhood is, in this view of society, an all-consuming and full-time, but unpaid, activity, embracing care and nurturance of dependent children and husband, through both domestic and more elusive emotional activities. Jessie Bernard points out the uniqueness of this 'institutionalization of motherhood' to industrial society:

> The way we institutionalize motherhood in our society − assigning sole responsibility for child care to the mother, cutting her off from the easy help of others in an isolated household, requiring round-the-clock tender loving care, and making such care her exclusive activity − is . . . new and unique.[15]

Fatherhood, by contrast, is not seen to entail regular social activities and relationships, but, in this vision of society, is used to refer to the act of procreation and more distant economic responsibilities. The Victorian 'paterfamilias' remains implicit in this view of fatherhood. It is indeed so implicit that no modern texts on the history of the family take up the notion.[16]

The New Right is trying to revive this model of the private family through both economic policies which assume such a set of relationships in the marketplace and social policies which increasingly celebrate motherhood as a crucial social activity for all women. Together, the New Right's policies are a powerful attempt to undo the policies of forty years of liberal or social democratic rule. Yet they are not all deliberate measures to transform family structures. Some are implicit, particularly those in the economic sphere, whereas other efforts are more explicit, particularly those that deal directly with women's and girls' sexual morality and social status in the family.[17]

In economic policy, the commitment to laissez-faire economics does not necessarily touch women's lives directly. Indeed, where women do not have family obligations, such as the care of dependent children, they are treated as individuals in their own right: just as if they were economic men. But when women acquire family obligations through sexual relations, upon marriage, birth or adoption, there is little by way of public support for their continuing to participate in the formal labour market. Indeed, their family obligations become a handicap to their participation in the labour force as equals with men. Illich puts the point forcefully:

> Women are discriminated against in employment only to be forced, when off the job, to do a new kind of economically necessary work without any pay attached to it . . . To a greater extent and in a different manner from men, women are drafted into the economy. They were and are deprived of equal access to wage labour only to be bound with even greater inequality to work that did not exist before wage labour came into being.[18]

Increasingly, social policies are used to prevent labour force participation of mothers and to impose moral obligations of care. There is also a growing emphasis on the necessity for women to become mothers in order to achieve adult social status. The current debates about infertility and the uses of reproductive technology reinforce notions of the centrality of parenthood in adult life. A passionate letter to *The Guardian* highlights the point:[19]

> May a childless spinster, now nearer to eighty than seventy intrude into the debate on infertility? It is not so long ago when generations of women because of the population imbalance were denied the opportunity of marriage and parenthood. This fact is almost forgotten today and their kind are, year by year, now dying out. Many of these women filled their lives with the care of other people's children, whether as nurses, teachers or social working (there were few alternatives open to them). It was upon the shoulders of these 'surplus women' that our expanding education and welfare services were largely supported. . . . Why, when the human condition itself imposes all manner of frustration and suffering, is this one above all others regarded by some today as so appalling that it must not and shall not be tolerated?

Involuntary childlessness in women is still seen as a tragedy and voluntary chidlessness as at least an oddity.[20] It is now becoming more, rather than less, difficult for women not to become mothers since health care resources are directed to infertility research and their attendant reproductive technologies.

Of course, mothers remain 'free to choose' whether or not to participate in paid employment, but are given little public or social support or encouragement to do so.[21] Those women who choose to take paid employment have to be able to afford to pay to replace themselves within the private family or have to be in desperate financial straits, where wages are a necessity. Either way, women's 'freedom to choose' is closely circumscribed by the joint operation of social and economic policies, to some extent deliberately and, in part, as an unintended effect.

One effect of laissez-faire economics, in the past, was vast social and economic inequalities between families. It was these inequalities in family circumstances that political parties of either left or right political persuasion sought to reduce through social and economic policies in which the state played a larger part. This formed the origins of the welfare state. The political values of those party to the post-war political consensus are indeed different and opposed to those of the New Right. Neither the Conservative nor Labour Party was committed to the notion of economic individualism (read 'male individualism') of the New Right. Their commitment was, and is, to a society, framed by traditional democratic values, within which the state plays an increasing part in managing the economy and setting standards and limits to individual action.

Parties of both left and right, in this schema, have taken a measure of responsibility for ensuring economic and social well-being by underwriting some of the costs and ill effects of economic production. Mishra has argued that, despite sharp ideological differences on 'social questions' between parties in terms of their relative commitments to collective or individual − market or voluntary − provision 'in practice, both more or less hugged the middle ground (known in Britain as "Butskellism")'.[22] He goes on to argue that 'no practical politician could seriously advocate a policy of dismantling the welfare state . . . state commitment to maintaining full employment, providing a range of basic services for all citizens and preventing or relieving poverty seemed so integral to post-war society as to be almost irreversible . . .'.[23] This commitment to welfare as an integral part of economic policy was not only made

in Britain but in most advanced industrial societies, including the
USA. Indeed, by the 1960s a new term was coined to describe the
interplay between social and economic policy – welfare capitalism.
Mishra goes on to claim that:

> Clearly if the USA, the Mecca of free enterprise and market capitalism,
> . . . was ready to embrace the notion of state responsibility for the
> nation's welfare, then the prospects for anti-collectivism were gloomy
> . . . Generalising across the western countries as a whole it could be
> said, without exaggeration, that in the 1960s, the correction of social
> imbalance through social programmes and services became almost a
> bipartisan policy.[24]

The expansion of the social or welfare services in the post-war
period certainly has not freed women from domestic and maternal
responsibilities but it has modified and mitigated the severest
conditions of motherhood. Zaretsky, for example, has argued
recently that 'the issue is not whether the welfare state eroded the
family, but rather in what form it preserved it. My argument is that
the family has been preserved as an economically private unit and
that most of the normative aspects of state policy are based on
that.'[25] Petchesky, in agreeing with Zaretsky, argues that 'the very
concept of welfare in the United States contains within it the idea
that the well-being of people and providing for their basic needs is
an essentially private matter, that the state should act as provider
only in situations of extremity or helplessness'.[26] But in the last two
decades in the USA the expansion of social welfare programmes has
provided new areas of 'entitlement', as Piven and Cloward argue,
as a result of demands by organized popular movements.[27] The
effect has been the creation of 'a political climate in which the *idea*
that basic human needs *ought to be met* through public, social
instruments has begun to achieve popular acceptance'.[28]

The 'bipartisan policy' of the 1960s was primarily about economic
growth, sustained by policies which allowed for some economic
redistribution between wealthy and poor families but which
maintained the private family relatively intact. Mishra summarized
it as:

> Distribution need not be a zero-sum game; private affluence and public
> generosity could go hand in hand. In any case, social expenditure
> involved horizontal rather than vertical redistribution of resources.
> . . . Far from being detrimental to the economy in any obvious way
> many social services – education being the prime example – were

in fact meant to help economic growth directly. Here, then, was a social arrangement with apparently few costs and many benefits which included maintaining social stability and fostering a sense of national community and solidarity. Not surprisingly, the consensus over social policy was widespread.[29]

Lord Stockton who, as Conservative Prime Minister Harold Macmillan, was actively involved in the construction of this particular 'bipartisan policy' and welfare consensus, has recently expressed these sentiments again. On 25 January 1985, the first day that the House of Lords' proceedings were televised, Lord Stockton argued for a return to policies that would guarantee 'one nation', reduce rather than stimulate class conflict and even suggested a national government as the way to achieve such ends. He condemned the Thatcher government's economic policy of monetarism, drawing a contrast with the USA and claiming that Reagan's recent success with economic recovery in the USA was due to his abandonment of monetarism in favour of taxation strategies designed to boost the economy.

Lord Stockton's speech is illustrative of the contrast between traditional, paternalistic conservatism and the New Right, at least concerning the question of economic policies. He is certainly critical of policies which do not modify the extremes of the workings of the free market, and which do not, then, provide at least a 'safety net' for poor families and a set of minimum standards of living below which no family should be allowed to fall. Mrs Thatcher's brand of conservatism, by contrast, holds the belief that such policies fetter the economy and contribute to economic decline. Perhaps more importantly, entitlements to public and social support are seen to cause family break-up because men lack the economic motivation to provide private, family support.

Lord Stockton's contrast between Thatcherism and Reaganism is important too. It is certainly the case that both Thatcher and Reagan started their terms of office committed to radical economic strategies, which contained particular visions of the place of the family. However, the constellation of political and ideological forces operating on Thatcher and Reagan, in office, have been different and have resulted in different practices, despite similarities in initial rhetoric. Peele opens her study of the Right in America with the argument that:

For the United States, developments on the right of the political spectrum reflect a fundamental questioning of many of the assumptions of post-war economic, social and foreign policy, and they constitute concrete evidence of the extent to which the landscape of the country's politics has changed even in the past twenty years. For Britain, those developments have had, or may yet come to have, echoes in the politics of that country . . . there is an obvious common interest in both democracies in such questions as the proper role of government in a free society and the correct balance between public and private provision of social services.[30]

But she argues later that there are far greater limits on Reagan's ability to carry through the range of conservative demands made upon him than there are on Thatcher's ability. She claims that the federal political machinery in the USA is fragmented and decentralized in contrast with the centralized British state, with the result that Reagan is less able to push through a conservative programme than Thatcher is. She argues that the particular US separation of powers between executive, legislature and judiciary inhibits Reagan from building up support for his free market principles and cuts in public expenditure. Yet she argues, at the same time, that the political 'atomism' of conservative and right-wing elements leads to different pressures over a variety of issues.

Reaganism, to Peele, has amounted to a complicated mix of various conservative elements, which has meant that economic policies were less ideologically coherent than the initial rhetoric which favoured either monetarism or 'supply-side economics' – that is tax cuts to encourage individual investment. Her conclusion is instructive:

> The Reagan administration has wanted to bring about a change of assumptions about the role of government in American life. By signaling a determination to cut the growth of federal expenditure in areas other than military expenditure, by signaling a hostility towards the civil rights policies of previous administrations . . . President Reagan has created a distinctive synthesis of conservative economics, populism and nationalism which has no exact counterpart in the politics of the right in Europe.[31]

Is it the case that Reagan and Thatcher's policies have in fact diverged during the course of their terms of office, and what are their differential effects, particularly on families and women's lives? There is considerable evidence to suggest that whilst the political pressures on both governments have been the same, especially from the Right over what might be called 'social and family issues', creating a new moral agenda, their effects in practice have been rather different. This is not only because of differences in political systems and political cultures, as Peele suggests, but also different economic positions in the world economy.

Reagan has not pursued, in as determined a fashion as Thatcher, a set of economic principles of monetarism, or free market economics, within a firm set of social arrangements. Rather, after two years in office, he altered the course of his domestic economic policies, providing a mix of tax cuts and incentives, which relied for their success on the exploitation of the USA's position in relation to Third World countries.[32]

The impact of the initial 'conservative program' was, as Mimi Abramovitz argues, 'to strike deeply at institutions that support the economic independence and security of women. They also reverse gains that women, along with minorities and organized labor have fought for and won since the 1930s.'[33] The effect has been dramatic. Mike Davis argues that the result has been a 'split level economy' in which the class structure takes the shape of an 'hourglass'.[34] In other words, there has been an increase in the numbers of both the very rich and the very poor, with a consequent squeezing of the traditional middle income groups. Davis points out that, in the USA in 1984, there were a million millionaires and a fast growing number of families composed of two-income, two-person households at the top of the hourglass and an equally fast-growing group of single-earner blue-collar families, single people in clerical occupations, women in many very low-paid jobs, the welfare poor and retired at the bottom. He argues that 'relative poverty is being mass produced, not only through the exclusion of third world men from the primary labour market, but *especially* through the dynamic incorporation of women into the burgeoning low wage sectors of the economy'.[35]

What Davis pays only fleeting attention to is the gender composition of the changed class structure. Abramovitz, Ehrenreich, Eisenstein and Petchesky all point to what an official US report discussed as 'the feminization of poverty'.[36] The National Advisory Council on Economic Opportunity observed in 1981 that 'the feminization of poverty has become one of the most compelling social facts of the decade'.[37] Ehrenreich has written that 'in 1980 two out of three adults who fit the federal definition of poverty are women, and more than half the families defined as poor were maintained by single women'.[38] She then cites the aforementioned report:

> All other things being equal, if the proportion of the poor in female
> householder families were to continue to increase at the same rate as
> it did from 1967 to 1978 the poverty population would be composed
> solely of women and children before the year 2000.

Reagan's economic and social policies have had the effect of
exaggerating these trends in family structure. On the one hand, as
Peele notes, his attempts to 'dismantle the welfare state' through
cut-backs in public spending have met with only limited success. But,
nevertheless, 'Reagonomics' as it became known, has accentuated
the poverty of lone mothers' lives. The major program that was cut
was Aid to Families with Dependent Children (AFDC), commonly
known as 'welfare', which reaches mainly lone mothers with
dependent children. In 1980 such mothers constituted 70 per cent
of welfare recipients.[39] In addition, 'in terms of race, 52.6 per cent
of the members of households were white, 43 per cent were black,
1.1 per cent were American Indian, 0.4 per cent were Asian'.
Associated medical programmes for such woman have also been
reduced in scope and effect. It could be argued that in these efforts
to dismantle the welfare state, referred to as 'the new Federalism',
there was at least implicit racism as well as sexism. Abramovitz
further argues, on the basis of the first two years of Reagonomics,
that:

> the social welfare cuts not only further the 'feminization' of poverty
> but they encourage women to leave paid work for unpaid labor in
> the home. Although the Administration holds that economic recovery
> requires an increased work effort by all, the call seems to be aimed
> primarily at men. Many features of the conservative program actually
> discourage paid employment among the 44 million working women
> who are nearly 50 per cent of today's labour force . . . through policies
> that (a) increase unemployment rates of all workers, (b) weaken work
> incentives contained in income maintenance programs, and (c)
> intensify women's household responsibilities by shrinking social
> services that free them for paid work outside the home . . . [40]

In particular she highlights the ways in which forms of employment
'protection' such as civil and women's rights have been relaxed. She
therefore sums up the approach:

> The Administration's outright assault on these government protections
> makes more sense when it is remembered that women, minorities and
> organized labor are being asked to bear the brunt of the economic
> recovery programs. If production costs of business are to be lowered

by cutting the standard of living of workers, minorities and women, their resistance to cutbacks must be forestalled and delegitimized.

On the other hand, some of Reagan's tax measures to ensure economic recovery were not directly aimed at undermining women's economic security. The effect, however, of tax changes ostensibly to liberalize the burden on women of child-care expenses was to reprivatize much of this 'work'. In 1981, the tax credit for child-care expenses, introduced in 1976, 'was liberalized'.[41] As Shaw puts it, in the 1984 tax year, 'the tax credit is 30 per cent [of total child care and housekeeping costs] for families with incomes under $10,000' and gradually decreases for richer families. The aim was 'to allow lower income families a more generous subsidy than higher income families . . . [but] few families are actually eligible for the full subsidy'.[42] Shaw also demonstrates the way the scheme actually works to the disadvantage of poorer families and adds:

> It also appears that in the case of household employment, many people are willing to work at lower wages in exchange for not having their earnings reported to the tax authorities. It may be that this 'hidden economy' is one of the reasons that the tax credit is not utilized by many low income families.

In addition to tax credits, the Economic Recovery Tax Act of 1981 gives tax incentives to employers to provide 'on-site' child-care centres, or to allow child-care expenses as a fringe benefit. In the latter case it usually operates through a so-called 'cafeteria plan' in which the employee can chose which of several benefits − longer vacations, pension benefits or subsidized child care − to take. However, the take-up of these schemes appears to have been limited and a recent tax reform plan proposed by the Treasury Department would make all fringe benefits subject to tax and eliminate most deductions. Shaw argues that these various government child-care policies have not played a major role in increasing the employment of mothers of young children but rather it is the increasing employment which made child-care subsidies 'a popular program for legislators to support'. But she goes on to argue that the schemes may account for the different profiles of women's employment in the USA and Britain. In the USA they may have allowed more women to consider working full-time. On the other hand, 'reflecting the American faith in private enterprise, policy makers appear to have expected that women's increasing employment and the partial subsidization of their child care costs would bring an expansion of child care provision to meet the increased demand'.[43] This does not yet appear to have happened. But:

> day care centers do, in fact, appear to have become a growth industry. Several for profit day care chains have been organized. The largest, Kinder-care, operates over 700 centers nationwide and aims at offering high quality care to affluent parents . . . A much larger number of child care centers are operated by churches using Sunday school facilities . . . Day care in the home of a child care provider is also common.[44]

In sum, the effects of Reagan's economic policies over the last four years have not been to squeeze women, especially mothers, out of paid employment but rather to squeeze women into low-wage, paid employment and to maintain child care in its 'privatized' form, either at home in the family or in profit-making private centres. This child-care 'work' accounts for some of the massive increases in low-wage service employment.

Nevertheless, Reagan's administration, in a variety of ways, has allowed for the expansion of facilities for children, albeit in the market-place. Another area of expansion is not only child care for pre-school children, but also for school-age children. In October 1984, as part of the Human Services Re-authorization Act that Reagan signed there was a commitment to a block grant for school-age child care and dependent- care resources and referrals. It would give each state an amount of funds in proportion to its population with a minimum of $50,000 for the least populated states. The school-age funds would be directed to planning, developing or improving facilities housed in public and private schools and operating by public agencies or private non-profit organizations.[45]

In addition, there has been a tremendous development in reproductive technologies in the USA, making motherhood available to women in circumstances hitherto unknown, particularly through *in vitro* fertilization. Given the commitment to private enterprises in all aspects of health and medical care in the USA, all these developments have taken place in the private market-place. The direction has been towards making motherhood more available. 'Most discussions of the new technology for the treatment of infertility have welcomed it as giving new choices to the infertile. But here too there is a negative side to consider: all of the new treatments for infertility have also created a new burden for the infertile – the burden of not trying hard enough.'[46] Indeed, it is the case that there is an enormous demand for 'test tube babies and the waiting lists in the US seem to be full for the next five years'.[47] But there is a growing critique of this uncritical growth industry in medicalized reproduction and its development of a market-place in motherhood. Reagan's economic initiatives have been to encourage, or not to discourage, the inexorable logic of capital into issues hitherto deemed to be 'private' and where market relations have been deemed to be immoral and inappropriate.

Thatcher's economic strategies have had an entirely different flavour. She has been far less eclectic in her approach to the management of the economy, having a clear vision that the only way to revitalize the economy was to remove what she considered unnecessary controls – such as the trade union role in collective bargaining. In the process of removing 'undesirable' controls, she has created her own brand of rigid controls, through increasing central government determination of the direction of industry, including the public sector and local authorities. Stewart, for example, notes the authoritarianism implicit in her attempt to appear to loosen controls over the local economy and local authorities.

> To understand the philosophy of the present Conservative government it is important not to be misled by the rhetoric of rolling back the power of the State: it is a rolling back in certain sectors only. There is a further important element that emphasises the *authority* of central government. Any other source of political authority however limited and constrained is seen as a challenge to the authority. It is in this context that one must interpret the continual emphasis by the Government on the unitary State.[48]

Indeed, the various shifts and changes in the machinery of government have removed 'democratic' controls and created rather more unaccountable, quasi-autonomous non-governmental organizations (Quangos). This in itself is curious, given Thatcher's initial commitment to remove inefficiency and waste through a review of quangos.[49] Like Reagan, her attempts to 'dismantle the welfare state', in Britain chiefly through the process of 'privatization', have created new forms of dependency upon the state. On the one hand, Thatcher's policies have, in fact, increased rather than decreased unemployment. Townsend notes that:

> just as the tax structure became less egalitarian in practice as well as in form, the dependent population increased – in largest measure 'artificially' through unemployment and premature retirement . . .

He goes on to argue that these shifts are taking place 'in accordance with the international changes taking place in class and not just political and market allegiances. . . it is a covert form of class warfare . . .'[50]

The form is two-fold. It is not just 'squeezing' the poor: it is also 'augmenting' the poor. Townsend also argues that the policies represent a major departure from the consensus politics of the post-war era.

> For the first time Government Ministers seem prepared to depart even from the most tenuous principles of one nation and consider seriously that certain sections of the British population are beyond redemption, have to be taught some rough lessons and are expendable. It would be difficult otherwise to explain certain authoritarian measures . . .[51]

He points out the particular form that poverty is taking, amongst not only the unemployed but 'other categories'.

> Between 1971 and 1981 the numbers of one-parent families increased by 71 per cent and now stands at nearly one million families. This is approximately one family in seven with children. The long-standing inequality between the sexes in access to resources and the institutional bias in favour of conventionally married couples contribute to the poverty which lone parents and their children experience.[52]

Although he is aware what the new and rapidly expanding area of poverty is, he is elliptical about the fact that the vast majority of lone parents are lone mothers. Rimmer notes that only one in nine single parents is a lone father.[53] Townsend, however, is indignant about the creation of the problem.

> For connected if complex reasons, therefore, different minorities in the population are being shepherded into states of dependency. A mass underclass is being created to serve the visions of a new international ruling class of haughty and socially distant political, managerial, professionals and technological leaders.[54]

As in the USA, the class and sex structure of the population is being rapidly transformed by government policies as well as the workings of the international economy. However, Thatcher is less benign than Reagan in the creation of this new class structure. She has a clearer vision of the place of families in her society than Reagan. By contrast with Reagan, she has provided fewer incentives to enable mothers in poverty to find paid employment to better themselves.

Two examples suffice: one is that entitlement to unemployment benefit has become more, rather than less, difficult for such mothers. Nowadays, mothers of pre-school children usually have to state their future child-care arrangements before they can sign that they are 'available for work', and therefore entitled to unemployment benefit. This measure fails to grasp the reality of such women's lives. The availability of public child care is virtually non-existent; private arrangements are scarce and subject to the vagaries of the local economic conditions. It is well-nigh impossible to 'plan' a specific mix of child care and paid employment, until the job presents itself. Jobs themselves are scarce and many mothers reluctant to make formal or 'public' arrangements on the off-chance that they may find a job. The measure, therefore, maintains child-care 'work' in the 'private' sphere in two senses: firstly as the mothers' own occupation and secondly as a private set of arrangements within the family or local community, dependent on reciprocity or exchanges of goodwill. Indeed, the Department of Employment's study of *Women and Employment* showed very clearly that most child care, even when done by someone other than the mother, is unpaid.[55] However, child care expenses can be offset against gross earnings for the purposes of calculating the earnings disregard for those women claiming supplementary benefit.

The second example comes from the tax system. In contrast with the USA, the tax system does not allow any child-care expenses to be deducted from taxable income except for those who have resident housekeepers − and this is a tiny number of working mothers. The Inland Revenue regards workplace nurseries as a fringe benefit and taxes the element of subsidy, in common with other fringe benefits, if the employee earns more than £8,500 a year.[56] But this view has only been revealed recently, much to the consternation of parents involved and the Equal Oportunities Commission (EOC). Fringe benefits have been taxable since the Second World War, but then the threshold was much higher. If the threshold had been maintained at its real value it would be about £22,000, thus excluding all but a tiny minority of employed mothers.

On the other hand, Britain has, since the early 1970s, provided child benefit − an amalgam of child tax allowances and family allowances, provided through the system of social security. However, under Thatcher, the value of such benefits has been seriously eroded and in current reviews of the whole system of social security there are serious proposals to tax and/or means-test child benefits. In other words, the costs and expenses of children are increasingly being transferred back to the 'private' family. Mothers will bear the burden of these costs. Joshi concludes, on the basis of her analysis of the Department of Employment's 1980 data, that 'family formation has a lasting effect for . . . it depressed women's life-time earnings on average by between twenty-five and fifty per cent'.[57] In particular, in Britain, mothers' employment tends to be fitted around family responsibilities, and the vast majority of mothers of dependent children are involved in part-time rather than full-time employment. There is no prospect of a public subsidy for either pre-school or school-age children at this point, it being judged entirely a private, family responsibility.

There is a more rigid attitude in Britain to sex segregation in employment and that a mother's proper place is not in paid employment but at home, caring for family members. This emphasis on the private family rather than the private market-place for child care may go some way towards explaining the divergences between Britain and the USA in their approaches to the control of the new reproductive technologies, creating new forms of motherhood. In the USA, there has been little attempt to control the private market in motherhood, allowing low-technology solutions such as surrogate motherhood through commercial agencies, to mushroom. The more scientific technological advances such as embryo freezing and transplants, referred to by Corea as 'egg snatching', have also developed apace.[58] In Britain, the concern about these techniques, orchestrated by the New Right, has been taken more seriously in the political arena. In July 1982, the government established a committee of inquiry under the chairmanship of Dame Mary Warnock to investigate the implications of such technological developments in human embryology and fertilization. It is also no accident that it chose an academic philosopher to chair the inquiry, since it was indeed concerned with the implications for the ethics of family life. In the event, the committee's report, although debated publicly and highly controversial, dealt only with practical ethics. It had very little to say about the implications for men and women's positions within the family or wider society. Warnock herself, in presenting the report, argued for a 'middle way', given the three dissenting views to aspects of the report. She wrote that 'we have tried in short to give due consideration both to public and to private morality'.[59] In fact, this led the committee to give undue deference to the medical profession and scientific community and their established scientific developments. On the other hand, in deference to an assumed public morality, the committee declared itself opposed to surrogate mother-hood on a commercial basis.[60] In this respect, it argued that maternity and child care should be 'natural' and based on unselfish notions of love. The introduction of a commercial element would sully this arrangement. The committee however made no comment on the commercial element involved in the donation of sperm for Artificial Insemination by Donor (AID) or the lack of a contract involved in the removal of a woman's eggs for the purposes of experimentation. Indeed, it did not oppose such developments, in the interests of medical and scientific advance, although it imposed a time-limit on research on human embryos, pragmatically choosing what is currently possible.[61] This has created an enormous controversy and has allowed a political space to New Right pressure groups to intervene successfully in the debate. As Leathard expresses it:

> by the autumn of 1984 . . . a . . . transformation was taking place in the politics of birth control. Public concern about the use of human embryos in research was expressed, in the view of three Warnock members, in the form of a question: 'When does life begin?' . . . The anti-abortion lobby soon spotted that it could capitalize on public doubts and apprehension over such problematic issues. So as the debate escalated in press and Parliament, a new pincer movement began to interlock anti-abortion, Gillick and Warnock.[62]

In order to understand this dramatic transformation and the increasingly effective role that moral Right pressure groups were beginning to play in British public policy debates, we need to understand the genesis and influence of these groups. The differences between Britain and the USA may to some extent be attributed to their histories concerning the extent of government intervention in family life, with Britain tending to be the more paternalistic. However, it should not be forgotten that the USA, too, has held firmly, since the nineteenth-century, to the doctrine of *'parens patriae'* in law, which holds that the state should intervene in family life as a strict and judicious parent.[63] The differences may well concern, therefore, what is seen as legitimate commercial practice, rather than the relations between public and private morality. In the USA women are afforded more 'natural' political and civil rights. In Britain, there is a stronger appeal to some 'natural' social order, predicated on the 'naturalness' of traditional family relationships.

F

In addition, of course, we need to understand the relative balance of power between the right-wing pressure groups and administration in power as well as the machinery of government.

In fact, the most influential conservative ideas on the British and US governments are very similar. In Britain, Ferdinand Mount and Roger Scruton represent the two best-known influences on Mrs Thatcher's social ideas, and theirs is a brand of relatively secular conservatism, albeit both patriarchal and paternalistic. Both Mount and Scruton have attempted to set out their intellectual ideas at length. Mount's book, *The Subversive Family* is both an attack on feminist approaches to the family and on those who argue for state intervention to sustain family life. His thesis is that the family is a 'natural' unit which has survived the vicissitudes of hundreds of years, but is best left unfettered by government regulations. Nevertheless, he has a clear view of the right and 'proper' family form – a heterosexual union, formed by marriage and nourished by children and grandchildren. He presumes that it is only this family that should be allowed free rein.[64]

> The defenders of the family . . . assert always the privacy and independence of the family, its biological individuality and its rights to live according to its natural instincts. It is for this reason that, even in societies where male supremacy is officially total, the family asserts its own *maternal* values . . .(my emphasis)

It was this vision that underpinned Mount's advice to the Family Policy Group, a secret Cabinet cabal to which he was advisor during 1982-3. The Family Policy Group, nicknamed 'the Family Patrol Group' by both Wicks and Edgar, aimed to establish clearer family responsibilities, both for children within families and in schools. One suggestion was a system of education vouchers redeemable at either state or private schools to increase 'parental choice'. Another was for children to be taught how to manage their pocket money. Yet another concerned control over children's sexual activities. The proposals were leaked to the press before many of them had reached the status of serious policies, although some of them have since been developed more fully, as in the official reviews of the social security system.

Scruton's vision is less liberal than that of Mount's, though equally 'moral' in its claims. Scruton argues for individual subservience to some ill-defined social authority, often the government. In an article about surrogate motherhood, entitled 'Ignore the body, lose your soul' he writes:

The liberal morality which tells us to permit the body's pleasures and to stifle the impulse of shame expresses, in effect, a peculiar metaphysical vision of the body as somehow detached from the self and outside the sphere of our true obligations . . . What a ludicrous mixture of moral truth and childlike superstition . . . Traditional sexual morality was an instrument whereby people came to terms with their incarnation and took moral responsibility for their flesh . . . We should never lose sight of the fundamental truth, that some uses of the body are sinful, and none more so than those which enable us to escape the obligations which the body itself imposes.[65]

In this appeal, he mixes religious and biological obligation. 'Anatomy is destiny' as a psychoanalytic principle and a secular version of the moral imperative is also Gilder's approach to these questions. Gilder, too, appeals to some patriarchal social authority as the ultimate in morality.[66] More systematically than Scruton and Mount, he exposes what he considers the ill-effects of liberal welfare policies. His book, *Wealth and Poverty*, was circulated by Reagan to members of his cabinet.[67] Gilder's concern is that the increase in women relying on social welfare benefits 'destroys the father's key role and authority'. Unable to feel 'manly in his home' he 'turns to the street for male affirmation'. In particular, this reduces man's motivation to work. 'The man has the . . . gradually sinking feeling that his role as provider, the definitive male activity from the primal days of the hunt through the industrial revolution and on into modern life has been largely seized from him; he has been cuckolded by the compassionate state.'[68] Gilder believes in a relatively harsh approach to dismantling the welfare state and to reviving the traditional patriarchal family. Eisenstein summarizes his views:

Disruption in family life creates disruption in the economy because men need to direct their sexual energies toward the economy and they only do so when they are connected by family duty. Marriage creates the sense of responsibility men need . . . A married man . . . is spurred by the claims of family to channel his otherwise disruptive male aggressions into his performance as a provider for his wife and children.[69]

Peele argues that:

capitalism, so far from being an unheroic bourgeois civilisation is celebrated by Gilder for its creativity and the capacity of entrepreneurs to engender [sic] wealth.[70]

33

3

Kristol, another neo-conservative in the USA, has also indicted the welfare state for having created trends which result in making 'the child fatherless; the mother husbandless; the husband useless'.[71]

As Peele notes, the neo-conservatives, such as Gilder and Kristol (often 'born-again social scientists' who began as communists or liberals), are not the only source of conservative influence in the USA. She identifies the other two as the religious Right and the New Right.

> Clearly the term 'new right' designates a self-conscious strand within American conservative politics . . . it is not, of course, a party or formal organisational grouping. Unlike the label 'neo-conservative' which many have sought to shed, the label 'new right' has not appeared to those who wear it to be such an unfashionable badge . . . The new right can be defined as a loose movement of conservative politicians and a collection of general-purpose political organisations which have developed independently of political parties.[72]

Given that many of these groups focus on 'single issues', especially questions of family and social issues, there is some overlap with the religious Right. Peele argues that it is precisely these issues that distinguish the new right-wing organizations from the old.

> What is important is the extent to which the new right has expanded the agenda of its concerns to include a number of moral and social issues − 'family issues' . . . which have not usually been explicit themes in conservative political argument in America . . . The emphasis . . . in the 1970s was in part a response to the perceived permissiveness of an earlier decade. But it has also had the effect of involving religious leaders much more directly in American political life.[73]

She suggests that this focus has the advantage of encouraging mobilization at the grass roots and 'this aspect of the new right's agenda and tactics is perhaps in the long-term of most significance' − and it may be much more difficult to stem than national politics.

Ehrenreich also sees family matters as crucial to the creation of the New Right out of the old Right. 'What was more innovative was to present feminism as a threat to women'. She continues:

> For the affluent male (and indirectly his wife) the right had always offered a program of economic self-interest: lower taxes, few regulatory obstacles to the predatory conduct of business, measures to restrict the tyranny of labour etc. The inspiration that helped to transform the 'old right' as represented by the John Birch Society to

the 'New Right' as represented by Schlaffly's STOP-ERA and a host
of single-issue organizations with 'pro-family' sympathies lay in the
realization that it was possible to appeal *directly* to affluent but
dependent women.[74]

She adds that:

> For the affluent man, the right offered a way to hold on to his class
> privileges in the face of encroaching Communists, criminals, workers,
> etc. For the affluent woman, the right offered a way to hold on to
> a man.[75]

Dworkin also attempts to develop this point, but she shows how
many prominent right-wing women eventually lost their loyalties to
the New Right, even if they did not fully convert to feminism.[76]
Petchesky also observes the decline in fervour of a quintessential
right-wing woman's commitment to the New Right following her
divorce.

As Peele notes, the significant feature of the New Right is its focus
on family and morality, intertwined issues that derive from the
involvement of religious sects and churches in right-wing causes and
politics.[77] Peele argues that the impetus for the involvement
stemmed from President Carter's initiative in planning a White
House Conference on the Family.

> If family policy for liberals entailed programs designed to provide
> safety-nets and support when the free-enterprise system failed to
> function efficiently . . . Conservatives wanted programs designed to
> strengthen traditional family relationships to bolster parental
> authority.[78]

The two key 'family' issues that the religious Right have pursued
have been abortion and religious schools, as well as religion, or
prayer, in school.[79] They appear to be very different issues but the
former entails questions not only of sexual immorality but also of
parental control. Religion in schools is seen partly as the antidote:
an attempt to reassert parental influence over children and to ensure
instruction in right and proper sex roles in the family as well as the
wider society. These issues have been debated publicly and
systematically in the USA throughout Reagan's period in office.

It has been argued that there are fewer pressure groups in Britain
sustaining public debate on either abortion or parental
responsibilities. Indeed, I was roundly chastised by Elizabeth Wilson

in her review of a previous article on this theme for having the audacity to compare Britain with the USA. Wilson wrote

> Pessimism is indeed currently a fashionable position in progressive circles . . . It does however lead at times to oversimplifications such as those found in Miriam David's discussion of the Moral Majority. She draws far too close a parallel between Britain and the United States and ignores the crucial difference: that in this country we simply do not have a fundamentalist religious movement of the kind found in North America to form the base of Mary Whitehouse types of activity on a mass scale. (How would Miriam David explain the recent 'permissive' judgement on contraceptive advice given to girls under 16?)[80]

Writing a year ago, Wilson may be forgiven for having been unaware of the activities of the religious and moral Right in Britain. As Leathard argues 'when political manoeuvres fail: *tactics move underground*'.[81] She adds that 'having failed through democratic means in Parliament the anti-abortionists tried a different tack: extra-parliamentary procedures'. She cites the abortive attempt to make sweeping and restrictive changes in abortion notification forms in 1982. She also mentions 'the use of moles and spies', citing the example of the prosecution by the Director of Public Prosecutions (DPP), of paediatrician Dr Leonard Arthur for murder, because he refused to take measures to keep a severely handicapped child alive in defiance of its parents' wishes. The case was brought to public attention by a member of Life, an anti-abortion pressure group. Arthur was found not guilty, but doctors were placed on the defensive. The moral Right in Britain clearly has not been quiet in the last four years but has pursued individuals rather than a sustained change of policy in Parliament.

The views of the religious and moral Right have been taken up, in some instances, by the government. For example, Patrick Jenkin, newly appointed Secretary of State for Social Services in 1979, let slip in a television debate on working mothers in October of that year:

> Quite frankly, I don't think that mothers have the same right to work as fathers do. If the Good Lord had intended us to have equal rights to go out to work, he wouldn't have created man and woman. These are biological facts.

Thatcher's appeal to Victorian values is about the bourgeois family in its traditional form. Hall and Davidoff claim that it is 'constructed on a specific type of family authority and sexual division of labour'.[82] Fitzgerald has also identified the rigidity inherent in Thatcher's approach to the family and particularly to the mother's place within it.[83]

There have been some successful attempts to alter the terms of family and public responsibility over particular social issues. For example, the rules governing the teaching of sex education in schools were altered in the 1980 Education Act as a result of pressure from Mary Whitehouse.[84] There was also a successful campaign to restrict the showing of 'video-nasties' at home, which unusually extended social control into family life.[85] But all of these issues have been presented in the British media, as the brain-children of particular individuals, rather than as an orchestrated set of campaigns. In fact, it could be argued that this is a more subtle but effective approach to the insertion of such moral questions into the political agenda and finally onto the statute books.

Just how successful have the New and moral Right pressure groups been in Britain and the USA? Despite all the rhetoric in the USA, the various forces of the Right have not been particularly successful in rescinding liberal legislation and policies on family matters. The most concerted attempt was the Family Protection Act, which *Congressional Quarterly* staff writers labelled 'a tidy wish list for the New Right'.[86] But despite its patriarchal terms and conditions, including both transforming schools' curricula to exclude women's studies and increasing parental authority over children, as well as male authority over women, it failed to receive Congressional approval. However, certain elements of it have become law. For example, the 'teenage chastity program' received approval in the summer of 1982. This has meant that federal funds for family planning agencies are only given to those that adopt a 'family centred' approach. This also means that such agencies require parental consent before dispensing contraceptives to 'unemancipated minors' i.e. girls under eighteen.[87] The same approach has been applied to abortions for minors and the Supreme Court has been forced to adjudicate on such issues. Petchesky writes that the Supreme Court's

> most recent decision concerning teenagers and abortion illustrates sharply its tendency to abandon or grossly distort isses of health and social needs and to stress the state's interest in preserving 'family integrity' and (in theory) favoring childbirth . . . It upheld the constitutionality of a Utah statute requiring a physician to notify 'if possible' a minor's parents prior to performing an abortion on her,

only in so far as the minor is 'living with and dependent on her
parents', 'unemancipated' and 'immature'.

The Supreme Court also sought to define maturity, stating that 'there
is no logical relationship between the capacity to become pregnant
and the capacity for mature judgment concerning the wisdom of an
abortion'.[88]

Petchesky also cites a more recent Supreme Court decision on 16
June 1983 in the Akron case, which re-emphasized the 'right to
privacy' in abortion decisions. The majority of judges argued that
'Akron has imposed a heavy, and unnecessary, burden on women's
access to a relatively inexpensive, otherwise accessible, and safe
abortion procedure.' Nevertheless, Petchesky argues that the courts
in this instance are not supporting women's rights but 'the interests
of a liberal state in population control and the medical profession
in its autonomy'.[89] To that extent, however, it seems unlikely that
the recent attempts by New Right groups to take direct action to
prevent abortion clinics from working are likely to win court
approval, despite Reagan having given his. Equally, congressional
initiatives, aimed at redefining the start of life, either in a
constitutional amendment or by restrictions of the courts'
jurisdiction, seem unlikely to succeed.

There is no doubt of the similarity between approaches in the USA
and in Britain. Victoria Gillick's sustained attempt to rescind official
guidelines to doctors (developed ten years ago) on the question of
prescribing contraceptives to girls under the age of sixteen, appears
to follow American initiatives. Gillick has been trying to reassert
parental authority over and above that of the state and, initially
unsuccessful, she succeeded on appeal. All three High Court judges
supported her appeal, arguing that it is illegal for doctors to give
contraceptive advice and treatment to girls under sixteen without
parental consent, save in exceptional circumstances. The previous,
permissive ruling was thereby overturned.

Mrs Gillick has presented herself as merely a concerned mother.
She created what Leathard called 'a disturbingly plausible facade
with the case for parental rights contained in the question: Would
you like your teenage daughter to be prescribed the pill without your
knowledge?'[90] In fact, she is well-known as a Roman Catholic anti-
abortion lobbyist and is alleged to have been a supporter of
'Powellight', an extreme right-wing, anti-immigration pressure
group.[91] The media portrayal of the issue in terms of one mother's

lonely fight is a far cry from reality. To appeal the lower court's decision required considerable financial, as well as emotional, backing.

The issue, however, has been persistently presented as one of parental rights, especially those of a mother's duties. There has been little discussion of girls' rights. It is perhaps best expressed by the *Daily Mail*'s headline the day that the Court of Appeal found in Mrs Gillick's favour: 'The Pill: Mother knows best'. Campbell, writing in the popular press, also argues this:

> The form of Gillick's action is a clue to her success. She hasn't gone for sex itself below the age of consent, nor even for parents or doctors aiding and abetting criminal activity, although both of these are factors. It's a question of control.
>
> Parental control is central to different wings of right-wing thinking. To the Responsible Society, Gillick's associates in this campaign, parental control is the instrument of moral rehabilitation. The society was formed during the heady days of the 1960s so-called sexual revolution, as a reaction against laxity and the youth culture phenomenon which was explicitly, not to say, militantly, sexual. The campaign was aimed at parents and their supposed loss of control. To retain it would be stamp out the erotic contagion.[92]

Butt has expressed these themes of control and the opposite − the rampant liberalism of the 'immoral left'.[1] He appears to misrepresent the issue and is seemingly unaware of those girls who do not have loving parents in whom to confide. On the contrary, some girls are the victims of incest and sexual abuse from the very people to whom Butt and Gillick would have given pride of place in consent over contraceptive advice.[93] Even if Gillick's campaign is lost, since the DHSS is mounting a strong appeal in the House of Lords, on the grounds not of children's rights, but of the clinical freedom of doctors, much of the campaign has had its desired effect. It has already confused and frightened young women and ensured that they avoid discussing their sexual activities publicly. As in the USA, the defeat of Gillick will be a pyrrhic victory. It will be a triumph of medical authority over parental authority, of the state's right to control families, in patriarchal ways.

This general theme of parental authority was certainly strong in the New Right's initiatives in the USA, as witnessed by attempts to ensure that federal funds go only to schools that allow voluntary school prayer, and in the giving of tax relief to religious schools, sometimes referred to as 'family schools'.[94] This theme of parental

rights over education has also been taken up in Britain. Here, the
emphasis on religion has not been so evident, partly because the
tradition of the separation of church and state has not existed here.
But the Thatcher government has tried a variety of measures to allow
for more parental choice over both state and private schools and
parental influence in school government. Hall has summarized the
flavour of the developments:

> The right have temporarily defined the terms and won the struggle
> because they are willing to engage. For a brief period in the 1960s
> and 1970s the involvement of parents with the school was the left's
> most democratic trump card. The dismantling of this into 'parental
> choice' and its expropriation by the right is one of their most significant
> victories. They stole an idea designed to increase popular power in
> education and transformed it into an idea of an educational
> supermarket.[95]

So even if the Gillick decision is reversed there are likely to be
many more attempts to reassert family or rather parental, and
especially parental, authority over children, particularly daughters.
Indeed, this theme remains in the political arena at present in Britain
with the success of Enoch Powell's Unborn Children (Protection)
bill. The bill seeks to prevent a human embryo from being created,
kept or used for any purpose other than enabling a child to be born
to a particular woman. In addition it would make it a criminal
offence to be in possession of an embryo except with the authority
of the Secretary of State for Social Services given expressly for that
purpose and no other. The bill has had two readings and its third
is now planned earlier than originally scheduled, for May 1985.

The bill has clearly been introduced by the anti-abortion lobby,
both Roman Catholic and Church of England. Two separate right-
wing pressure groups – The Society for the Protection of the Unborn
Child (SPUC) and Life – have expressed jubilance about it. So
although it has been raised in the aftermath of the Warnock debate
on reproductive technologies the bill is clearly an attempt to revive
traditional moral and family issues. It places the Thatcher
government in a moral dilemma. In the debate on the bill, Health
Minister Kenneth Clarke argued that the government remained
neutral about embryo experimentation. He did announce plans to
bring in a bill to make commercial surrogate motherhood illegal,
but argued for a delay on a major bill on human fertilization. If
Powell's bill is successful, the government will have a substantial

medical and scientific lobby to placate. The moral Right has certainly managed finally to seize centre stage on these broad issues of the morality of maternity.

It is clear that these moral questions of family life have become central political issues. The Right has stolen the initiative because it is able to express with certainty issues which both liberals and the Left have been unable to clarify. Indeed, there is still a conflict between the themes of family authority and state authority, whether expressed through medical, educational or social agencies. However, it remains unlikely that the inertia built into the liberal state will readily be changed by these lobbying tactics of the moral Right. Whether or not it is able to alter the rules and machinery of government, it is digging deep into social rules apparently accepted and agreed on in the post-war period.

Perhaps more significant are the subtle transformations of women's lives, not by policy issues at the national or federal level or by pressure-group tactics and lobbying, but at the local and community level. Denied access to employment on a full-time basis, mothers are increasingly expected to participate in community and voluntary work. In Britain this takes the form of unpaid labour in schools, in befriending schemes for poor mothers rearing young children, in voluntary work in playgroups, nurseries and so on.[96] In the USA, there has also been a renewed commitment to voluntary and community child-care centres, usually church-run. In addition, the curricula of schools are transforming boys' and girls' expectations of their future lives. In Britain, a host of new educational and training initiatives stress the 'vocational' element, but as far as those girls deemed to be "less able" are concerned, the emphasis is on unpaid or low-paid vocations. The new initiatives include, for girls, education for family life, parent education or preparation for parenthood.[97] All these imply a particular conception of family life and parental responsibility. Women as mothers are expected to be able to depend economically on a husband and have dependents to care for as their main occupation and preoccupation. How they organize their family lives is a matter of their own responsibility, but is to be done in conditions in which they receive no public support or financial help. Girls who choose not to conform will, in the future, pay a heavy price – moral disapprobation, unwanted and unsupported pregnancy and motherhood, education in 'parental skills' to demonstrate their 'inadequacies'.

Rhetoric or reality, family life is certainly undergoing enormous

changes in the current period. The new 'underclass' which is being
created through shifts in international economies is chiefly an
underclass of mothers alone, rearing dependent children, in
conditions not of their choosing. Until these transformations are
recognized for the effects they are having on women's lives, policies
to counter them may not address the real problems. Women's lives
may still be burdensome and controlled. Women will be denied the
moral autonomy and judgments afforded men in our society. In that
sense, women at the point of maternity become infantilized and
denied public and social support for what is usually regarded as an
awesome and aweful task by the Right − the care of their children.

Notes

1 Ronald Butt, 'Not only moral but right', *The Times*, 7 Mar. 1985.
2 Butt, *Not only moral.*
3 Rose Shapiro, 'The moral minority on the move', *Marxism Today*, vol. 29, no. 2, Feb. 1985, pp. 7-12.
4 Miriam David, 'Thatcherism is anti-feminism', *Trouble and Strife*, vol. 1, no. 1 (Sept. 1983); and Miriam David, 'The New Right in the USA and Britain: A new anti-feminist moral economy', *Critical Social Policy*, vol. 2. no 3 (Spring 1983), pp. 31-46.
5 Anna Coote and Bea Campbell, *Sweet Freedom: The struggle for women's liberation* (Picador, London, 1982).
6 Peregrine Worsthorne in *The Sunday Times*, 27 Feb. 1983.
7 Rosalind Petchesky, *Abortion and Woman's Choice: The state, sexuality and reproductive freedom* (Longman, New York, London, 1984), p. 247; Zillah Eisenstein 'The sexual politics of the New Right: on understanding the crisis of liberalism', *Signs: Journal of Women and Culture*, vol. 7, no 3 (1982) pp. 567-88; Barbara Ehrenreich, *The Hearts of Men* (Pluto, London, 1983); David, 'The New Right in the USA and Britain'.
8 Petchesky, *Abortion and Woman's Choice*, p. 247.
9 Centre for Educational Research and Innovation (CERI), *Caring for Young Children* (OECD, Paris, 1982), p. 12.
10 Ibid., pp. 19-20.
11 Petchesky, *Abortion and Woman's Choice*, p. 247.
12 David, *The New Right*, p. 32.
13 Miriam David, 'Teaching and preaching sexual morality, *Journal of Education*, vol. 166, no. 1 (Mar. 1984), pp. 48-77.

14 David, *The New Right*; David, *Teaching and preaching*; Eisenstein, *The Sexual Politics*.

15 Jessie Bernard, *The Future of Motherhood* (Penguin, New York and London, 1975), p. 9.

16 Margaret Combs, unpublished M.Phil. thesis on the Parents' National Educational Union (PNEU), Aston University, Birmingham, 1985, p. 24-5.

17 Antony Fitzgerald, 'The New Right and the family', in *Social Policy and Social Welfare*, eds. M. Loney et al. (Heinemann, London, 1983).

18 Ivan Illich, *Gender* (Marion Boyars, London, 1983), p. 46.

19 Alice Eden, letter to *The Guardian*, 27 Jul. 1984.

20 See further discussions in C. New and M. David *For The Children's Sake* (Penguin, London, 1985).

21 Ibid.

22 Ramesh Mishra *The Welfare State in Crisis: Social thought and social change* (Wheatsheaf, Brighton, 1984), p. 4.

23 Ibid.

24 Ibid.

25 Eli Zaretsky quoted in Petchesky, *Abortion and Women's Choice*, p. 278.

26 Petchesky, *Abortion and Woman's Choice*, p. 248.

27 Frances Fox Piven and Richard Cloward, *The New Class War* (Pantheon Books, New York, 1982).

28 Petchesky, *Abortion and Woman's Choice*, p. 249.

29 Mishra, *The Welfare State*, p. 4-5.

30 Gillian Peele, *Revival and Reaction: The Right in contemporary America* (The Clarendon Press, Oxford, 1984), p. 1.

31 Ibid., p. 194.

32 A. Palmer and I. V. Sawhill, *The Reagan Experiment*, (Brookings Institution, Washington D.C., 1983).

33 Mimi Abramovitz 'The conservative program is a woman's issue', *Journal of Sociology and Social Welfare*, vix (Sept. 1982), pp. 399-442.

34 Mike Davis, 'The political economy of late imperial America' *New Left Review*, 143 (Jan./Feb. 1984), pp. 6-39.

35 Ibid., p. 19.

36 Abramovitz, *The conservative program*; Ehrenreich, *The Hearts of Men*; Eisenstein, *The sexual politics*; Petchesky, *Abortion and Woman's Choice*.

37 Abramovitz, *The conservative program*, p. 401.

166   David

38 Ehrenreich, *The Hearts of Men*, p. 172.
39 Andrew Hacker, *U/S: A Statistical Portrait of the American People* (Penguin, London, 1983), p. 190.
40 Abramovitz, *The conservative program*, p. 405.
41 Lois Shaw, 'Child care policy in the United States of America', paper prepared for EOC Day Conference on *Child Care Policies*, Mar. 19, 1985.
42 Ibid., p. 4-5.
43 Ibid., p. 14.
44 Ibid., p. 15.
45 *School-Age Child Care (SACC)*, vol. 2, no. 3, (Apr. 1985), a publication newsletter from Wellesley College, Centre for Research on Women, Wellesley, Mass.
46 Barbara Katz Rothman, 'The meanings of choice in reproductive technology', in *Test Tube Women: What Future for Motherhood*? R. Arditti, R. Duelli Klein and Shelley Minden, (eds.). (Pandora, London, 1984), p. 31.
47 Arditti et al., *Test Tube Women*, p. 52.
48 John Stewart, 'Storming the town halls', *Marxism Today*, (Apr. 1984), p. 8-9.
49 Sir Leo Pliatzsky, *Report on non-Departmental Public Bodies*, cmnd 7797 (HMSO, London, Jan. 1980).
50 Peter Townsend, *Why Are the Many Poor?* pamphlet no. 500 (Fabian Society, London, 1984), p. 23.
51 Ibid., p. 25-6.
52 Ibid., p. 17.
53 L. Rimmer, *Families in Focus* (Study Commission on the Family, London, 1981), p. 40.
54 Townsend, *Why*, p. 17.
55 Jean Martin and Ceridwen Roberts, *Women and Employment: A lifetime perspective* (HMSO, London, 1984).
56 Hilary Land, *Paying for child care*, paper prepared for EOC conference on Child Care Policies, 12 May. 1985.
57 Heather Joshi, *Women's Participation in Paid Work: Further analysis of the women and employment survey* research paper no. 45 (Department of Employment), London, 1984).
58 Corea, 'The egg snatchers' in Arditti et al. eds *Test Tube Women*, p. 37.
59 DHSS, *Report of the Committee of Inquiry into Human Fertilisation and Embryology* (Warnock Report), cmnd 9314 (HMSO, London, 1984).

60 Ibid., p. 85.
61 Ibid., p. 84.
62 Audrey Leathard, 'The politics of birth control 1985', paper prepared for British University, Mar. 1985, p. 10.
63 Norton Grubb and Marvin Lazerson, *Broken Promises* (Basic Books, New York, 1982).
64 Roger Scruton, *The Meaning of Conservatism* (Penguin, London, 1980); Ferdinand Mount, *The Subversive Family: An alternative history of love and marriage* (Jonathan Cape, London, 1982).
65 Roger Scruton, 'Ignore the body: lose your soul', *The Times*, 5 Mar. 1985.
66 George Gilder, *Wealth and Poverty* (Basic Books, New York, 1981; Buchan & Enright, London, 1982).
67 Eisenstein, *The Sexual Politics*, p. 574.
68 Abramovitz, *The conservative program*, p. 416.
69 Eisenstein, *The sexual politics*, p. 576.
70 Peele, *Revival and Reaction*, pp. 33-4.
71 Nigel Ashford, 'The neo-conservatives', *Government and Opposition*, vol. 16, no. 3 (1981), p. 357.
72 Peele, *Revival and Reaction*, p. 51-2.
73 Ibid., p. 71-2.
74 Ehrenreich, *The Hearts of Men*, p. 161.
75 Ibid., p. 161.
76 Andrea Dworkin, *Right-Wing Women* (Perigree Books, New York, 1982), p. 29.
77 Peele, *Revival and Reaction*, p. 80.
78 Ibid., p. 93.
79 David, *Teaching and preaching*.
80 Elizabeth Wilson, review of Jane Lewis (ed.), *Women's Welfare: Women's Rights* (Croom Helm, London, 1983) in *Journal of Social Policy*, vol. 13, pt. 1, (Jan. 1984), p. 101.
81 Leathard, *The politics of birth control 1985*, p. 7.
82 C. Hall and L. Davidoff, 'Home Sweet Home', *New Statesman*, vol. 105, no. 2723, 27 May 1983; special supplement on Victorian values.
83 Fitzgerald, *The New Right and the family*.
84 M. E. David, 'Sex, education and social policy: a new moral economy', in *Gender, Class and Education*, eds. S. Walker and L. Barton (Falmer Press, Lewes, 1983), pp. 141-61.
85 M. Barker, *The Video Nasties* (Pluto, London, 1984).
86 David, *The New Right*.

87 Petchesky, *Abortion*, p. 308.
88 Ibid., p. 314.
89 Ibid., p. 319.
90 Leathard, 'The politics of birth control 1985', p. 3.
91 'The racist past of a morality campaigner', *Searchlight*, Feb. 1984, p. 3.
92 Bea Campbell, 'A battle for control', *City Limits* 1-7 Feb. 1985, p. 9.
93 Carol Lee 'Victory for Mrs Gillick is a tragedy for thousands of young people', *The Guardian*, 30 Jan. 1985, p. 22.
94 David, *Teaching and preaching*.
95 S. Hall, 'Education in crisis', in *Is There Anyone Here From Education*? eds A. M. Wolpe and J. Donald (Pluto Press, London, 1983), pp. 2-11.
96 Miriam David, 'Motherhood and social policy − a matter of education?' *Critical Social Policy*, 12 (Spring 1985), pp. 28-44.
97 Ibid.

Chapter Six

The New Right, Social Order and Civil Liberties

ANDREW BELSEY

Civil Liberties and the Thatcher Government

In March 1985 the British government of Margaret Thatcher opposed proposals designed to make the procedures of the European Convention on Human Rights more effective. This was not unexpected from a government that has put a much higher priority on enforcing 'law and order' than on the protection and enhancement of human rights and civil liberties. In spite of the Thatcher government's use of the rhetoric of freedom at home, and its attempts to criticize selected (mainly Eastern bloc) regimes abroad for their poor human rights records, it has maintained Britain's achievement of being one of the worst offenders against the European Convention.[1]

In recent years British law and practice has been found defective by Convention standards in many cases, including those concerning telephone tapping, corporal punishment, the freedom of the press, and the treatment of prisoners, immigrants, sexual minorities and mental patients. The provisions of the Convention have proved a source of embarrassment to all recent British governments, Labour as well as Conservative. As commentators have pointed out, the Thatcher government's approach to civil liberties was built upon the poor record of the previous Labour administration.

The sad fact is, though, that civil liberties are under constant pressure, irrespective of the political complexion of the government in power, and always have been. But it would be foolish to suppose that therefore things are always the same, and complacent not to recognize the particular and severe challenge to civil liberties mounted by the New Right doctrines from which the Thatcher government draws much of its ideological sustenance. A number of recent events, such as the 'state trial' of Clive Ponting, the policing of the strike in the coal industry, and revelations about the security services, suggest that civil liberties are now under greater threat than ever before. Behind these and other cases are a number of general issues.[2]

Under the Thatcher government there has been a considerable emphasis on law enforcement and therefore on increasing police powers, as shown by the passing of the Police and Criminal Evidence Act, 1984. This strengthens the powers of the police to seize evidence, and to arrest, stop, search and detain. At the same time police practice has changed. The coal strike of 1984-5 produced what a few years ago would have been unthinkable in mainland Britain: police road-blocks at which travellers had the choice of turning back or being arrested.[3] The police's actions were at best anticipations of the new Police Act, as the section permitting 'road checks' had not then come into operation, and even if it had it is doubtful whether some of the police actions would have been within the scope of road checks authorized by the Act. However, once the police had discovered the use of widespread road-blocks in an industrial dispute it was not hard to predict that their use would not be limited to this issue, and indeed not long afterwards similar road-blocks were used to prevent members of the peace movement reaching the Molesworth Cruise Missile Site.[4] Another innovation of doubtful legality which has been used against both strikers and anti-nuclear protesters is the imposition of bail conditions which prevent free movement and prohibit certain types of political activity. What have recently appeared in Britain then are forms of exile and curfew, methods of social control normally associated with politically unsavoury regimes overseas.

It is not too fanciful to see policing becoming both more peremptory and more militarized. Behind this change lies the Prevention of Terrorism Act, which pioneered the use of exile in the UK, and more generally the export to the British mainland of Northern Ireland police methods and equipment: riot shields, batons, tear gas, plastic bullets and surveillance.[5] Another aspect of the militarization of society and of law enforcement is the use of 'national security' to justify breaches of civil liberties. This appeared not only in the banning of trade unions at Government Communications Headquarters (GCHQ) in 1984 but also in the trials of Sarah Tisdall in 1984 and Clive Ponting in 1985, when ministers implied that even though the information leaked was not classified, the presence of leakers in the Civil Service is itself a threat to national security. Further, it appears to be taken for granted in official circles that secret surveillance and jury vetting – in other words, special measures designed to increase the chances of a conviction – will be used by the state in such cases. Unfortunately judges have proved to be no guardians of civil liberties, as on these issues they have accepted that national security is involved if the government says it is, an acceptance that gives an extraordinary privilege to executive actions.[6] The attempt by the judge in the Ponting case to equate the interests of the state with the policies of the government would, if generally agreed to, give an even greater privilege, and would have the effect of making Britain like South Africa, where opposition to government policies can lead to charges of treason. Although the judge was widely condemned by both Left and Right, he was supported by the Attorney-General.[7]

Much of the current erosion of civil liberties can be traced to the government's opposition to freedom of information and its use of official secrecy.[8] The Official Secrets Act is used not only to keep people in ignorance, and therefore unable fully to exercise their democratic rights, but more especially to protect further an already unaccountable security service consisting of MI5 and the Special Branch. The revelations of Cathy Massiter, an ex-MI5 agent, suggest not only that the security services spy on legal organizations like trade unions, the Campaign for Nuclear Disarmament, Friends of the Earth, and the National Council for Civil Liberties, but also that information on CND collected by MI5 was improperly passed to a government minister, the Secretary of State for Defence, Michael Heseltine, who used it illegitimately for party-political purposes to mount an attack on CND.[9] The government's response to the allegations was not encouraging. It arranged for a very hurried report by the 'Judicial Monitor of the Interception of Communications', Lord Bridge, which found that there had been no 'improperly authorised interceptions' and therefore completely ignored the questions of non-authorized interceptions and improper use of intercepted material.[10] The government also issued a White Paper prior to introducing legislation bringing the practice of interception within the provisions of the European Convention on Human Rights.[11] But the main aim of the very careful drafting is clearly to prevent people from ever discovering whether or not their telephone has been tapped.

A further, large area of erosion of civil liberties has been the general and continuous marginalization and harassment of dissenting and minority groups. For example, people in Wales who hold nationalist (and more especially republican) views have been victimized and subjected to political trials.[12] Members of ethnic minority groups have been subjected to victimization and discrimination, and the use of the category 'illegal immigrant' effectively removes all protection of civil and legal rights.[13] Immigration and nationality laws continue to discriminate against women. The government's attitude to women's rights in general is extremely negative, seeing women as properly occupying a naturally subordinate position in society, preferably providing free labour in the home and receiving only low wages if they insist on working outside the family. Gay people too still suffer considerable discrimination and harassment.

Rather than concerning itself with civil liberties, the Thatcher government has promoted certain rights, where these are understood in terms of 'a re-definition of "individual rights" in the direction of those "rights" which run counter to the interests of the labour movement (rights of individuals not to be disturbed by demonstrations, pickets, riots, trade unions, rights of employers to hire and fire at will, rights of tenants to buy their council houses, etc.)'. This limited economic conception of rights is supported by a rhetoric of law and order, which includes demands for crime prevention, detection and punishment, together with the necessary means and a more general insistence on the imposition of social discipline. It is an insistence on a form of policing that will ensure the preservation of 'public order' by the prevention of 'disorder'.[14]

The New Right

While the erosion of civil liberties under the Thatcher government is not entirely attributable to New Right ideology, it is not unconnected with it. Like a great deal of social and political theory the New Right is very exercised by the problem of social order, its creation and maintenance, and its views on this have considerable consequences for a wide range of civil liberties issues.

This is true whether the New Right is considered under its 'neo-liberal' or its 'neo-conservative' aspects. I take these terms to refer to two ideal types, each produced by means of a list of important points or principles. Thus neo-liberalism can be seen as the politics constructed from the five points: (1) the individual; (2) freedom of choice; (3) market society; (4) laissez-faire; (5) minimal government. Neo-conservatism first of all takes these points in reverse order and then reverses each one, so it is the politics constructed from (1) strong government; (2) social authoritarianism; (3) disciplined society; (4) hierarchy and subordination; (5) the nation. The contrast between the two sides is illustrated in figure 6.1.

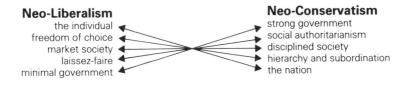

Neo-Liberalism
the individual
freedom of choice
market society
laissez-faire
minimal government

Neo-Conservatism
strong government
social authoritarianism
disciplined society
hierarchy and subordination
the nation

New Right political practice, such as Thatcherism, involves both sides. On the one hand it draws on the conservative discourse of authority and discipline and on the other on the liberal discourse of freedom and justice. The two sides seem quite distinct, but in political practice there is much cross-over and no clear separation can be made. It is a mistake to ignore either side and the intermingling in practice. Bosanquet's analysis in *After the New Right*, for example, is misleading because not only does he banish authoritarian neo-conservatism from the New Right but also he grossly underestimates the authoritarian and conservative aspects of neo-liberalism. In fact 'law' and 'order' are very important concepts in each version of the New Right. It is not surprising therefore that there is considerable cross-over between the two sides. Each has a fairly clear conception of order, and each has a conception of law as that which is necessary to enforce order.

I shall take it as reasonably uncontroversial that the more authoritarian elements of the New Right with their rigid approach to social order are hostile to civil liberties and that this hostility is apparent in political practice. It might be thought, though, that the self-proclaimed 'libertarian' elements of the New Right, with their claims to be representatives of 'liberty', would take a more relaxed attitude to the problem of social order and be the friends of civil liberties. I shall suggest, however, that the theoretical position of the liberals means that they are no more the friends of liberty than are the authoritarians, and that the appropriation of the word 'libertarian' by elements of the New Right is a grotesque confidence trick.

Neo-Conservatism and Social Order

Conservatives have, of course, always concerned themselves with what they regard as the problem of social order. Scruton begins his book on conservatism (which can be considered as exemplary of neo-conservatism) by quoting from Peel's *Tamworth Manifesto* of 1834: conservatism appeals to those whose aims are 'the maintenance of order and the cause of good government'. And for the conservative these aims are not separable: it is at least a necessary condition of good government (and perhaps a sufficient one) that it maintains social order. And, to put it bluntly, it maintains order by imposing it: 'the conservative attitude seeks above all for government, and regards no citizen as possessed of a natural right that transcends his obligation to be ruled'.[15]

The key concepts of conservative political theory are tradition, authority and allegiance. Tradition has a double role: it is both history in the sense of the past, the succession of gradual and wise changes that have resulted in the present social order, and history in the sense of representations of the past, the symbolic forms of myth and ritual which perform a justificatory role, making the established social order seem inevitable. But no such ideological system could be sufficient on its own, so in the end social order must be maintained by authority. For there to be the necessary regime of total authority the liberal notion of the separation of society and state must be abandoned. However, the conservative version of authority turns out to be nothing but power dressed up in symbolic robes. And 'power seeks to coerce and rule'.[16]

The object of total state power is the allegiance of the citizen. But this is no 'liberal' allegiance, freely consented to for good reasons. The individual of liberalism does not exist. The only reality the (always male) individual has is as the subject of, and the creation of, the state:

> It is basic to a conservative view of things . . . that the individual should seek and find his completion in society, and that he should find himself as part of an order that is greater than himself, in the sense of transcending anything that could have been brought about through his own enactment. He must see himself as the inheritor, not

the creator, of the order in which he participates, so that he may derive from it . . . the conceptions and values which determine self-identity.[17]

State, society and individual come together in the nation, an organic entity the interests of which must predominate in order to ensure its own continuation and preservation. 'For if the power of the state is threatened, so too is its authority, and with it the structure of civil society.' In practical terms this means that 'there must be provision against sedition, laws which enable the power of the state to reassert itself against antagonists'.[18] In fact though, everyone is a potential antagonist, and so the individual must be totally dominated by and subjected to the state, and cannot claim any rights against it.

This totalitarian social and political theory of neo-conservatism is hardly likely to be conducive to the healthy existence of civil rights and political liberties. Thus, beginning the analysis with the basic concept of freedom, 'for the conservative, the value of individual liberty is not absolute, but stands subject to another and higher value, the authority of established government'. Now, no sensible political theory would make freedom an absolute, but for the neo-conservative it is not just not an absolute, it is non-existent: 'Freedom is comprehensible as a social goal only when subordinate to something else, to an organization or arrangement that defines the individual aim'.[19]

Having abandoned freedom, the conservative can then abandon the democratic franchise. Democracy is a 'contagion' and 'can be discarded without detriment to the civil well-being as the conservative conceives it'. The House of Commons should give way to the House of Lords, especially the Law Lords. It is judges who should rule; the sovereignty of parliament should be superseded by the sovereignty of law.[20]

One of the most pressing tasks for the judges is to re-establish the law of sedition:

> This decline in the very *idea* of sedition has been brought about not by popular agitation, but by the politics of power. The fact is, not that our society believes in freedom of speech and assembly, but rather that it is afraid to announce its disbelief. This disbelief is so entrenched in English law . . . that it is impossible to doubt that it could be eradicated without wholly overturning the social order which the law enshrines.

And among the targets of an enforced law of sedition would be 'what is said at every radical demonstration, and at many a Trades Union Congress'.[21]

Various other civil liberties issues come in for equally sophisticated treatment at the hands of the neo-conservative. For example, 'illiberal sentiments' towards ethnic minorities should not be subject to law, for 'they are sentiments which seem to arise inevitably from social consciousness: they involve natural prejudice, and a desire for the company of one's own kind. That is hardly sufficient ground to condemn them as "racist"'. Then on 'law and order': 'Are we to take our example from the cruel and emphatic law of Islam, and institute flogging and maiming as expressions of civic virtue? The answer cannot be abstractly determined.' And as for strikes in the public sector, they are 'tantamount to rebellion'. The solution is to 'reward extravagantly those servants who are essential; but make them servants. As for the others, let them strike, and permanently.'[22]

The obnoxiousness of such views does not need drawing attention to. But what about their danger? The representative of neo-conservatism quoted here, Roger Scruton, may be a self-appointed one-person conservative think-tank and an acknowledged 'philosopher' of the Conservative Party, but can one academic produce an intellectual and political upheaval that spells the end of civil liberties? Or can several? Of course not; there is no simple cause-and-effect relationship. But the danger that emerges from Scruton and the other neo-conservatives is not on that account negligible; far from it, in fact. They may not yet be satisfied that the Thatcher government has given up its commitment to 'freedom', but they must be delighted by the way it has responded to demands for the re-establishment of 'authority' and 'the smack of firm government'.[23] New Right authoritarianism can be seen triumphant, not least in the government's approach to immigration, law enforcement, freedom of movement and assembly and the trade unions. Furthermore, the politicians find it easy to echo the ideologues' discourse. Thus when Scruton writes that 'a society really does have enemies . . . those enemies seek to undermine it, and . . . it is the duty of the government . . . that they should be prevented by every means to hand',[24] one can hear an ancestral voice prophesying war on first 'the enemy without' and later 'the enemy within'.

Hayek's Historical Mythmaking

There is no mystery about the conservative attitude to civil liberties. What though about the neo-liberals? This requires a more lengthy analysis of the chosen representative, F. A. Hayek. (Whether he really is representative of neo-liberalism is a question that will be taken up later.) Hayek is not afraid of bold paradox. He offers the (from him) surprising assertions that 'In a sense, we are all socialists', 'In a sense, it is rather surprising that all people in the world are not socialists', and 'Emotionally, ninety-nine per cent of the population of the world are socialists'.[25] These claims are not all the same — indeed they are somewhat opposed — but Hayek seems to think they are all the same. Or more likely he just doesn't care. What is puzzling about some of his latest writings is not just the repetition but the variation. He tells the same story many times: each time most of the details and some of the principles differ. This hardly raises confidence in the credibility of his project. In what follows I shall attempt to reconstruct his theme and ignore most of the variations. I do not believe that the version of history that emerges will restore confidence.

The reason why we are all socialists lies in our evolutionary history. Once upon a time human beings lived a life of hunting and gathering in groups of between thirty and fifty people. This form of life lasted from a half to one million years. During this time appropriate instincts and emotions became fixed in human beings through their physiological constitution.

The two main emotional instincts of primitive society were solidarity: 'common purposes pursued together with our fellows', and altruism: duty to 'the visible needs of our known friends'. It is central to Hayek's whole project that altruism be defined in this limited way: it can be only attention to 'the known needs of known other people'; the unknown needs of unknown people cannot be relevant as either cause or effect.[26]

These instincts were appropriate to primitive society because in such small groups living close to the edge of survival it was possible for everyone to know everyone else, recognize their needs and work together to achieve common ends. Hayek assumes (without any proper discussion or explanation) that these instincts amount to socialism. Since they are instinctive, inside human beings in some way, they are still with us and we still think of them as 'good

H

instincts'. In this sense we are all socialists.[27]

The problem is, socialism was fine for primitive society, but if its members had stayed with it, human beings would still be hunting and gathering and civilization would not have occurred. However, there was a decisive historical break.[28] Someone, somewhere, probably in the Mediterranean lands, traded. Finding *him*self (naturally) with some surplus product, instead of distributing it among his fellows as the dictates of primitive morality demanded, he thought of it as private property, and exchanged it for some other product from somewhere else.

These first traders, or rather, the first money-lenders, are the real heroes of history, for they 'contributed to the development of an ethics that made the worldwide exchange society possible'. From their efforts developed commercial morality, an exchange economy and the market society. What eventually emerged was 'civilization' or, as Hayek puts it in one place, '[our] worldwide, peaceful, and prosperous society'.[29] Not that there was no opposition: the remnants of the old order − tribal leaders, religion − opposed the new developments; Christianity, for example, long opposed usury.

In spite of opposition a new moral and economic tradition emerged: barter, private property, contract, competition, interest. All this cut right across instinctive emotions and required their suppression: 'we have to recognize that the development of civilization was based on our gradually learning new rules of conduct that involved restraining and taming those primordial instincts'. The new behaviour in the market was reflected in new abstract rules of conduct, prescribing norms concerning private property and the family. The final result was a 'spontaneous order produced by the market through people acting within the rules of the law of property, tort and contract'.[30]

For between two and three thousand years the new market order persisted, becoming no longer new but traditional. It was the order of small-scale capitalism, the petit-bourgeois world of the independent farmer, craftsman, journeyman and merchant. Everyone who took part in it learnt and accepted its rules, but not because they understood how the rules achieved their purpose or even what their purpose was. The rules were not theorized at all; they were simply part of common sense. 'They were just traditional rules that everyone accepted.'[31]

The family, the patriarchal family, was important to the new order, for the enterprises were family-based. The 'familial organisation

. . . was the unit of all economic activity, [and] the heads of the households saw society as a network of family units connected by the markets'. And it was the familiar duty of 'the responsible head of a family . . . to build up capital, both for his family and his business'. Even more importantly, people learnt the rules of the new order 'by being either masters of a small enterprise or members of that master's family or immediate servants and thus immediately taking part in the market process'. Thus the family is 'an instrument for the transmission of important cultural values'.[32]

These values were clearly not explicit rules at all; it was behaviour that was being learnt; the rules were no more than tacit knowledge. Indeed, the rules could not have been explicitly learnt, for they were not articulated. People remained in ignorance of the basis of the market order; they did not understand it. So it was clearly neither designed nor planned in any conscious or rational sense.

The moral rules of market society evolved by 'a process of cultural selection, analagous to the process of biological selection'. 'Nobody ever invented them. They were not the result of design. The new manners of conduct were not adopted because anyone thought they were better. They were adopted because someone who acted on them profited from it and his group gained from it.' 'The morals of property and the family were spread, and came to dominate a large part of the world, because those groups who by accident accepted them prospered and multiplied more than the others.' So the market order allowed people both to survive and be successful.[33]

In the end, however, just when it might have seemed that the now traditional order was triumphantly secure, it faltered, as the result of two challenges. The first was philosophical. Enlightenment rationalism, building on Cartesian scepticism, taught that it was intellectually and morally wrong to believe or accept anything that did not have sufficient rational justification. But this was just what commercial morality lacked; no one understood it; it was just what passed as traditional or conventional wisdom. At the same time there was a second challenge mounted by organizations, whether in the private or the public sector, which began to outgrow and outpace the traditional small enterprises of market society. Though elsewhere Hayek claims that the large corporation is merely the product of the market process, he is distressed by the emergence of Organization Man. This new figure identified with the organization and learnt to help his fellows to work together to achieve the purpose of the organization. Entrepreneurial Market Man began to be swamped by bureaucratic Organization Man, whose values were, it turned out, nearer to the old primitive instincts of tribal socialism than to the rules of market society. In the new organizations there was no passing on of market values at the master's workbench or table. So much for the story. Now, the message. Socialistically-minded thinking is not only anachronistic, it is dangerous. For it threatens to destabilize and destroy the system that has produced modern civilization and enabled it to support a large population on earth. Only a market system can produce the goods to feed, clothe and meet the other needs of the people of the world.

What is to be made of this fabulous tale? Is it meant to be taken seriously? The problem is not just the many small variations; it is the contradictions. Thus, for example, Hayek says that 'the myth' of primitive communism 'has been completely refuted by anthropological research'.[34] His story is hardly plausible, not only on anthropological grounds but also on historical, psychological, biological, economic or logical grounds. It is especially weak in its uncritical use of terms like 'instinct', 'evolution' and 'selection'. It exhibits a historical nostalgia for a lost golden world, and manages, in its phrase '[our] worldwide, peaceful, and prosperous society', to obscure the realities of recent world history. It is almost as if Hayek wants to avenge Hegel by standing Marx on his head. Hayek's history is materialist, indeed economically determinist. But it is the relations of consumption and exchange with which he is concerned and which he takes to define modern society. This is hardly surprising in an economy of small enterprises. The motive force of history is trade; the consumer is merely the trader writ small. But the relations of production, classes, class struggle, the ruling class, surplus value, exploitation, ideology, all these have of course completely disappeared.

Whatever view is taken of the nature of historical understanding, it is difficult to see Hayek's version as other than myth.[35] And like most myth it is not innocent. It is offered as foundation for Hayek's theory of society and as support for his solution to the problem of social order. To the extent that Hayek's theory of history is unsatisfactory, so too will be his justification of social order.

Hayek on Social Order

I shall claim that in spite of appearances, in spite of the rhetoric of freedom, in spite of being a 'liberal', Hayek has a conception of order having much in common with the authoritarian tradition in social theory, and is therefore no stranger to the authoritarian New Right.

There can be no doubt that Hayek is centrally concerned with the problem of order. He points out that it is the main concept of his book. He refers to 'the market order', 'the spontaneous order of the market', 'the spontaneous order of society', and uses many similar phrases. In fact, he dislikes the term 'society' (in spite of constantly promoting it in his, and Adam Smith's, expression 'the Great Society'), and now prefers to call the totality of human social (i.e. market) relations 'the extended order of human action' or just 'the extended order'.[36] It is Hayek's project to ensure the maintenance of this order, which, although he again dislikes the term, can be called capitalism.

The basis of the capitalist order is, however, paradoxical, to say the least. In Hayek's mythical state of nature (as opposed to Hobbes's, for instance) the primitive emotions and moral instincts are 'good'.[37] But these instincts must be suppressed if civilization is to emerge: 'we have to recognize that the development of civilization was based on our gradually learning new rules of conduct that involved restraining and taming those primordial instincts'.[38] There have been many theories of civilization which claim that it depends on the suppression of primitive urges, but these have been bad, dangerous instincts like impulsiveness, egoism and aggression. It does at least make sense, whatever else might be thought of such theories, to suppose that civilization depends on the substitution of the good for the bad. But for Hayek it is the other way round: civilization depends on the replacement of the good by the bad, the elimination of the good instincts and the imposition of market morality which 'we very much dislike, and even hate'.[39] But this is paradoxical; it just does not make sense to talk of solidarity and altruism as 'primordial instincts to be restrained and tamed', as if they were vicious and dangerous. The language is simply not appropriate.

It's no wonder, then, that there is a problem of order in capitalist society, given its contradictory foundations. In spite of having evolved through selection by survival and success, it is in constant danger from the lurking remnants of primitivism. Disorder is always threatening. It would be hardly surprising if it turned out that order has to be constantly imposed. But where is the spontaneity then?

There is also another difficulty that Hayek wishes to draw attention to, that of knowledge, or rather ignorance. In primitive society the problem of order was solved by the existence of the appropriate instincts. The numbers were small, the tasks rudimentary, so there was no problem with ignorance or lack of communication. 'Planning' was appropriate.

But not so for modern society. This is because it is impossible to bring together the required knowledge. Our thinking must instead take cognizance of and begin from 'our incurable ignorance of most of the particular circumstances which determine the course of this great society'. The market, however, overcomes mere human ignorance: 'I've come to believe that both the aim of the market order, and therefore the object of explanation of the theory of it [?], is to cope with the inevitable ignorance of everybody of most of the particular facts which determine this order'.[40]

Whatever exactly this means (and frequently with Hayek it is not clear; the syntax is askew) one question emerges: how can the market order have an aim? For the market is impersonal, and the idea of *order* is constantly contrasted with that of *organization*, which being the product of human design can be purposive. In spite of the fact that Hayek does not explain how the market can have an aim, or why another contradiction has been introduced, this is no mere slip, for the implied teleology is an essential part of the system. The market is to be seen as a reified demander of service and obedience.

In one of his most revealing sentences, Hayek says that 'the market is essentially an ordering mechanism'.[41] A great deal of meaning can be unpacked from this pun. First of all, the market creates an order in the sense of system: order rather than chaos. Secondly, a system is governed by regularities, which serve as the basis for predictions. Thirdly, the parts of the system are arranged in order, so it is a structured, hierarchical system and not a homogeneous one. Fourthly, the market creates a structure by co-ordinating the activities of human beings. Finally, the market orders in the sense that it tells people what to do; it issues orders and requires obedience.

At first this final authoritarian aspect of the market is concealed by presenting it merely as a 'guide' that 'signals' the correct way forward: 'It is a basic fact that we as scientists have to explain the results of the actions of men, which produces [*sic*] a sort of order by following signals inducing them to adapt to facts which they do not know'.[42] But there is more to it than this, as Hayek soon reveals. Neo-classical economists, he says, neglected 'the "guide" or "signal function" of prices. This was due to the survival of the simple causal explanation of values and prices, assuming that values and prices were determined by what had been done before than as a signal [*sic*] of what people ought to do'.[43]

The fractured syntax reveals a sudden switch from a causal liberalism to a teleological authoritarianism. In the liberal theory, autonomous individuals have demands and make choices to satisfy them; this creates and maintains the market and determines prices. But here the market and its price system have been objectified, and people merely follow its signals as if they were trains on a track. Where is individual freedom now?

So the teleologically-viewed market issues instructions and requires obedience. 'A system of market-determined prices is essentially a system which is indispensable in order to make us adapt to events and circumstances of which we cannot know.' The point of this adaptation is the achievement of a purpose: 'the distribution of market rewards is the mechanism by which individuals are told what to do in order to make their maximum contribution to the total product'. The ultimate project is 'the obedience to purely abstract rules of conduct that leads to the formation of a social order'.[44] And not just to its formation, but its perpetuation. The point is that all behaviour is *for the sake of* the market order of capitalism.

In this way, capitalist social relations can be maintained only if people will follow the orders of the market, only if they will submit to 'the discipline of abstract rules'.[45] The problem is, atavistic feelings derived from primitive instincts, i.e. the demand for social justice, keep simmering away and threaten to boil over and disrupt the efficient running of the capitalist world. These feelings must therefore be suppressed and market discipline maintained. Market behaviour must be enforced by the abstract rules, reappearing this time no longer as descriptions of the operations of the market but as the stern commands of the law. So because of its inherent instability, the 'spontaneous' market order will require a strong state to uphold it.

Hayek's General View of Society

Hayek displays a basically authoritarian concern for order — capitalist order — and for its enforcement. The resulting general picture of society and social relations is harsh and stark. 'The Great Society can only be an abstract society — an economic order from which the individual profits by obtaining the means for all his ends, and to which he must make his anonymous contribution. This does not satisfy his emotional, personal needs.'[46] This contradiction is driven home many times. The so-called 'Great Society' is not a face-to-face society, not a concrete, human society, not a cohesive society, not a society that can be based on love. The basis of social relations must be abstract rules; as law the rules are to keep people apart, in their private domains. This is a strange view of social relations.

So the individual stands naked in the market-place, alone and isolated. There is no help to be had from government, as this must not be allowed to interfere in the market. Nor can the individual turn for comfort to fellow citizens: this would be atavistic regression, 'a sign that intellectually and morally we have not yet fully matured to the needs of the impersonal comprehensive order of mankind'.[47]

Such bleak individualism is not appealing or attractive, as even Hayek is aware. So he reverts to what textual critics call the 'dangerous supplement', a supplementary argument introduced to support the main argument when it runs into trouble, but which thereby actually undermines it. Hayek's dangerous supplement is the voluntary organization, which he recommends as a means of overcoming the harsh abstractness of the market order. How the isolated individuals are to form such associations without excessive indulgence in primitive emotions is not clear. Furthermore, Hayek realizes the dangerousness of his supplement and more or less withdraws it. The power of such organizations raises problems; they have necessary limits and may have to be restricted by law, for 'though spontaneous order and organization will always coexist, it is still not possible to mix these two principles of order in any manner we like'.[48] The activities of organizations as well as individuals have to be co-ordinated by the spontaneous order, and organizations are integrated into the order in a hierarchical way. So only organizations which fit into market society can be allowable. Among associations which will be suspect on this criterion will clearly be what Hayek refers to as the 'wasteful apparatus of para-government . . . consisting of trade associations, trades unions and professional organizations'.[49] So clearly, within the bleak individualism of market society, the scope for voluntary association will be severely limited in the interests of unfettered capitalism.

Implications for Civil Liberties

In general there is obviously little comfort in Hayek's views of social order and social relations for those concerned with the erosion of civil rights and political liberties. And in spite of offering himself as the champion of liberty, there is little in Hayek's approach to various specific issues to increase the comfort.

Hayek's conception of freedom is negative. Freedom is simply the absence of coercion. Freedom is contrasted with slavery; it implies 'the possibility of a person's acting according to his own decisions and plans, in contrast to the position of one who was irrevocably subject to the will of another, who by arbitrary decisions could coerce him to act or not act in specific ways'.[50] How is it possible to know whether a person is free? Only by examining the extent of coercion. The greatest human freedom exists when there is the greatest absence of private coercion. Some coercion is permissible, so long as it is the exclusive right of a just government which uses it according to law to enforce the law.

To have individual freedom then, it is necessary to live in a free society, one in which coercion is limited in this way. To understand freedom requires the understanding of a free society. This is one which is governed according to law, without arbitrary, private coercion. Law is a system of abstract general rules laying down the duties of people indifferently and impartially.

Freedom, then, 'refers solely to a relation of men to other men, and the only infringement on it is coercion by men'.[51] Hayek's definition of freedom and the resulting limitation of coercion to human agency, is of central importance to the whole project. Only individuals, organizations and governments can coerce and be a restriction on freedom. In the absence of such coercion there must be freedom. The abstract order of market society, being a spontaneous order, is not an agency in this sense, and therefore cannot be coercive.

This position has an interesting consequence. It means that to the extent that Britain is a market society, the homeless, destitute dosser on the Embankment is as free as the aristocratic revellers in Park Lane. But since the Soviet Union is not a market society, the Soviet worker going about his or her daily activities unhindered is as unfree as the inmate of a Siberian labour camp. The market tells people what to do but in an impersonal way so no one loses any freedom. Socialism tells people what to do but in a personal way so everyone loses all freedom.

This is supposed to show that capitalist society is a free society. But this is a rather limited view of freedom. There is only freedom to obey the market. There is no choice, no other option. The order of the market is supposed to be spontaneous. But if this breaks down, it will be enforced.

A person, then, is free to the extent that she or he lives in a free society. To be in a disadvantaged position in a market society is not a limitation of freedom, so long as the disadvantage is the product of spontaneous order. Nor can such a disadvantaged position be regarded as unjust. For 'only human conduct can be called just or unjust . . . A bare fact, or a state of affairs which nobody can change, may be good or bad, but not just or unjust'. This means that 'so long as it remains a spontaneous order, the particular results of the social process cannot be just or unjust'.[52]

So justice is not a concept that can be applied to any particular social position. Justice is acting in accordance with the law, a set of abstract general rules of conduct. What Hayek wants to establish especially is that the distribution of wealth and income in capitalist society cannot be evaluated according to justice, which 'clearly has no application to the manner in which the impersonal process of the market allocates command over goods and services to particular people'. The aim is to demolish any conception of 'social' or 'distributive justice' which leads to socialism. Any attempt to redistribute income must rely not on general rules but specific imperatives, and this not only will create disorder but is coercive and unjust.[53]

Hayek realizes that there is a problem of appearance, though, which seems to be unjust: 'It has of course to be admitted that the manner in which the benefits and burdens are apportioned by the market mechanism would in many instances have to be regarded as very unjust *if* it were the result of a deliberate allocation to particular people'.[54] This raises an important point. What is missing from Hayek's analysis is any conception of dominant interests in the market, of unequal power that can produce unequal results. Although no egalitarian, Hayek does suppose that there is some sort of equality in the market, although he does not want to push this too far to any formal notion of equality of opportunity. He believes that the market order means a great reduction of power in society, so no interest can operate the market for its own benefit (though there is constant danger from socialist thinking in general and trade unions in particular). So if the rich stay rich or get richer, and the poor stay poor or get poorer, this is not because those who are already rich have more power in the market and can turn it to their advantage. It is a matter partly of skill and partly of luck. It does not raise moral questions.

Since a spontaneous market order leads to both freedom and justice, there is little need for politics as it has developed in recent democratic ages. What is required is a constitution which will entrench the rules of market order. This leaves little scope for government: jurisdiction rather than parliament should be sovereign. 'The judge is . . . an institution of a spontaneous order.'[55]

What remains of parliamentary functions should be divided into two. A legislative assembly will be responsible for legislation proper, for maintaining, revising and interpreting the law in the sense of the abstract general rules of market order. Members of, and electors to, this assembly will have to have reached the age of 45, and the members will serve for fifteen years. There will be no party politics allowed in this assembly.

A governmental assembly of lesser status will be responsible for day-to-day policy and administration. It will be organized on party lines. Although there will be no age restriction here, the franchise will not be completely open. It would not be unreasonable if 'employees of government and all who received pensions and other support from government should have no vote'.[56]

All this is part of Hayek's 'Model Constitution' and is still of course his private fantasy. But it is worth noting that his suggestion that the unemployed, among others, should have no vote has also been heard coming from the mouths of politicians. Other consequences of Hayek's 'constitutionalism' are even more alarming. Since the constitution entrenches capitalism, socialism would be unconstitutional. Indeed, measures would have to be taken which would 'stop' socialism, or even advocacy of a mixed economy. What exactly this would mean for freedom, free speech, freedom of association is not spelled out in any detail by Hayek, but the drift is clear enough. But it is paradoxical in Hayek's own system. The governmental assembly will be party-political: will socialists be allowed to be candidates or members? Suppose they constituted a majority; would they be allowed to form a government? Hayek does not sort out these contradictions. But his ideas are no less a threat for being vague, no less a danger to hard-won political freedoms and rights.

Hayek reserves some of his severest strictures for the trade unions. They just do not seem to understand the facts of life (or the market order) and are not only ignorant but malicious. There are several strands to his attack. First of all, Hayek retains an idealized picture of the market order according to which it consists of small family businesses (although he is simultaneously aware of the existence of large corporations). In such small-scale capitalism, in true seventeenth-century fashion, the 'servants' are part of the 'master's' household, so all relations are on an individual basis and there is no need for collective bargaining.

But, he maintains, even in a large firm there is no need for bargaining at all as wages will be fixed by the market. Activities of unions that try to change or influence the market order are unjust and ought to be curbed. Unions are sectional interests, blackmailing the government and the public, and having sufficient organized political power to distort democracy and obtain unjust special privileges. Finally, their activities are futile and counter-productive, since they actually reduce the real level of wages and cause inflation.

Hayek's hatred of the trade unions depends on his belief that they have coercive power but large firms and corporations do not: 'it is inexcusable to pretend that . . . the pressure which can be brought by the large firms or corporations is comparable to that of the organization of labour'. The real problem is 'not the selfish action of individual firms but the selfishness of organized groups', so 'the real exploiters in our present society are not egotistic capitalists or entrepreneurs . . . but organizations which derive their power from the moral support of collective action and the feeling of group loyalty'.[57] Firms and corporations are part of the spontaneous order: unions are not. It is on the basis of this one-sided and implausible argument that trade unions must be restricted or even banned.

It has already become apparent that only organizations compatible with the market order of capitalism will be allowed. Other organizations would be unconstitutional, especially those advocating socialist measures. Indeed, the very idea of 'social justice' must be fought. Hayek does not say how, but since this belief 'is at present probably the gravest threat to most other values of a free civilization',[58] presumably any weapon should be used to fight off such a pernicious danger. Clearly, support for any non-market system would have to be regarded as subversive, seditious. So there is little scope for free speech and association in the spontaneous order of market society, i.e. in capitalism.

Hayek's illiberal line continues on the subject of immigration and race relations, as freedom would upset the market order. Thus the existence of social security in a country like Britain 'necessitates certain limitations on the free movement of men across frontiers'. Furthermore, 'There exist . . . other reasons why such restrictions appear unavoidable so long as certain differences in national or ethnic traditions (especially differences in the rate of propagation) exist'. 'Sentiment' is not yet ready for multiculturalism, and positive measures through legislation are unwise.[59] What all this amounts to is a moderate but unsubtle dose of cultural racism.

In summary, Hayek's conception of freedom is a strange one. Very restricted politics and democracy, no freedom of speech, assembly or organization, a racist approach to nationality, and above all no choice but to be part of a harsh, inhuman market order. It is not a question of rights or liberties but of obligations to obey the rules of market society.

So if Hayek is a neo-liberal, he is a conservative neo-liberal. He, of course, refuses to call himself a conservative, and some conservatives reject him. But much of his position is indistinguishable from that of Scruton (who in fact quotes him approvingly)[60] – for example, his emphasis on tradition and national character, his willingness to make use of myths, superstitions and other beliefs that he knows to be false,[61] and above all his disparagement of democratic politics, his elevation of the law and his senatorial conception of constitutionalism. Indeed, Scruton's description of the constitution as 'what guides, limits and authorizes power, and thus manifests itself primarily through law, through the "style" of law, and through the position of the citizen as defined by law' could have been written by Hayek, just as Hayek's claim that 'It is this submission to undesigned rules and conventions whose significance and importance we largely do not understand, this reverence for the traditional, that the rationalistic type of mind finds so uncongenial, though it is indispensable for the working of a free society' would be, with the exception of the word 'free', entirely congenial to Scruton.[62]

So Hayek brings together conservatism and liberalism. He believes that the foundation of society is in tradition. It is just that he believes that the tradition is one of market morality and behaviour. This is a fairly standard conservative position, going back at least to Burke. Of course, Hayek's conservatism would not be totally congenial to the neo-conservatives; it is still far too liberal. Scruton, for example, would find absurd the claim that the conservative tradition is the one of the petit-bourgeois trader – he seeks a much more aristocratic foundation for the nation's heritage. But though the arguments may differ the passion for order and enforcement is the same.

Neo-Liberalism, the Limits of Government and Civil Liberties

If Hayek is not a typical neo-liberal, where do the supposedly genuine ones stand on civil liberties? Are they the real friends of liberty?

The neo-liberals are a disparate lot. But their general position is clear and obvious. The market is free and must be paramount. It will decide and must not be interfered with. So the purpose of law is to protect the workings of the market. The market is a natural process and cannot be coercive; its allocations do not raise problems of justice or morality: 'Most differences of status or position or wealth can be regarded as the product of chance at a far enough remove'.[63] There is reduced scope for government, and for democratic politics.[64]

Thus, to take an example, governments must not suppose that they should rush in to legislate about discrimination in employment. On this subject Friedman's position is that employers have the right to discriminate, provided they are prepared to pay the market costs of discrimination, but that in seeking competitive advantage they will try to avoid costs by not discriminating.[65] But this is totally unrealistic; in a discriminatory society it is the employer who fails to discriminate who bears a cost.

Unfortunately though, this is typical of the neo-liberals' refusal to take such issues seriously. Because they see everything in terms of the individual they are unable to acknowledge structural or institutional racism or sexism – even when they themselves exhibit it. For example, in equivocating between the individual and the household as the unit of social and economic analysis,[66] Friedman assumes a patriarchal model of the family. So women get a poor deal from the neo-liberals – they are not even allowed to be individuals.

The same charge can be brought against other New Right theorists such as Mount,[67] who have attempted to find a domain of private, individual freedom in the family. Hayek too suggests that sexual behaviour should be a matter of private conduct and stresses the importance of privacy. It is true that the views of such thinkers are clearly different from those of the neo-conservatives such as Scruton who cannot permit a domain of private conduct outside the control of the state. But both Mount's and Hayek's opinions about sexuality and the family are extremely patriarchal. Moreover, Hayek is not completely convinced that such an important matter as 'propagation' should not be subject to a veto by society.[68] So the record of the neo-liberals on civil liberties is not very encouraging. On very few occasions will one of them go so far as to criticize the police. They tend to get more worked up about seat belts as a threat to individual freedom.[69]

The same strange sense of priorities is to be found among Conservative politicians. They are not exactly neo-liberals, but they like to use the rhetoric of 'rolling back the state'. They are happy to push aside a parliamentary debate on telephone-tapping so that they can continue their defence of individual freedom against fluoridization: 'very few of the right-wing Tory MPs who are outraged by one part fluoride per squillion gallons of drinking water seem greatly distressed by the organs of the state chipping in on your telephone conversations – or mine, or Mrs Joan Ruddock's'.[70]

Those who use the neo-liberals' language of 'getting the state off the backs of the people' believe that the market economy provides freedom and must be protected by law. But it is the emphasis on law that allows neo-liberalism to slide over into the authoritarianism of the neo-conservatives to produce Thatcherism. The New Right coalition is happy to see a strong state protecting the market order. What is at issue is not civil liberties but setting the capitalist free.

So those who claim to speak for freedom suddenly become very authoritarian when faced by what they see as challenges to their conception of law and order. An example is set by the Home Secretary himself, Leon Brittan, who can make a speech full of fine Hayekian phrases about freedom and justice, while presiding over immigration practices operated with 'insensitivity, incompetence and illegality'.[71] It is this double standard which demonstrates the authoritarian reality of neo-liberalism and which lies behind Britain's breaches of the European Convention on Human Rights.[72]

But not only do neo-liberals not take civil liberties seriously, they do not even properly consider the consequences of their own views on the role of government. They believe it sufficient to refer to Adam Smith's inherently controversial claim that the three functions of government are only (1) defence against external enemies; (2) maintaining a system of law and order; (3) promoting public works which are not profitable for any individual.

But this leads not only to double standards but to much doublethink. While the neo-liberals want to limit the third function as much as possible, they assume the other two are uncontroversial and fail to bring out their implications. They claim to be interested in reduced government spending but have no objection to spending £10 billion on the defensively-useless Trident system, and do not protest about the fact that fifty per cent of Britain's expenditure on research and development is devoted to military projects, in spite of the massive distortion that this spending must imply for any conception of a free market. They are not alarmed when soldiers arrest civilians (*not* in Ireland) and are authorized to shoot them.[73] No neo-liberal protest is heard about the militarization of society, with its secrecy and manipulation, which is one of the gravest threats to freedom.[74]

The neo-liberals know the propaganda value of words like 'freedom', 'liberty', 'choice'. They believe that the constant reiteration of these words demonstrates their commitment to individual freedom and to rolling back the frontiers of government. But it is only freedom to take part in the capitalist system, and they have no objection to an increase in state power to enforce their 'freedom'. Any claim that the neo-liberals are 'libertarian', are the friends of liberty, must be regarded with the deepest suspicion.

Conclusion

Whatever theoretical differences there are between the two sides of the New Right, in practice they come together on the issues of social order and civil liberties. The neo-conservatives are explicitly the champions of order and the enemies of freedom. The neo-liberals are no less concerned with order, and so their proclamation of freedom is merely a rhetorical device. Hayek's teleological conception of the market order of capitalism straddles the two sides and makes him a central figure, as his popularity with Conservative politicians suggests. For the neo-conservative the individual is confronted by the power of the state, for the conservative neo-liberal the power of the law and for the neo-liberal the power of the market. In each case the aim is order and discipline.

So in political practice, such as that of Thatcherism, there is much cross-over between the two sides of the New Right. This interchange and mutual support is simply another example of traditional conservative pragmatism. The neo-liberals want a strong system of law to protect the market, and do not object to authoritarian measures to enforce it. In spite of constant appeals to the naturalness or spontaneity of the market system of capitalism, its order has to be enforced. The neo-conservatives do not believe in the inevitability of the market, but find its harsh discipline a politically useful means of imposing authority. When the two sides meet in practice the main aim is pragmatic: indiscriminately to take weapons from both sides to obtain power, to keep power and to suppress challenges.

The New Right is at its most insidious in the neo-liberals, for the neo-conservatives make no secret of their authoritarian aims. The neo-liberals, with their proclamation of freedom, suppress any conception that for many people a decent life means a constant struggle against the 'impersonal' decisions of the market. However, the unemployed, single parents, the disabled, the elderly, ethnic minorities, women, are unlikely to be impressed by the news that their disadvantaged positions are sure signs of their freedom, and by the insistence that any attempt to organize collective assistance for them will rob them of their liberty.

Civil liberties, human and political rights, are never given away but have to be struggled for against entrenched interests. Neo-liberals deny that there are such interests or anything like a ruling class in capitalism. For them there is just the market which will decide, and no need for civil liberties. These are disruptive of the market since − or so the neo-liberals claim − the existing imbalance in the market is not unjust but is free and equal, natural and spontaneous. But to resist further assaults on civil liberties is not to claim that existing rights and processes are adequate. They are not. Parliament often fails. Social-democratic institutions and consensus practices have not succeeded in protecting the real victims of the capitalist order. But although not perfect, hard-won civil rights and political liberties need to be defended against further depredations by the new authoritarians. Among the guardians of liberty is vigilance − and not the vigilantes of the New Right.

194   Belsey

Notes

1 See the reports by Malcolm Dean, *The Guardian*, 18, 20, 25 Mar. 1985.

2 The best survey of the current state of civil liberties is Peter Wallington (ed.), *Civil Liberties 1984* (Martin Robertson, Oxford, 1984). See also Stuart Hall, 'The great moving Right show' and Martin Kettle, 'The drift to law and order', in *The Politics of Thatcherism*, eds. Stuart Hall and Martin Jacques (Lawrence and Wishart, London, 1983), pp. 19-39, 216-34; Patricia Hewitt, *The Abuse of Power: Civil Liberties in the United Kingdom* (Martin Robertson, Oxford, 1982).

3 *Civil Liberties and the Miners' Strike: First report of the independent inquiry* (National Council for Civil Liberties, London, 1984); Bob Fine and Robert Millar (eds.), *Policing the Miners' Strike* (Lawrence and Wishart, London, 1985).

4 *The Times*, 8 Feb. 1985.

5 Catherine Scorer and Patricia Hewitt, *The Prevention of Terrorism Act: The case for repeal* (National Council for Civil Liberties, London, 1981); Peter Hain, *Political Trials in Britain* (Penguin, London, 1985), ch. 10.

6 Clive Ponting, *The Right to Know: The inside story of the 'Belgrano' affair* (Sphere, London, 1985); John Griffith, 'When judges roll over onto their backs', *New Statesman*, 15 Mar. 1985, pp. 25-7. See also Hain, *Political Trials*, ch. 4.

7 Bernard Crick, '3 out of 10 for McCowan', *New Statesman*, 22 Feb. 1985, pp. 16-17; leading article, *The Times*, 25 Feb. 1985.

8 Des Wilson (ed.), *The Secrets File: The case for freedom of information in Britain today* (Heinemann, London, 1984).

9 'MI5's official secrets', produced by *20/20 Vision* and shown on Channel 4 television on 8 Mar. 1985, Programme Script, pp. 2, 9, 38-41. The fate of this programme makes an interesting case-study in civil liberties. After it was banned from the screen by the Independent Broadcasting Authority, extracts from the script were published in *The Guardian* and *Tribune* (both 1 Mar. 1985). Only after the Government had indicated that there would be no prosecutions under the Official Secrets Act did the IBA allow the programme to be shown.

10 *The Daily Telegraph*, 7 Mar. 1985. For a justifiably sceptical response to the Bridge inquiry, see Hugo Young, 'Incredibly sheer

perfection of Lord Bridge's secret world', *The Guardian*, 18 Mar. 1985.

11 Home Office, *The Interception of Communications in the United Kingdom*, Cmnd. 9438 (HMSO, London, 1985).

12 *Operation Fire!* (Welsh Campaign for Civil and Political Liberties, Cardiff, 1980); John Davies, Lord Gifford and Tony Richards, *Political Policing in Wales* (WCCPL, Cardiff, 1984).

13 Paul Gordon, 'Outlawing immigrants, 1: Anwar Ditta and Britain's immigration laws', and Pal Luthra and Paul Gordon, 'Outlawing immigrants, 2: the Bestways passport raid and Britain's internal immigration controls', in *Causes for Concern: Questions of Law and Justice*, eds. Phil Scraton and Paul Gordon (Penguin, London, 1984), pp. 114-34, 135-53. For a longer perspective, see Zig Layton-Henry, *The Politics of Race in Britain* (Allen and Unwin, London, 1984).

14 Bob Fine, 'Law, order and the police', in *Socialist Arguments*, eds. David Coates and Gordon Johnston (Martin Robertson, Oxford, 1983), pp. 107-29, esp. p. 118; Kettle, 'The drift to law and order', p. 226.

15 Roger Scruton, *The Meaning of Conservatism* (Penguin, London, 1980), pp. 15, 16. For a fuller analysis, see my article, 'The REAL meaning of conservatism', *Radical Philosophy*, 28 (1981), pp. 1-5.

16 Scruton, *Conservatism*, p. 58.

17 Ibid., p. 66.

18 Ibid., p. 91.

19 Ibid., p. 19.

20 Ibid., pp. 53, 16, 57-63.

21 Ibid., p. 18. Scruton later suggested that Arthur Scargill should be prosecuted for sedition (*The Times*, 9 Oct. 1984). The suggestion was taken up by Conservative MP Peter Bruinvels, who formed the 'Law and Order Society' and raised over £100,000 for the purpose of bringing a sedition charge against Mr Scargill (*The Guardian*, 15 Mar. 1985).

22 Scruton, *Conservatism*, pp. 68, 84, 112.

23 See David Edgar, 'Bitter harvest', in *The Future of the Left*, ed. James Curran (Polity Press, Cambridge, 1984), pp. 39-57, esp. pp. 44-5.

24 Scruton, *Conservatism*, p. 18.

25 F. A. Hayek, *Knowledge, Evolution and Society* (Adam Smith Institute, London, 1983), pp. 41, 43.

26 Ibid., pp. 30, 38, 30.
27 F. A. Hayek, *Law, Legisation and Liberty: A new statement of the liberal principles of justice and political economy* (3 vols, Routledge and Kegan Paul, London, 1982), vol. I: *Rules and Order;* vol. II: *The Mirage of Social Justice*; vol. III: *The Political Order of a Free People*, vol. III, p. 169; Hayek, *Knowledge, Evolution and Society*, p. 29.
28 Hayek, *Knowledge, Evolution and Society*, p. 31. Elsewhere, though, Hayek seems to realize that there must have been a much more gradual process of change, e.g. *Law, Legislation and Liberty*, vol. III, p. 159.
29 Hayek, *Knowledge, Evolution and Society*, pp. 31-2, 39.
30 Hayek, *Knowledge, Evolution and Society*, p. 38; *Law, Legislation and Liberty*, vol. II, p. 109.
31 Hayek, *Knowledge, Evolution and Society*, p. 41.
32 Hayek, *Law, Legislation and Liberty*, vol. II, p. 135; *Knowledge, Evolution and Society*, pp. 34, 40; *Law, Legislation and Liberty*, vol. II, p. 87.
33 Hayek, *Knowledge, Evolution and Society*, pp. 47, 32, 46-7.
34 Hayek, *Law, Legislation and Liberty*, vol. I, p. 108.
35 Elsewhere Hayek is severe on historians who fail to separate history from myth: F. A. Hayek, 'History and politics', in *Capitalism and the Historians*, ed. F. A. Hayek (Routledge and Kegan Paul, London, 1954), pp. 3-29, esp. p. 4.
36 Hayek, *Law, Legislation and Liberty*, vol. I, p. 35; *Knowledge, Evolution and Society*, pp. 19, 43, 44, 45.
37 Elsewhere he says they are animal: *Law, Legislation and Liberty*, vol. III, p. 160.
38 Hayek, *Knowledge, Evolution and Society*, p. 38.
39 Ibid., p. 45.
40 Ibid., pp. 18-19.
41 Ibid., p. 19.
42 Ibid., p. 20.
43 Ibid., p. 36.
44 Ibid., pp. 35, 54, 42.
45 Hayek, *Law, Legislation and Liberty*, vol. II, p. 133.
46 Ibid., vol. III, p. 146.
47 Ibid., vol. II, p. 149.
48 Ibid., vol. I, p. 48.
49 Ibid., vol. III, p. 13.
50 F. A. Hayek, *The Constitution of Liberty* (Routledge and Kegan

Paul, London, 1960), pp. 11-12.
51 Ibid., p. 12.
52 Hayek, *Law, Legislation and Liberty*, vol. II, pp. 31, 32.
53 Ibid., vol. II, pp. 70, 63-4, 128-9.
54 Ibid., vol. II, p. 64.
55 Ibid., vol. I, p. 95.
56 Ibid., vol. III, p. 119.
57 Ibid., vol. III, pp. 89, 96.
58 Ibid., vol. II, pp. 66-7.
59 Ibid., vol. III, p. 56; vol. II, pp. 58, 131.
60 Scruton, *Conservatism*, p. 111.
61 F. A. Hayek, 'The moral tradition that reason must recognise', *The Guardian*, 17 Sept. 1984.
62 Scruton, *Conservatism*, p. 52; Hayek, *Constitution of Liberty*, p. 63.
63 Milton Friedman, *Capitalism and Freedom* (University of Chicago Press, Chicago, 1962), pp. 165-6.
64 Milton Friedman and Rose Friedman, *Free to Choose* (Penguin, London, 1980), p. 126.
65 Friedman, *Capitalism and Freedom*, p. 108 ff.
66 Ibid., p. 12.
67 Ferdinand Mount, *The Subversive Family* (Cape, London, 1982).
68 Hayek, *Law, Legislation and Liberty*, vol. II, p. 57; vol. III, p. 63.
69 Ferdinand Mount, 'From Swing to Scarman', *Spectator*, 28 Nov. 1981, p. 4; Geoffrey Wheatcroft, 'When nanny says "belt up"', *Sunday Telegraph*, 20 Jan. 1983.
70 Ian Aitken, 'Tories who are fluoriding high before the fall', *The Guardian*, 8 Mar. 1985.
71 Leon Brittan, 'The moral case for the market economy', speech to the Bow Group, 6 Dec. 1984; David Pannick, 'Out of court', *The Guardian*, 1 Apr. 1985.
72 Colin Leys, 'The rise of the authoritarian state', in *The Future of the Left*, ed. Curran, pp. 58-73.
73 Duncan Campbell, 'The pink card that allows troops to kill', *New Statesman*, 14 Dec. 1984, p. 4.
74 See Andrew Belsey, 'Secrecy, expertise and democracy', in *Objections to Nuclear Defence: Philosophers on deterrence*, eds. Nigel Blake and Kay Pole (Routledge and Kegan Paul, London, 1984), pp. 168-81.

Select Bibliography

Ackroyd, C. et al., *The Technology of Political Control*, 2nd edn (Pluto, London, 1980).

Barker, M., *The New Racism* (Junction Books, London, 1981).

Barker, M., *The Video Nasties* (Pluto, London, 1984).

Barnett, A., *Iron Britannia* (Allison and Busby, London, 1982).

Barry, N., *Hayek's Social and Economic Philosophy* (Macmillan, London, 1979).

Bell, D., *The Cultural Contradictions of Capitalism* (Basic Books, New York, 1978).

Berry, C., 'Conservatism and human nature', in *Politics and Human Nature*, ed. I. Forbes and S. Smith (Frances Pinter, London, 1983).

Billig, M., *L'internationale raciste. De la psychologies à la 'science des races'* (Maspero, Paris, 1981).

Booker, C., *The Seventies* (Allen Lane, London, 1980).

Bosanquet, N., *After the New Right* (Heinemann, London, 1983).

Brittan, S., *How to End the Monetarist Controversy* (Institute of Economic Affairs, London, 1981).

Brittan, S., *The Role and Limits of Government* (Temple Smith, London, 1983).

Brittan, S., *The Economic Consequences of Democracy* (Temple Smith, London, 1977).

Bruce, S., *One Nation Under God?: Observations on the new Christian Right in America* (Department of Social Studies, Queens University, Belfast, 1984).

Buchanan, J. et al., *The Economics of Politics* (Institute of Economic Affairs, London, 1978).

Butler, E., *Hayek* (Temple Smith, London, 1983).

Congdon, T., *Monetarism* (Centre for Policy Studies, London, 1978).

Cormack, P. (ed.), *Right Turn* (Leo Cooper, London, 1978).

Cowling, M. (ed.), *Conservative Essays* (Cassell, London, 1978).

Crawford, A., *Thunder on the Right* (Pantheon, New York, 1980).

Curran, J. (ed.), *The Future of the Left* (Polity Press/New Socialist, Cambridge, 1984).

David, M., 'The New Right in the USA and Britain: a new anti-feminist moral economy', *Critical Social Policy,* vol. 2., no. 3 (Spring 1983), pp. 31-46.

Dawkins, R., *The Selfish Gene* (Oxford University Press, Oxford, 1976).

Edgar, D., 'Bitter Harvest', in J. Curran (ed.), *The Future of the Left* (Polity Press/New Socialist, Cambridge, 1984).

Eisenstein, Z., 'The sexual politics of the New Right: on understanding the crisis of liberalism', *Signs: Journal of Women and Culture*, vol. 7, no. 3, (1982), pp. 567-588.

The Empire Strikes Back (Centre for Contemporary Cultural Studies, Hutchinson, London, 1982).

Ferraresi, F. (ed.), *La Destra radicale* (Feltrinelli, Milan, 1984).

Fine, Ben et al., *Class Politics: An Answer to its Critics* (Leftover Pamphlets, London, 1984).

Fine, Bob and Millar, R. (eds.), *Policing the Miners' Strike* (Lawrence and Wishart, London, 1985).

Friedman, M., *Capitalism and Freedom* (University of Chicago Press, Chicago, 1962).

Friedman, M., *Inflation and Unemployment* (Institute of Economic Affairs, London, 1977).

Friedman, M. and Friedman, R., *Free to Choose* (Penguin, London, 1980).

Gilder, G., *Wealth and Poverty* (Buchan and Enright, London, 1982).

Glazer, N., *Affirmative Discrimination* (Basic Books, New York, 1975).

Gramsci, A., *The Prison Notebooks* (Lawrence and Wishart, London, 1971).

Hain, P., *Political Trials in Britain* (Penguin, London, 1985).

Hall, S. and Jacques, M. (eds.), *The Politics of Thatcherism* (Lawrence and Wishart, London, 1983).

Hall, S. et al., *Policing the Crisis* (Macmillan, London, 1978).

Hayek, F. A., *The Road to Serfdom* (Routledge and Kegan Paul, London, 1944).

Hayek, F. A., *The Constitution of Liberty* (Routledge and Kegan Paul, London, 1960).

Hayek, F. A., *A Tiger by the Tail* (Institute of Economic Affairs, London, 1972).

Hayek, F. A., *Law, Legislation and Liberty* (Routledge and Kegan Paul, London, 1982).

Hayek, F. A., *Full Employment at Any Price?* (Institute of Economic Affairs, London, 1975).

Hayek, F. A., *Knowledge, Evolution and Society* (Adam Smith Institute, London, 1983).

Hodgson, G., *The Democratic Economy* (Penguin, London, 1984).

Jaggar, A. M., *Feminist Politics and Human Nature*, (Harvester, Sussex, 1983).

Jessop, B. et al., 'Authoritarian populism, two nations, and Thatcherism', *New Left Review*, 147 (1984), pp. 32-60.

Johnson, P., *Enemies of Society* (Weidenfeld, London, 1977).

Johnson, P., *The Recovery of Freedom* (Basil Blackwell, Oxford, 1980).

Joseph, K., *Stranded on the Middle Ground* (Centre for Policy Studies, London, 1976).

Joseph, K. and Sumption, J., *Equality* (John Murray, London, 1979).

Keegan, W., *Mrs Thatcher's Economic Experiment* (Allen Lane, London, 1984).

King, R. and Nugent, N., *Respectable Rebels* (Hodder and Stoughton, London, 1979).

Kristol, I., *On the Democratic Idea in America* (Harper and Row, New York, 1973).

Kristol, I., *Two Cheers for Capitalism* (Basic Books, New York, 1978).

Labour Research, vol. 73, no. 2. (Feb. 1984); and vol. 74, no. 2, (Feb. 1985).

Mannheim, K., 'The utopian mentality' in *Ideology and Utopia* (Routledge and Kegan Paul, London, 1936).

Miles, M. W., *The Odyssey of the American Right* (Oxford University Press, New York, 1980).

Mises, L. von., *Socialism* (Routledge, London, 1936).

Mount, F., *The Subversive Family: An alternative history of love and marriage* (Jonathan Cape, London, 1982).

Nash, G. H., *The Conservative Intellectual Movement in America* (Basic Books, New York, 1976).

Nell, E. J. (ed.), *Free Market Conservatism: A critique of theory and practice* (Basil Blackwell, Oxford, 1984).

New Internationalist, 133 (Mar. 1984).

Nozick, R., *Anarchy, State and Utopia* (Basil Blackwell, Oxford, 1974).

Nugent, N. and King, R., *The British Right* (Saxon House, Farnborough, 1977).

The Omega File (Adam Smith Institute, London, 1983-4).

Peele, G., *Revival and Reaction: The right in contemporary America*, Clarendon Press, Oxford, 1984.

Pines, B. Y., *Back to Basics* (William Morrow, New York, 1982).

Plant, R., *Equality, Markets and the State* (Fabian Society, London, 1984).

Plenel, E. and Rollat, A., *L'Effect Le Pen* (La Déconverte/Le Monde, Paris, 1984).

Ponting, C., *The Right to Know: The inside story of the 'Belgrano' affair* (Sphere, London, 1985).

Podhoretz, N., *Breaking Ranks* (Harper and Row, New York, 1979.

Riddell, P., *The Thatcher Government* (Martin Robertson, Oxford, 1983).

Rusher, W. S., *The Making of the New Majority Party* (Green Hill, Illinois, 1975).

The Salisbury Review

Scraton, P. and Gordon, P. (ed.), *Causes for Concern: Questions of law and justice* (Penguin, London, 1984).

Scruton, R., *The Meaning of Conservatism* (Penguin, London, 1980).

Seidel, G., *The Holocaust Denial* (Beyond the Pale Collective, Leeds, 1986), forthcoming.

Seidel, G. (ed.), *La Nature de la Droite*, (provisional title) (Editions Tierce, Paris, 1986), forthcoming.

Seidel, G. (ed.), *'L'autre,* l'étranger, présence et exclusion dans le discours', MOTS, no. 8. (special number), (Mar. 1984).

Steinfels, P., *The Neo Conservatives* (Simon and Schuster, New York, 1979).

Taguieff, P., 'La stratégie culturelle de la Nouvelle Droite en France (1968-1983)', *Vous avez dit fascismes?* (Arthaud/Montalba, Paris, 1984), pp. 13-152.

Thompson, E. P., *Writing by Candlelight* (Merlin, London, 1980).

Tyrrel, R. E. (ed.), *The Future That Doesn't Work* (Doubleday, New York, 1975).

Wallington, P. (ed.), *Civil Liberties 1984)* (Martin Robertson, Oxford, 1984).

Watkins, K. W. (ed.), *In Defence of Freedom* (Cassell, London, 1978).

Wilson, D. (ed.), *The Secrets File: The case for freedom of information in Britain today* (Heinemman, London, 1984).

Wilson, E. O., *Sociobiology: The New Synthesis* (Harvard University Press, Cambridge, 1975).

Wilson, J. Q., *Thinking about Crime* (Basic Books, New York, 1975).

Index

abortion 153, 157-162
Abramovitz, M. 145-6
accountability 83-5, 91, 102
Action Française 126
Adam Smith Institute (ASI) 3, 7, 9,
    39, 82-3, 90, 97, 102
Adam Smith Institute – Omega
    Reports 8, 21, 82-91, 98-103
on defence policy 99-102
on education 84-5
on employment policy 89-90
on energy policy 87-89
on foreign policy 99-101
on health policy 13-14, 86-7
on housing 90
on local government 83-4, 87
on planning 90-1
on social security 85-6, 89
Akron case 160
Allende, S. 100
Aims of Industry 3, 59
American Enterprise Institute 66
Amis, K. 70
anti-feminism 21, 69, 129, 136, 145,
    154, 156
anti-semitism 115, 117, 123-6, 133-4
anti-socialism 14, 17, 26-7, 40-2,
    44-5, 49, 97, 129, 187
Aquinas, T. 94
Ashworth, C. 128

Association of Self-Employed
    People 62
Arthur, L. 158
Audit Commission 87
Austrian school of economics 3,
    27-8, 31, 40-4

Barker, M. 111-112, 114, 116
Barrès, M. 126
Bell, D. 64
Besley, A. 3, 7, 21
Benoist, A. de 108, 123
Bernard, J. 139
Berry, C. 94
Beveridge, W. 28
Biffen, J. 70
Biggs-Davison, J. 123-5
Bishop, M. 122
Böhm-Bawerk, E. von 31
Booker, C. 73
Bosanquet, N. 2-4, 81, 173
Boyson, R. 55
Bozell, B. 56
Bridge, Lord 171
British Movement 113-14
British National Party 113-14
Brittan, L. 191
Brittan, S. 25
Bruinvels, P. 195
Buckley, W. F. 58

Bukharin, N. 27
Bush, G. 66
Burke, E. 68, 71, 93-4, 110, 189
Butt, R. 72, 74, 136, 161

Campaign for Nuclear
    Disarmament 123, 171
Campaign Against Racism in the
    Media 111
Campbell, B. 161
Carter, J. 157
Casey, J. 81, 93-4, 110-17, 119,
    129-30
Centre for Policy Studies 3, 39, 62,
    71, 82
childcare 147-8, 151-2
Christianity 20, 76, 92, 97, 110,
    123-6, 133, 156-8, 161-2
Churchill, W. S. 59
civil liberties 7, 16, 21, 102, 169-72,
    185-93
Cloward, R. 142
Club de l'Horloge 127
Coard, B. 122
Cold War 7, 12, 14, 29, 99-101
Commission for Racial Equality
    118-120
Committee for the Survival of a
    Free Congress 65
Conservative Caucus 65
Conservative Friends of Israel 123
Conservative Party 3, 7-10, 21-2,
    47-51, 59-63, 111, 141, 176,
    191-2
Conservative Philosophy Group 4
Corea, G. 152
Cosgrove, P. 70
Cowling, M. 93, 99
Cowling, M. (ed) Conservative
    Essays 4, 91, 100, 108
culture 107-31

David, M. 5, 7, 21, 122, 158
Davidoff, L. 158
Davis, M. 145

Dector, M. 73
Disraeli, B. 4
Drew, E. 67, 69
Dworkin, A. 157
Dworkin, R. 124

economic individualism 30
Economic League 3
economic planning 41-2, 50, 182
Economic Recovery Tax Act 147
Edgar, D. 5, 7-9, 16, 21, 154
education 14, 17, 84-5, 89, 98,
    116-22, 127, 157, 159, 161-3
Ehrenreich, B. 145, 156
Eisenhower, D. 59
Eisenstein, Z. 145, 155
Eliot, T. S. 110
Engels, F. 123-4
Equal Opportunities Commission
    151
European Convention on Human
    Rights 169, 171, 191
European Parliament: Committee
    of Inquiry into the rise of
    Racism and Facism 132
exchange rates 3, 33-5

Falkland Islands 55, 99, 115, 130
Falwell, J. 65
family 7, 24, 31, 47, 56, 136-168,
    190-1
    in Hayek 178-9, 190-1
    in neo-conservatism 56, 71, 74-6,
        93-6, 153-6
    in neo-liberalism 7, 47, 85, 93, 98,
        190
family structure 137-139, 150
    Asian 113, 146
    West Indian 112-13, 121-2, 146
    lone parent families 138-9, 146,
        150
    Family Policy Group 75, 92, 154
Family Protection Act 159
Federation of Conservative
    Students 7